MARY BERRY'S

DESSERTS AND CONFECTIONS

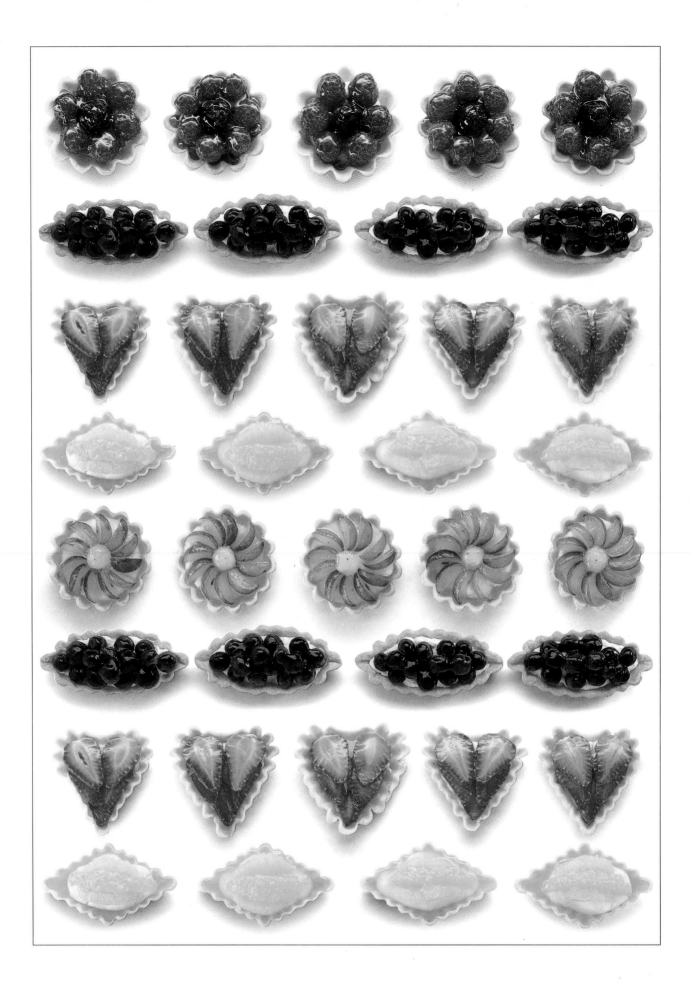

MARY BERRY'S

DESSERTS AND CONFECTIONS

DORLING KINDERSLEY
LONDON • NEW YORK • STUTTGART

A DORLING KINDERSLEY BOOK

Created and Produced by
CARROLL & BROWN LTD
12 Colas Mews
London NW6 4LH

CARROLL & BROWN LTD

Editorial Director	Jeni Wright
Art Director	Denise Brown
Designers	Wendy Rogers Sally Powell Joanna Pocock

First published in Great Britain in 1991
by Dorling Kindersley Limited
9 Henrietta Street, London WC2E 8PS

Reprinted 1993

Copyright © 1991 Dorling Kindersley Limited and The Hearst Corporation

A CIP catalogue record for this book is available from the British Library
ISBN 0 - 86318 - 654 - 8

Reproduced by Colourscan, Singapore
Printed and bound in Singapore by Toppan

CONTENTS

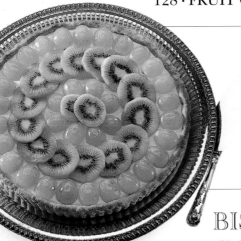

FOREWORD

W hat's for pudding? A question so often in our minds. This is a collection of good-looking, good-tasting recipes that I hope will answer just that question.

Whether you are planning a grand finale to a special meal, seeking new ways to serve old family favourites, choosing for a coffee morning or bridge tea, or wanting to tempt the young with snacks when they come home from school, in this book you will find a wide range of fabulous choices.

Included in my collection are wonderful variations on perennials like Lemon Meringue Pie, Apple Pie, Brandy Snaps and Crêpes Suzette, or if you are interested in mastering the classics like Apple Strudel and Crème Brûlée, you will discover how easy they are to prepare using the recipes in this book. However, if simple dishes are your choice, try a Peach, Raspberry or Kiwi Fruit Fool or Cherries en Gelée. If, like me, you delight in hearing 'Mmm!' and 'Ooh!' as you serve dessert, Chocolate Truffle Cake and Swiss Chocolate Torte won't disappoint, and I will guarantee that the Swan Cream Puffs and Meringue Mushrooms will please children from six to ninety-six.

I happen to believe that desserts can be good for you as well as just plain good. They can add heartiness to a light menu and lighten a substantial one. Desserts can supply nutritional foods, such as milk, fruit or grain products, which may be missing from the rest of the day's meals. Even if you, or members of your family, are watching your waistlines, you can enjoy desserts in thinner slices or smaller servings, and still conform to healthy eating guidelines.

Full-colour photographs of every recipe show you what to expect, and step-by-step instructions, many of them illustrated, guide you through each technique in preparation. To make great desserts more glorious, there are dozens of garnishes, decorations and serving tips to help you make every dish as pleasing to the eye as it is to the palate.

All the hard work that the designers and editors at Carroll & Brown have expended on my behalf shows clearly in this book. A *very* special 'thank you' goes to Jeni Wright, the project editor, who spent many hours working with me on perfecting the collection. All that remains is for me to wish you 'Bon Appétit', with the hope that this dessert collection gives you as much pleasure to prepare and enjoy, as it did for me to put it together.

Mary Berry

SPECIAL DESSERTS

7-74

SPECIAL DESSERTS

In this chapter are desserts that call for a show-off setting – your prettiest glass bowls to reveal textures, and dainty china plates and dishes to enhance colours. Mousses, soufflés, custards and creams are generally soft and smooth, easy to serve and to eat, and stunningly varied in colour and flavour. Many, like Tiramisù, take their shape from the dish in which they are served; others, like Zuccotto, from the mould in which they were placed to set or to firm up. Jewel-toned fresh fruit desserts can put the taste of summer on your table any time, thanks to the year-round availability of many familiar fruits, and add exotic new varieties to the list of dessert possibilities. Rounding out this chapter are tender crêpes and blinis, and meringue desserts as appealing as Meringue Mushrooms and as elegant as Strawberry and Almond Dacquoise.

CONTENTS

MOUSSES AND SOUFFLÉS

Light, fluffy mousses and soufflés – made from fruit, chocolate, nuts and cream – are right for any occasion, from everyday meals for family and friends to special events when you want to impress. And, because cold mousses can be made ahead, they're perfect for entertaining.

REAL CHOCOLATE MOUSSE

8-10 servings

Can be made day before and kept in refrigerator

4 egg yolks

450 ml / ³/₄ pint milk

60 g/2 oz caster sugar

1 tablespoon powdered gelatine

225 g/8 oz plain chocolate, chopped

450 ml / ³/₄ pint double or whipping cream

Whipped cream and finely chopped pistachios (see right) to decorate

1 In large non-stick saucepan, beat egg yolks, milk and sugar until blended. Evenly sprinkle gelatine over mixture; leave to stand for 5 minutes to soften gelatine slightly. Stir in chopped chocolate.

2 Cook over low heat, stirring frequently with wooden spoon, for about 15 minutes or until gelatine dissolves completely, chocolate melts and mixture thickens and coats the spoon well (do not boil or mixture will curdle).

3 Pour mixture into bowl; cover and refrigerate until mixture mounds slightly when dropped from a spoon, about 1¹/₂ hours, stirring occasionally.

4 In medium bowl, whip double or whipping cream until stiff peaks form. With rubber spatula or wire whisk, fold whipped cream into chocolate mixture.

5 Pour mousse into 8-10 individual soufflé dishes or 1 large serving bowl; cover and refrigerate for 4 hours or until mousse is set.

6 Before serving, decorate mousse with whipped cream and finely chopped pistachios.

Piping whipped cream: *using piping bag with medium star tube, pipe whipped cream in shell shape at edge of each chocolate mousse.*

Chopping pistachios: *with sharp knife, on cutting board, finely chop shelled pistachios. Use to sprinkle over whipped cream and chocolate mousse.*

Chopped pistachios and whipped cream add flavour as well as colour to this wickedly rich chocolate mousse

RASPBERRY LAYERED MOUSSE

🥄 8 servings

⏱ Can be made day before and kept in refrigeraor

450 g/1 lb frozen raspberries

175-225 g/6-8 oz caster sugar

2 tablespoons powdered gelatine

2 eggs

300 ml/½ pint milk

600 ml/1 pint double or whipping cream

14 ginger nut biscuits, crushed (about 150 g/5 oz)

Raspberries and mint leaves to decorate

1 Sprinkle raspberries with half of the sugar; set aside to thaw.

2 Place sieve over non-stick saucepan. With back of spoon, press and scrape raspberries and juice through sieve to purée; discard pips.

3 Sprinkle half of the gelatine over raspberry purée in saucepan; leave to stand for 5 minutes in order to allow gelatine to soften slightly.

4 Over medium heat, cook raspberry mixture until gelatine dissolves completely, stirring frequently.

5 Pour into bowl, cover and refrigerate until mixture mounds slightly when dropped from a spoon, about 1 ½ hours, stirring occasionally.

6 Meanwhile, in another non-stick saucepan, beat eggs, milk and half of the remaining sugar until blended. Evenly sprinkle remaining gelatine over mixture; leave to stand for 5 minutes in order to soften gelatine slightly.

7 Cook gelatine mixture over low heat, stirring frequently, for 10 minutes or until gelatine dissolves completely and mixture coats a spoon well (do not boil or it will curdle).

8 Pour into bowl, cover and refrigerate until mixture mounds slightly when dropped from a spoon, about 1 ½ hours, stirring occasionally.

9 About 10 minutes before gelatine mixtures are ready, in large bowl, whip double or whipping cream with remaining sugar until stiff peaks form.

10 With rubber spatula or wire whisk, gently fold half of the whipped cream into each of the gelatine mixtures.

11 In large serving bowl, layer half of the biscuits, then custard cream, rest of biscuits, then raspberry cream. Cover and refrigerate until set, about 3 hours.

> *TO SERVE*
> Decorate mousse with raspberries and mint leaves.

The different layers of Raspberry Layered Mousse can be seen if the dessert is made in a glass bowl

MARBLED MOUSSE CAKE

 8 servings

Can be made day before and kept in refrigerator

60 g/2 oz plain chocolate, broken into pieces

450 ml/ ¾ pint milk

3 egg yolks

200 g/7 oz caster sugar

2 tablespoons powdered gelatine

1 teaspoon vanilla essence

600 ml/1 pint double or whipping cream

200 g/7 oz plain chocolate flavour cake covering

1 Place pieces of plain chocolate in bowl over pan of gently simmering water and heat, stirring frequently, until melted and smooth; remove pan from heat.

2 In large non-stick saucepan, blend milk, egg yolks and 150 g/5 oz sugar. Evenly sprinkle gelatine over mixture; leave to stand for 5 minutes to soften gelatine slightly. Cook over low heat, stirring often, for about 15 minutes or until gelatine dissolves completely and mixture coats a spoon well (do not boil or mixture will curdle).

3 Pour half of the egg yolk mixture into small bowl; add melted chocolate. With wire whisk, beat just until blended. Into remaining egg yolk mixture, stir vanilla essence.

4 Cover and refrigerate both mixtures until they mound slightly when dropped from a spoon, 20-25 minutes, stirring occasionally.

5 In large bowl, whip double or whipping cream with remaining caster sugar until stiff peaks form.

6 With rubber spatula or wire whisk, gently fold half of the whipped cream into each chilled egg yolk mixture.

7 Alternately spoon chocolate and vanilla mousse mixtures into 23 cm/9 inch springform cake tin. Swirl mixtures together with a palette knife, to create a pretty marbled design. Cover and refrigerate for 4 hours or until set.

8 Meanwhile, cut sheet of non-stick baking parchment into 30 x 18.5 cm/12 x 7½ inch rectangle; place on baking sheet. Melt 150 g/5 oz chocolate cake covering in a bowl over a pan of gently simmering water, stirring frequently.

9 Spread melted cake covering over paper rectangle (see Box, right); refrigerate until firm.

10 Cut chocolate rectangle into strips (see Box, right); peel off paper. Place chocolate strips on baking sheet; refrigerate.

11 Make chocolate curls: with heat of hands, slightly soften remaining chocolate cake covering. Draw blade of vegetable peeler along smooth surface of chocolate to make wide chocolate curls. Place curls on plate; refrigerate.

12 Remove chocolate strips from refrigerator; leave to stand for 5 minutes to soften. Remove side of springform tin; place mousse cake on cake stand or plate. Cover side with chocolate strips (see Box, below).

13 With cocktail stick, gently pile chocolate curls in centre of mousse cake.

MAKING CHOCOLATE FRAME

Spreading melted chocolate: with palette knife, quickly spread warm melted chocolate over non-stick baking parchment rectangle to cover evenly; refrigerate until firm, about 30 minutes.

Cutting chocolate into strips: with sharp knife, cut chocolate rectangle lengthways into five 4 cm/1 ½ inch wide strips.

Cake covering is used for making this chocolate 'frame' because it moulds easily to the shape of the mousse

Covering side of cake: place chocolate strips one at a time round cake. Press each strip gently with palette knife to fit shape of mousse, overlapping slightly.

Chocolate 'frame' is made by carefully shaping strips of chocolate round mousse, overlapping them so that frame is made up of more than one layer

For this dramatic presentation, glacé cherries are placed at regular intervals round top edge of mousse cake and grated chocolate is sprinkled round edge of plate

EASY CHOCOLATE ALMOND MOUSSE

 4-6 servings

Can be made day before and kept in refrigerator

300 ml/ ½ pint double or whipping cream

1 tablespoon powdered gelatine

175 g/6 oz plain chocolate, broken into pieces

4 ice cubes

175 ml/6 fl oz milk

60 g/2 oz caster sugar

¾ teaspoon almond essence

Whipped cream and toasted flaked almonds (see Box, right) to decorate

TOASTING FLAKED ALMONDS

In frying pan or saucepan over medium heat, cook small quantity of almonds until golden, stirring frequently with wooden spatula.

Leave almonds to cool before using.

1 Pour half of the double or whipping cream into non-stick saucepan. Evenly sprinkle gelatine over cream; leave to soften for 5 minutes.

2 Cook over medium heat until tiny bubbles form round edge of pan and gelatine dissolves completely, stirring frequently.

3 Pour hot mixture into blender or food processor with knife blade attached; add chocolate pieces. Cover and blend until chocolate melts.

4 Add ice cubes to chocolate mixture.

5 Add milk, sugar, almond essence and remaining double or whipping cream; blend until smooth.

6 Pour mixture into 4-6 glasses or bowls; cover and refrigerate for 4 hours or until set.

7 Decorate each mousse with whipped cream and top with toasted flaked almonds.

HOT BANANA SOUFFLÉS

 4 servings

Allow 30 minutes preparation time

---

3 medium-sized bananas (about 450 g/1 lb)

---

2 teaspoons lemon juice

---

4 egg whites

---

25 g/³/₄ oz icing sugar plus extra for sprinkling

---

1 Preheat oven to 230°C/450°F/gas 8.

2 Brush inside of four 300 ml/½ pint soufflé dishes lightly with oil.

3 Peel and slice bananas; place slices in bowl, add lemon juice and mash well with fork.

4 In large bowl, with electric mixer on full speed, beat egg whites until soft peaks form; gradually sift in 25 g/³/₄ oz icing sugar, beating until sugar completely dissolves and whites stand in stiff peaks.

> **TO SERVE**
> When soufflés are done, remove from oven; sift tops lightly with icing sugar and serve immediately.

5 With rubber spatula or wire whisk, gently fold beaten egg whites into banana mixture, one-third at a time.

6 Spoon mixture into soufflé dishes; set dishes in baking tray for easier handling.

7 Bake for 15 minutes or until soufflés are puffed and browned.

Hot soufflés look so good when they come out of the oven, puffed and high like these. Don't delay when serving!

ORANGE LIQUEUR SOUFFLÉ

6 servings
Allow 2 hours preparation and cooking time

60 g/2 oz butter

50 g/1 ²/₃ oz plain flour

350 ml/12 fl oz milk

45 g/1 ¹/₂ oz caster sugar, plus extra for sprinkling

4 egg yolks

5 tablespoons orange liqueur

1 tablespoon grated orange zest

6 egg whites

Icing sugar for sprinkling

Whipped cream for serving (flavoured with orange liqueur or orange juice if liked)

1 In large non-stick saucepan over low heat, melt butter; stir in flour until blended. Gradually stir in milk; cook, stirring constantly, until mixture boils and thickens; boil for 1 minute.

2 Remove saucepan from heat. With wire whisk, beat caster sugar into milk mixture. Rapidly beat in egg yolks all at once until well mixed. Cool mixture to lukewarm, stirring occasionally. Stir in orange liqueur and grated orange zest.

Making indentation in soufflé mixture for top hat effect

3 Brush inside of 1.2 litre/2 pint soufflé dish with butter; sprinkle lightly with caster sugar.

If you sprinkle inside of buttered soufflé dish with caster sugar it will melt during baking and soufflé will not stick to dish

4 Preheat oven to 190°C/375°F/gas 5. In large bowl, with electric mixer on full speed, beat egg whites until stiff peaks form. With rubber spatula or wire whisk, gently fold beaten egg whites, one-third at a time, into egg yolk mixture.

5 Spoon mixture into prepared dish. With back of metal spoon, about 2.5 cm/1 inch from edge, make 4 cm/1¹/₂ inch deep indentation all round in soufflé mixture (centre will rise slightly higher than edge, making top hat effect when soufflé is done).

6 Bake soufflé for 30-35 minutes until knife inserted under top hat comes out clean.

7 When soufflé is done, remove from oven and sprinkle top lightly with sifted icing sugar; serve immediately. Hand whipped cream in bowl to spoon on to each serving, if you like.

The 'top hat' effect of this baked soufflé is created by making an indentation with a spoon in soufflé mixture before cooking

SUCCESSFUL SWEET SOUFFLÉS

Hot sweet soufflés consist of a thick sauce of butter, flour, milk, sugar, egg yolks and flavourings folded with stiffly beaten egg whites. For success every time, follow these simple guidelines.

• Always cook butter and flour first, to get rid of the raw taste of uncooked flour. When adding milk, take care to do it very gradually.

• Boil milk mixture for 1 minute so that smooth sauce is formed.

• Beat in egg yolks vigorously with pan off the heat.

• Fold egg whites gently into sauce, taking care not to stir whites.

• Bake soufflé on rack slightly below centre of oven so that mixture itself is centred and has sufficient room to rise.

• Do not open oven door before end of baking time; cold air could cause soufflé to fall.

FRESH APPLE SOUFFLÉ

4 servings

Allow about 1 hour preparation and cooking time

3 medium-sized cooking apples (about 450 g/1 lb)

45 g/1 ½ oz caster sugar

½ teaspoon almond essence

5 egg whites

Icing sugar for sprinkling

1 Peel apples; cut into quarters; with sharp knife, remove cores.

2 Cut apples into bite-sized chunks. In large saucepan over high heat, heat apples and *4 table-spoons water* to boiling. Reduce heat to low; cover and simmer for 8-10 minutes, stirring occasionally, until apples are tender. Stir in caster sugar and almond essence. Pour apple mixture into bowl; set aside to cool.

3 Preheat oven to 230°C/450°F/gas 8. In large bowl, with electric mixer on full speed, beat egg whites until stiff peaks form.

4 With rubber spatula or wire whisk, gently fold egg whites into cooled apple mixture until evenly incorporated.

5 Spoon mixture into 1.5 litre/2 ½ pint soufflé dish. Bake for 15 minutes or until soufflé is puffy and lightly browned. Remove soufflé from oven; sift icing sugar lightly over top and serve immediately.

Although not strictly speaking a soufflé, this simple, low-calorie dessert of apples, sugar and egg whites has a similar light and fluffy texture

CUSTARDS AND CREAMS

Velvety smooth, soft and pleasing, custards and creams are easy and quick to make. Most can be prepared ahead, making them excellent for menus in which other dishes require last-minute attention. Fruit Fools are the exception; they must be made just before serving, but preparation takes only about 20 minutes. In these pages you will find desserts ranging from simple family favourites like Crème Caramel to sophisticated party desserts like Zuccotto.

AMERICAN CREAM POTS

6 servings

Can be made day before (up to end of step 6) and kept in refrigerator

4 eggs

600 ml/1 pint milk

45 g/1 ¹/₂ oz caster sugar

1 teaspoon vanilla essence

6 tablespoons maple syrup

1 x 315 g/11 oz can mandarin orange segments, drained, to decorate

1 In large jug or bowl, with wire whisk, beat eggs, milk, sugar and vanilla essence until well blended.

2 Pour milk mixture into six 175 ml/6 fl oz mousse pots.

3 Arrange mousse pots in 30 cm/12 inch frying pan; fill pan with water to come halfway up sides of pots. Cover pan.

4 Over medium heat, heat water in pan to boiling point.

5 Simmer custards about 10 minutes or until beginning to set around edges. Remove pan from heat, then leave custards to stand in covered pan for 15 minutes until fully set.

6 Remove pots of custard from pan; refrigerate until well chilled, about 2 hours. If not serving immediately, cover each chilled dessert tightly and refrigerate.

7 Just before serving, pour 1 tablespoon maple syrup on top of each pot of custard.

8 To serve, top each custard with mandarin orange segments.

Maple syrup and canned mandarins are a quick and clever 'American' way to dress up a simple egg custard

CHOCOLATE CUPS

 8 servings
Allow about 2 hours preparation and chilling time

175 g/6 oz plain chocolate flavour cake covering, broken into pieces

300 ml/ ½ pint double or whipping cream

1 x 400 g/400 ml can Devon custard

Few drops of orange food colouring (optional)

1 large banana

Cocoa powder

1 Place paper cake cases in each of eight 6 cm/2 ½ inch holes in deep bun tin.

2 In small bowl set over saucepan of gently simmering water, gently heat chocolate cake covering, stirring frequently, until melted and smooth.

3 Starting from top rim of each paper case, carefully drizzle melted chocolate cake covering, 1 teaspoon at a time, down inside of case. About 3-4 teaspoons of melted chocolate will line each paper case.

4 If necessary, spread chocolate over inside of case with back of teaspoon.

5 Refrigerate until firm, about 30 minutes. With cool hands, remove 1 cake case at a time from refrigerator; gently but quickly peel paper case from each one, leaving chocolate cup.

6 Place empty chocolate cups on chilled dessert platter and refrigerate.

7 In small bowl, whip double or whipping cream until stiff peaks form.

8 With rubber spatula or wire whisk, fold whipped cream into custard until blended. Add food colouring, if used.

9 Slice banana and divide equally between cups. Spoon filling into cups. Refrigerate for at least 30 minutes or until filling is well chilled.

> *TO SERVE*
> *Lightly sprinkle cocoa through small sieve over creamy filling in Chocolate Cups.*

Beneath this creamy custard is a surprise filling of sliced banana

CRÈME CARAMEL

6 servings
Can be made day before and kept in refrigerator

120 g/4 oz granulated sugar

5 eggs

60 g/2 oz caster sugar

Few drops of vanilla essence

750 ml/1 ¼ pints milk

Cracked Caramel (page 253), Cape gooseberries or lime julienne and citrus fruit segments to decorate

1 Preheat oven to 150°C/300°F/gas 2. Put granulated sugar and *4 tablespoons water* in heavy saucepan and dissolve over low heat. Bring to the boil; boil, without stirring, until syrup is pale golden brown. Remove from heat and quickly pour into 6 small ramekins, or oval- or heart-shaped moulds.

2 Mix the eggs, caster sugar and vanilla essence together in a large bowl.

3 Warm milk in saucepan over low heat until it is hand hot, then pour it on to egg mixture, stirring constantly.

4 Brush butter on sides of ramekins or moulds above caramel. Strain custard into ramekins or moulds and place in a roasting tin. Pour in hot water to come halfway up sides of ramekins or moulds.

5 Bake in oven for about 45-60 minutes until set. Remove from oven and leave to cool, then refrigerate until set and well chilled, at least 12 hours or overnight.

6 Just before serving, loosen custards from ramekins or moulds with small knife. Turn each custard out on to a chilled dessert plate, letting syrup drip over custard and down sides. Add decoration of your choice.

Cracked Caramel

Cracked Caramel Decoration: *with end of rolling pin, carefully crack hardened caramel into small pieces.*

Cape Gooseberry Decoration (also called physalis and Chinese lantern): *carefully peel back inedible husk to resemble flower petals.*

Lime Julienne Decoration: *with vegetable peeler, remove zest from lime, leaving bitter white pith behind. Cut zest into fine strips.*

Lime Julienne

Cape Gooseberry

CRÈME BRÛLÉE

 6 servings

Can be made day before up to end of step 3

Crème Brûlée

600 ml/1 pint single cream
4 eggs
60 g/2 oz caster sugar
1/2 teaspoon vanilla essence
45 g/1 1/2 oz demerara sugar

To serve

Cut-up fresh fruits (strawberries, pineapple and banana)
Canned mandarin-orange segments
Fresh mint sprigs

1 Preheat oven to 150°C/300°F/gas 2.

2 Blend cream, eggs, caster sugar and vanilla in large bowl. Pour into baking dish.

3 Stand dish in roasting tin containing 2.5 cm/1 inch hot water; bake in oven for about 1 hour or until just firm. Leave to cool, then refrigerate for at least 4 hours.

4 About 1 hour before serving, preheat grill to high. Work demerara sugar through sieve over chilled cream mixture.

5 Brown under a hot grill for 3-4 minutes until sugar has melted. The melted sugar will form a crisp crust over custard. If crust is done too early, the sugar will become soft and lose its crisp texture. Leave to cool.

6 To serve, arrange some sliced fruit in centre of Crème Brûlée with mint sprigs. Serve remaining fruit separately.

Working demerara sugar through sieve so it will be free of lumps; it should then brown evenly under the grill

To serve Crème Brûlée, tap top with metal spoon to crack crust and reveal creamy custard underneath

BRÛLÉE TOPPING

If your grill isn't very efficient and you find it difficult to get an even layer of brûlée on the top of the custard cream, instead of sprinkling demerara sugar over the top of the custard and browning it under the grill, try this alternative method.

Caramel Topping

Make a caramel as you would for crème caramel: put *90 g /3 oz granulated sugar* and *3 tablespoons water* in a heavy saucepan and heat gently until the sugar has dissolved. Bring to the boil and boil, without stirring, until the syrup is pale golden brown. Remove from the heat and quickly pour over the top of the chilled custard cream; syrup will turn instantly into a hard caramel. Chill in the refrigerator for 3-4 hours to soften caramel a little.

BURGUNDY CREAM

6 servings

Allow 2 ½ hours preparation and chilling time

500 ml/16 fl oz red grape juice

100 g/3 ½ oz caster sugar

3 tablespoons arrowroot, dissolved in 4 tablespoons water

250 ml/8 fl oz red Burgundy wine

Custard Cream (see Box, right)

1 In large saucepan, mix red grape juice, caster sugar and arrowroot dissolved in water. Cook over medium heat, stirring constantly, until mixture begins to thicken and comes to the boil, about 5 minutes.

2 Add wine and cook for 5 minutes longer, stirring constantly.

3 Pour wine mixture into 6 wine glasses or dessert bowls; cover and refrigerate until well chilled, about 2 hours.

4 Meanwhile, prepare Custard Cream and refrigerate it.

TO SERVE
Top each serving with a few spoonfuls of Custard Cream.

CUSTARD CREAM

To make custard cream, in medium non-stick saucepan, combine *400 ml/14 fl oz single cream, 3 tablespoons caster sugar, 1 tablespoon cornflour* and *1 egg yolk.* Cook over medium-low heat, stirring constantly, until mixture coats a spoon well, about 15 minutes (do not allow mixture to boil otherwise it will curdle).

Remove custard from heat. Stir in *½ teaspoon vanilla essence*; pour into bowl. To keep skin from forming on top of custard as it cools, press dampened grease-proof paper directly on to surface.

'CHEAT' BUTTERSCOTCH SQUARES

Makes 15 squares

Allow 5 ½ hours preparation and chilling time

120 g/4 oz slivered almonds

150 g/5 oz plain flour

120 g/4 oz butter or margarine

100 g/3 ½ oz icing sugar, sifted

225 g/8 oz full-fat soft cheese, softened

450 ml/ ³/₄ pint double or whipping cream

2 x 69 g/2.4 oz packets butterscotch-flavour dessert whip

450 ml/ ³/₄ pint milk

Made from a packet mix, whipped cream and soft cheese, these butterscotch squares are unbelievably yummy

Each square is sprinkled with toasted chopped almonds

1 With sharp knife, finely chop two-thirds of slivered almonds; coarsely chop remaining slivered almonds into two or three pieces to use as decoration.

Mixing ingredients for shortbread base with fingertips until crumbly

2 Preheat oven to 180°C/350°F/gas 4.

3 In medium bowl, with fingers, mix flour, butter or margarine, finely chopped almonds and 30 g/1 oz icing sugar until crumbly.

4 With fingers, press mixture firmly into 33 x 23 cm/13 x 9 inch baking dish.

5 Bake shortbread base for 15-20 minutes until golden brown. Cool in dish on wire rack.

6 While shortbread is cooling, in same bowl with spoon, beat soft cheese and 60 g/2 oz icing sugar until light and fluffy.

7 In medium bowl, whip double or whipping cream until stiff peaks form.

8 With rubber spatula, fold one-third of the cream into soft cheese and icing sugar mixture; spread over shortbread base. Reserve remaining whipped cream.

9 In large bowl, with wire whisk, prepare dessert whip according to packet instructions, but prepare both packets together and use only 450 ml/ ³/₄ pint milk in total. Spread dessert whip over soft cheese layer.

10 Fold remaining icing sugar into reserved whipped cream; spread over dessert whip. Refrigerate until firm, about 4 hours.

11 Toast coarsely chopped almonds until golden; cool. Cut dessert into 15 squares, remove from dish, then sprinkle with almonds.

DECORATING WITH SAUCES

There's more to serving a sauce than just spooning it over a pudding. It can be made into an eye-catching decoration that's quick and surprisingly easy to do; all that's needed is a bit of imagination coupled with a steady hand.

Fruit purées, bottled fruit and chocolate syrups, custard, cream and sweet sauces can all be used effectively. The decoration on Black Cherry and White Chocolate Trifle (page 32), for example, is a delicate 'feathering' of raspberry jam on snowy whipped cream. Simple bottled chocolate syrup piped on to custard is all that's needed to decorate Cherries en Gelée (page 50) so attractively.

The designs on these two pages should help to get you started. Each combines two different ingredients of contrasting colour yet compatible flavour. Choose from a wide variety of ingredients – colourful fruit sauces and purées, glistening jams and jellies, rich dark chocolate, golden custard.

Cream Wisps
Spoon raspberry purée on to plate. With small writing tube, pipe dots of double cream in a circle 2.5 cm/1 inch in from edge of purée. Draw tip of knife or skewer through 1 edge of each dot to form the shape of a wisp. Use to frame scoops of ice creams and sorbets.

Chocolate Spider Web
Spoon lightly whipped cream on to plate. With small writing tube, pipe 2 concentric circles of chocolate syrup or melted and cooled chocolate on to cream. With tip of knife or skewer, quickly draw lines in spoke fashion; alternate direction of each spoke, first from centre to edge, then from edge to centre. Use as a decoration for moulded desserts and individual portions of cakes and tarts.

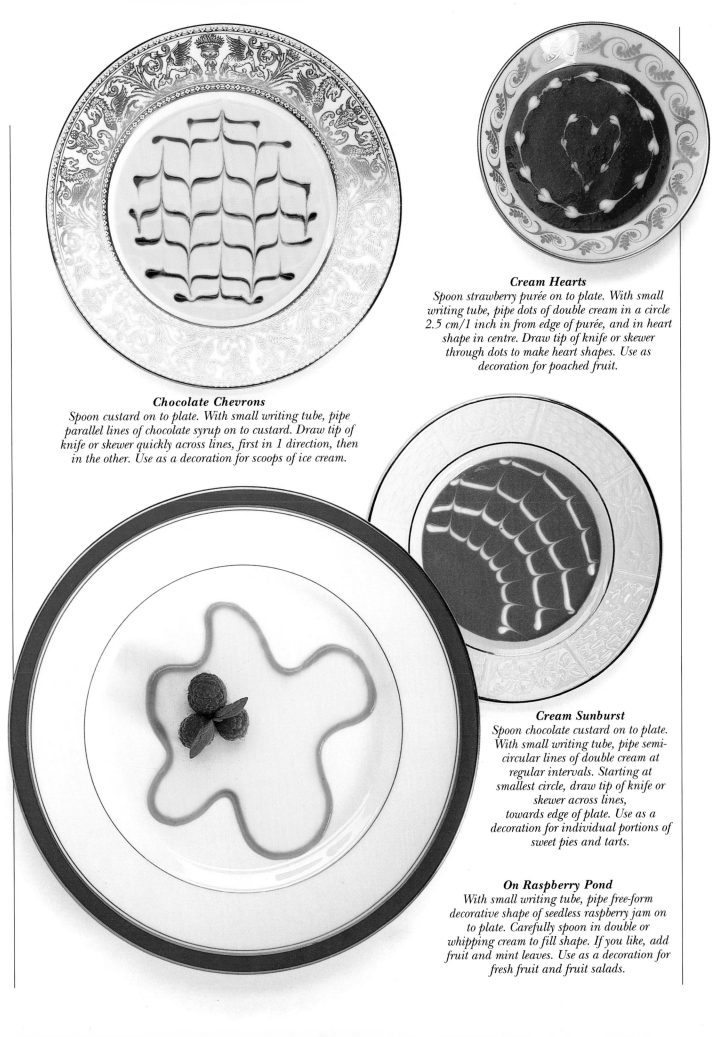

Chocolate Chevrons
Spoon custard on to plate. With small writing tube, pipe parallel lines of chocolate syrup on to custard. Draw tip of knife or skewer quickly across lines, first in 1 direction, then in the other. Use as a decoration for scoops of ice cream.

Cream Hearts
Spoon strawberry purée on to plate. With small writing tube, pipe dots of double cream in a circle 2.5 cm/1 inch in from edge of purée, and in heart shape in centre. Draw tip of knife or skewer through dots to make heart shapes. Use as decoration for poached fruit.

Cream Sunburst
Spoon chocolate custard on to plate. With small writing tube, pipe semi-circular lines of double cream at regular intervals. Starting at smallest circle, draw tip of knife or skewer across lines, towards edge of plate. Use as a decoration for individual portions of sweet pies and tarts.

On Raspberry Pond
With small writing tube, pipe free-form decorative shape of seedless raspberry jam on to plate. Carefully spoon in double or whipping cream to fill shape. If you like, add fruit and mint leaves. Use as a decoration for fresh fruit and fruit salads.

ZUCCOTTO (FLORENTINE CREAM CAKE)

This delicious dessert comes from Italy, where it is traditionally made in a special pumpkin-shaped mould (zuccotto means 'little pumpkin' in Italian). Here *a large glass mixing bowl is used, and it works just as well as a special zuccotto mould, giving an equally good shape, as you can see in the photograph.*

Turned out upside-down, this luscious dinner party dessert looks pumpkin-shaped, which is why the Italians call it 'zuccotto', or 'little pumpkin'

4 Beat melted chocolate into butter and sugar mixture with remaining liqueur until smooth, thick and creamy.

5 In small bowl, whip 300 ml/ ½ pint double cream with 2 teaspoons coffee essence until stiff peaks form. Fold in grated chocolate.

6 Cover cake triangles in bowl with whipped cream mixture.

 8-10 servings
Can be made day before and kept in refrigerator

1 Madeira cake, measuring about 23 x 12.5 cm/ 9 x 5 inches

6 tablespoons almond liqueur

135 g/4 ½ oz plain chocolate

120 g/4 oz icing sugar, sifted

60 g/2 oz butter, softened

450 ml/ ¾ pint double cream

4 teaspoons coffee essence

2 tablespoons slivered almonds, chopped

30 g/1 oz caster sugar

1 Line medium-sized bowl with cling film. Cut Madeira cake into 1 cm/ ½ inch thick slices; cut each slice diagonally in half to make 2 triangles.

2 Sprinkle 3 tablespoons almond liqueur on triangles of cake. Line bowl with triangles; reserve remaining triangles.

3 Break 90 g/3 oz chocolate into pieces and melt in bowl over pan of gently simmering water. Coarsely grate remaining chocolate. In bowl, beat icing sugar and softened butter until creamy.

Covering cake in bowl with whipped cream mixture

7 Spoon chocolate and almond liqueur mixture into centre of dessert and smooth top.

8 Neatly cover top of dessert with remaining cake triangles.

9 Cover bowl and refrigerate for at least 4 hours.

10 Meanwhile, in small saucepan over medium heat, cook chopped slivered almonds until golden, stirring frequently; cool.

11 In small bowl, whip remaining double cream with caster sugar and remaining 2 teaspoons coffee essence until soft peaks form.

12 Turn dessert out on to chilled platter; discard cling film. Cover dessert with whipped cream; sprinkle toasted chopped almonds on top.

DECORATIVE FINISHES FOR ZUCCOTTO

You can decorate the Zuccotto very simply, with toasted chopped almonds as in the main photograph (page 26), or you can sift cocoa powder or icing sugar over the top for an equally attractive finish. Another more decorative idea, which echoes the almond and coffee flavours of the Zuccotto, is this Daisy Design, and it only takes a few extra minutes to do.

Daisy Design
A simple daisy made from blanched or toasted almonds and chocolate 'coffee beans' is quick and effective to make: gently press 'coffee bean' into whipped cream icing for centre of daisy, then press slivered almonds round sweet for petals. If you like, make 1 large daisy centred on top of Zuccotto, or several small daisies placed round sides.

Toasted slivered almond

Slivered blanched almond

Chocolate 'coffee bean'

TO SERVE
Cut Zuccotto into slices and arrange on dessert plates to reveal different layers inside.

STRAWBERRY ORANGE CHARLOTTE

8 servings

Can be made day before and kept in refrigerator

2 tablespoons powdered gelatine

175 ml/6 fl oz orange juice

4 egg yolks

350 ml/12 fl oz milk

1 x 400 g/14 oz can sweetened condensed milk

225 g/8 oz frozen strawberries

60 g/2 oz caster sugar

4 tablespoons strawberry jam

4 tablespoons orange liqueur

25 g/³/4 oz cornflour

2 x 100 g/3 ¹/2 oz packets sponge fingers (boudoir biscuits)

450 ml/³/4 pint double or whipping cream

1 tablespoon icing sugar

Strawberries to decorate

1 In non-stick saucepan, sprinkle gelatine over orange juice; leave to stand for 5 minutes. Cook over medium heat until gelatine dissolves, stirring often.

2 In medium bowl, with wire whisk, beat egg yolks, milk and condensed milk until blended. Beat egg yolk mixture gradually into gelatine mixture. Cook over medium-low heat, stirring constantly, until mixture thickens and coats a spoon well, about 15 minutes (do not boil or it will curdle).

3 Pour custard mixture into large bowl; cover and refrigerate until mixture mounds slightly when dropped from a spoon, about 1 ¹/2 hours, stirring occasionally.

4 Meanwhile, sprinkle strawberries with caster sugar; thaw. In food processor or blender, blend strawberries and their juice with jam until smooth.

5 Pour mixture into medium saucepan; stir in liqueur, cornflour and 4 tablespoons water. Cook over medium-high heat, stirring constantly, until mixture boils and becomes thick; boil for 1 minute. Remove from heat.

6 Line bottom and sides of 23 cm/9 inch springform cake tin with sponge fingers.

7 If necessary, trim sponge fingers to fit tin so they will line bottom and stand upright round sides. Brush sponge fingers on bottom of tin with 4 tablespoons strawberry mixture (see Box, below). Cover tin tightly; set aside. Pour remaining strawberry mixture into bowl; allow to cool, stirring mixture occasionally.

8 In small bowl, whip 350 ml/12 fl oz double or whipping cream until stiff peaks form. With rubber spatula or wire whisk, fold whipped cream into custard mixture.

9 Spoon half of the custard mixture over sponge fingers in bottom of springform tin. Spoon 150 ml/ ¹/4 pint of strawberry mixture over custard layer. Add remaining custard mixture (see Box, below). Drop heaping spoonfuls of remaining strawberry mixture on top of custard. Using palette knife, swirl mixtures together to create a marbled design (see Box, below). Refrigerate until firm, at least 4 hours or overnight.

10 When ready to serve, carefully remove side of springform tin from charlotte; place charlotte on cake plate or stand. In small bowl, whip remaining double or whipping cream with sifted icing sugar until stiff peaks form. Spoon into piping bag with medium star tube; pipe in pretty design round top edge of charlotte. Cut strawberries in half and use to decorate charlotte attractively.

MAKING MARBLED DESIGN

Brushing sponge fingers on bottom of tin: evenly spread 4 tablespoons strawberry mixture over sponge fingers.

Adding custard mixture: over second layer of strawberry mixture, spoon remaining custard mixture.

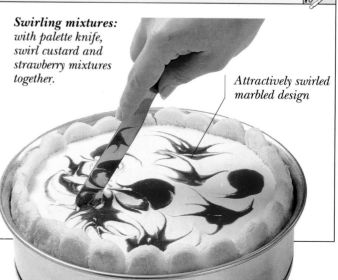

Swirling mixtures: with palette knife, swirl custard and strawberry mixtures together.

Attractively swirled marbled design

Strawberry Orange Charlotte looks very pretty with a satin ribbon tied round its middle

TIRAMISÙ

🥄 10 servings

🕐 Can be made day
before and kept in
refrigerator

*450 g/1 lb mascarpone
cheese (see Box, below
right)*

*75 g/2 ¹/₂ oz icing sugar,
sifted*

*125 ml/4 fl oz coffee
liqueur*

*90 g/3 oz plain chocolate,
grated*

*450 ml/ ³/₄ pint double or
whipping cream*

2 teaspoons coffee essence

*18 sponge fingers (boudoir
biscuits)*

1 In large bowl, with
wire whisk or fork,
beat mascarpone cheese,
60 g/2 oz icing sugar,
3 tablespoons coffee
liqueur and two-thirds of
grated chocolate. (Set
aside remaining chocolate
for top of dessert.)

*Large rosettes of whipped
cream look good piped round
edge of dish and sprinkled
with grated chocolate*

2 In small bowl, whip
300 ml/¹/₂ pint double
or whipping cream until
stiff peaks form. With
rubber spatula or wire
whisk, fold cream into
cheese mixture.

3 In small bowl, stir
coffee essence,
remaining coffee liqueur
and *2 tablespoons water.*

4 Place 4 sponge
fingers in bottom of
large glass bowl; brush
with 2 tablespoons of
coffee essence mixture.
Spoon one-third of cheese
mixture over sponge
fingers. Repeat with
sponge fingers, coffee
essence mixture and
cheese mixture to make
2 more layers. Top with
remaining sponge fingers,
gently pressing them into
cheese mixture. Brush
sponge fingers with
remaining coffee essence
mixture. Sprinkle remain-
ing grated chocolate over
dessert, reserving 1 tablespoon for decoration.

5 In small bowl, whip
remaining cream with
remaining icing sugar
until stiff peaks form.

*Sweetened mascarpone
cheese, cream and
coffee liqueur are
layered with coffee-
soaked sponge fingers
in this heady Italian
dessert*

6 Spoon whipped cream
into piping bag with
large star tube. Pipe large
rosettes on top of dessert.

7 Sprinkle reserved
grated chocolate over
whipped cream rosettes.
Leave dessert in refrigerator until chilled and
flavours are blended (this
will take at least 4 hours).

TO SERVE
*Serve Tiramisù well chilled
in a glass serving bowl so
that its different layers
can be seen.*

MASCARPONE CHEESE

Mascarpone, a fresh, double-cream cheese, is one of
the great Italian cheeses available in cheese shops,
delicatessens and many supermarkets.
It is buttery-smooth in texture and slightly nutty or
tangy in flavour. As well as being used in recipes, it is
superb with fresh seasonal fruit or fruit purées.

Mascarpone Cheese Substitute

If mascarpone cheese is
not available when
making Tiramisù, substi-
tute *450 g/1 lb full-fat soft
cheese, softened;* in step 1,
in large bowl, with electric
mixer or hand whisk, beat
soft cheese and *3 table-*
spoons milk until mixture
is smooth and fluffy.
Increase amount of icing
sugar for cheese mixture
to 80 g/2 ³/₄ oz; beat in
with coffee liqueur, then
stir in grated chocolate
until evenly blended.

RASPBERRY ORANGE TRIFLE

 8-10 servings

Can be made day before and kept in refrigerator

1 x 300 g/10 oz Madeira cake

2 tablespoons orange liqueur

2 tablespoons orange juice

450 ml/³/4 pint double cream

225 g/8 oz fresh or frozen (thawed and drained) raspberries

350 g/12 oz seedless raspberry jam

2 x 400 g/400 ml cans Devon custard

2 teaspoons orange-flower water

1 large orange

1 tablespoon powdered gelatine

60 g/2 oz plain chocolate, broken into pieces

Raspberries and lemon leaves to decorate

1 Cut cake horizontally into 3 layers; brush cut sides with liqueur mixed with orange juice.

2 Whip two-thirds of cream; fold in raspberries.

3 Spread bottom layer of Madeira cake with 1-2 tablespoons raspberry jam; top with middle layer. Spread 3 tablespoons jam over middle layer.

4 Replace top of Madeira cake. Slice layered cake crossways into 12 slices.

5 In large bowl, mix custard and orange-flower water. Grate zest from orange and add to custard mixture; reserve orange for decoration.

6 In small bowl, sprinkle gelatine over *5 tablespoons water*; leave to stand for 5 minutes to soften gelatine. Stand bowl in pan of gently simmering water and heat gently until gelatine completely dissolves. Cool slightly, then fold into custard mixture.

7 In small bowl over pan of gently simmering water, heat chocolate, stirring frequently, until melted and smooth; remove from heat.

8 Into large glass bowl, pour one-third of the custard. Drizzle with half of the raspberry jam, then pour over another third of the custard. Drizzle with half of the melted chocolate.

9 Carefully arrange some of the layered Madeira cake slices round side of bowl.

10 Cut remaining Madeira cake slices into chunks and layer in bowl; drizzle with remaining chocolate, then spoon raspberry and cream mixture over top.

11 Pour remaining custard mixture over to cover cake. Spoon remaining raspberry jam over to cover custard.

12 Cover bowl and refrigerate until well chilled, about 4 hours.

13 Whip remaining cream until stiff peaks form; use to pipe swirls on top of trifle. With knife, remove any remaining zest and white membrane from orange and cut out segments. Decorate trifle with orange segments, raspberries and lemon leaves.

BLACK CHERRY AND WHITE CHOCOLATE TRIFLE

Give your dinner table a festive look when you serve this stunning trifle for dessert. No-one will be able to resist its luscious layers of fruit, custard, cream and sponge.

Made ahead of time and kept in the refrigerator, its delicious flavour improves, so it's the perfect dessert for easy yet luxurious entertaining.

🍴 **8 servings**
🕐 **Can be made day before and kept in refrigerator**

White Chocolate Custard (see Box, page 33)

350 g/12 oz trifle sponges

1 x 397 g/14 oz can black cherry fruit filling for pies, flans and desserts

5 tablespoons kirsch

450 ml/³/4 pint double or whipping cream

30 g/1 oz icing sugar, sifted

About 2 tablespoons seedless raspberry jam

Chopped pistachio nuts to decorate

1 Prepare White Chocolate Custard; refrigerate until cool, about 1 hour.

2 Cut trifle sponges into 2 cm/³/4 inch chunks. In small bowl, stir black cherry fruit filling and kirsch until evenly combined.

3 In large glass serving bowl, place half of the trifle sponge chunks.

4 Spoon half of the cherry fruit filling mixture over sponge.

5 Top fruit filling mixture with half of the White Chocolate Custard. Repeat layering with sponge, fruit filling mixture and custard. Cover and refrigerate for at least 4 hours.

6 In small bowl, whip double or whipping cream with icing sugar until stiff peaks form. Reserve about one-third of the whipped cream; spread remaining cream over trifle.

7 Warm raspberry jam in small pan until just melted, then spoon into small piping bag with small writing tube (alternatively use paper piping bag with tip cut to make 3 mm/¹/8 inch hole) and decorate top of trifle (see Box, below).

8 Spoon reserved whipped cream into piping bag with large star tube. Pipe round edge of trifle (see Box, below). Decorate with pistachios.

DECORATING TOP OF TRIFLE

Filling piping bag: *into small piping bag with small writing tube, spoon raspberry jam*

Making feather design: *draw tip of knife across lines at 1 cm/¹/2 inch intervals, alternating first in one direction and then in the other*

Piping parallel lines: *on whipped cream on trifle, pipe raspberry jam in parallel lines, about 1 cm/¹/2 inch apart*

Piping cream: *using piping bag with large star tube, pipe reserved whipped cream decoratively round edge of trifle*

WHITE CHOCOLATE CUSTARD

In large non-stick saucepan, combine *100 g/3 ¹/₂ oz caster sugar* and *30 g/1 oz cornflour*; slowly stir in *1 litre/1 ³/₄ pints milk* until smooth. Cook over medium heat, stirring constantly, until mixture boils and thickens; boil for 1 minute. Remove saucepan from heat. In cup, with fork, beat *4 egg yolks*; stir in about 150 ml/ ¹/₄ pint hot milk mixture. Slowly pour egg mixture back into milk mixture, stirring rapidly to prevent lumping; cook over medium-low heat, stirring constantly, until mixture thickens and coats a spoon well. Remove saucepan from heat. Stir in *175 g/6 oz white chocolate, broken into pieces*, until chocolate melts and mixture is smooth. In order to prevent skin from forming as custard cools, press dampened greaseproof paper directly on to surface of hot custard.

Piped and feathered raspberry jam looks most effective on top of snowy white whipped cream

With its festive colours, this pretty trifle would make a fitting finale for a Christmas meal

BUTTERMILK BAVARIAN WITH PEACH SAUCE

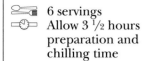
6 servings

Allow 3 ½ hours preparation and chilling time

750 ml/1 ¼ pints buttermilk

75 g/2 ½ oz caster sugar

2 tablespoons powdered gelatine

3 tablespoons lemon juice

1 teaspoon grated lemon zest

150 ml/ ¼ pint double or whipping cream

1 x 822 g/1 lb 13 oz can peach slices in syrup

2 teaspoons cornflour

Shredded lemon zest to decorate

1 In non-stick saucepan, stir 350 ml/12 fl oz buttermilk with sugar until blended. Evenly sprinkle gelatine over buttermilk mixture; leave to stand for 5 minutes to soften gelatine slightly.

If you use a deep fluted mould to set the Bavarian in, it will look extra good when it is turned out for serving

2 Cook over medium heat, stirring frequently, until gelatine dissolves completely. Remove saucepan from heat. Into buttermilk mixture, stir lemon juice, lemon zest and remaining buttermilk.

3 Cover and chill until buttermilk and lemon mixture mounds slightly when dropped from a spoon, about 45 minutes, stirring occasionally.

4 In small bowl, whip double or whipping cream until stiff peaks form.

5 In large bowl, with electric mixer on medium speed, beat chilled buttermilk and lemon mixture until foamy, about 30 seconds.

The sprinkling of shredded lemon zest on top of the Bavarian echoes the lemon flavour in the dessert itself

6 Add whipped cream to buttermilk and lemon mixture; beat until mixture is smooth and creamy, about 30 seconds.

7 Pour mixture into 1.5 litre/2 ½ pint mould; cover and refrigerate until dessert is firm, about 2 hours.

8 Meanwhile, prepare peach sauce: into small saucepan, drain syrup from peaches; set peaches aside. Into peach syrup, stir cornflour; cook over medium heat until mixture thickens and boils, stirring constantly; boil for 1 minute. Gently stir in peaches. Cover sauce and refrigerate.

TO SERVE
Turn Bavarian out on to chilled platter. Arrange peaches on top and round bottom. Spoon sauce over; decorate with shredded lemon zest.

FRUIT FOOLS

4 servings (each flavour)
Allow about 20 minutes preparation for each flavour

PEACH

3 medium-sized ripe peaches

30 g/1 oz caster sugar

300 ml/ 1/2 pint double or whipping cream

1/8 teaspoon almond essence

Mint leaves to decorate

1 Peel, halve and stone peaches. Reserve 1 peach half for decoration. Cut remaining peaches into chunks.

2 In food processor or blender at medium speed, blend peach chunks and sugar together until smooth.

3 In small bowl, whip double or whipping cream together with almond essence until stiff peaks form.

4 With rubber spatula or wire whisk, fold almond-flavoured whipped cream into peach purée.

TO SERVE
Spoon mixture into parfait glasses or dessert dishes; decorate with reserved fruits and mint leaves.

RASPBERRY

225 g/8 oz frozen raspberries

60 g/2 oz caster sugar

300 ml/ 1/2 pint double or whipping cream

1/8 teaspoon almond essence

Raspberries and mint leaves to decorate

1 Sprinkle raspberries with sugar; set aside to thaw. Over large bowl, with back of spoon, press and scrape thawed raspberries with their juice firmly against medium-mesh sieve to purée; discard pips left in sieve.

2 In small bowl, whip double or whipping cream together with almond essence until stiff peaks form.

3 With rubber spatula or wire whisk, fold almond-flavoured whipped cream into raspberry purée.

Raspberry Fool

Peach Fool

KIWI FRUIT

3 large kiwi fruit

30 g/1 oz caster sugar

300 ml/ 1/2 pint double or whipping cream

1/8 teaspoon vanilla essence

Mint leaves to decorate

1 Peel kiwi fruit. Cut 1 kiwi fruit crossways in half. Reserve 1 half for decoration. Cut remaining kiwi fruit into chunks.

2 In food processor or blender at medium speed, blend kiwi fruit chunks and sugar together until smooth.

3 In small bowl, whip double or whipping cream together with vanilla essence until stiff peaks form.

4 With rubber spatula or wire whisk, fold vanilla-flavoured whipped cream into kiwi fruit purée.

Kiwi Fruit Fool

CHOCOLATE BOX WITH BERRIES AND CREAM

This spectacular, luscious-looking dessert is simple to make when you follow the easy step-by-step directions below, yet your guests cannot fail to be impressed with your apparently expert skills. And the striking *combination of rich dark chocolate with the lightness of the fresh strawberries and cream gives an opulent appearance which makes this dessert the perfect choice for any special occasion or celebration.*

6 servings

Can be made day before (up to end of step 6) and kept in refrigerator

175 g/6 oz plain chocolate flavour cake covering, broken into pieces

30 g/1 oz cocoa powder

175 g/6 oz full-fat soft cheese, softened

60 g/2 oz butter, softened

175 g/6 oz icing sugar, sifted

2 tablespoons milk

450 ml/³/4 pint double or whipping cream

700 g/1 ½ lb strawberries

Mint leaves to decorate

1 Turn 23 cm/9 inch square baking tin upside down; mould foil over outside of tin to make a smooth box shape. Turn right way up and remove tin; place foil box inside tin and press out any wrinkles so chocolate box will come away from foil smoothly.

2 In small bowl over pan of gently simmering water, heat pieces of plain chocolate cake covering, stirring frequently, until melted and smooth.

3 Pour melted chocolate into foil-lined tin and swirl round sides and bottom, keeping edges as even as possible (see Box, below). Refrigerate for 1 minute, then swirl chocolate round inside of tin a second time, to reinforce sides of chocolate box. Refrigerate until firm, about 30 minutes.

4 Meanwhile, prepare filling: dissolve cocoa powder in *2-3 tablespoons boiling water*. In large bowl, with electric mixer, beat soft cheese and butter until smooth (do not use margarine or filling will be too soft to cut). Add icing sugar, cocoa and milk; beat until light and fluffy.

5 In small bowl, whip 350 ml/12 fl oz double or whipping cream until stiff peaks form. With rubber spatula or wire whisk, fold whipped cream into soft cheese mixture.

6 Remove chocolate box in foil from tin (see Box, below), then gently peel foil from sides and base. Place chocolate box on platter. Spread soft cheese filling evenly in chocolate box. Refrigerate until filling is well chilled and firm, about 2 hours.

7 In small bowl, whip remaining double or whipping cream until stiff peaks form. Spoon into piping bag fitted with large star tube.

8 Pipe whipped cream in 2.5 cm/1 inch wide border on filling inside chocolate box. Cut larger strawberries in half and arrange over entire top of soft cheese filling. Decorate top of dessert with mint leaves. Serve remaining strawberries with dessert.

MAKING CHOCOLATE BOX

Pouring chocolate: *slowly pour warm melted chocolate into foil-lined baking tin*

Swirling chocolate: *gently tilt tin from side to side so chocolate swirls round sides and bottom*

Removing chocolate box: *carefully lift foil to remove chocolate box from tin*

The combination of strawberries with long stalks and fresh mint leaves makes this sensational dessert look colourful and stunning

MERINGUES

Light and delicate, crisp and sweet, meringue serves as the case for a classic Pavlova, makes layers for gâteaux such as dacquoise, and becomes tiny shells to hold fillings of cream, fruit and frozen mixtures. Meringue can also be shaped into mushrooms, to make stunning petits fours, while small meringues, spooned or piped into dollops like whipped cream, can top puddings or decorate cakes and gâteaux – bake them as for Miniature Meringue Shells (page 40).

PAVLOVA

 8 servings

Can be made day before (up to end of step 4) and kept in cool place

3 egg whites

175 g/6 oz caster sugar

1 teaspoon vinegar

1 teaspoon cornflour

5 kiwi fruit

300 ml/ ½ pint double or whipping cream

1 Place a sheet of non-stick baking parchment on a baking sheet and mark a 20 cm/8 inch circle on it, using plate or cake tin as guide.

2 Preheat oven to 150°C/300°F/gas 2. In large bowl, with electric mixer on full speed, beat egg whites until soft peaks form. Gradually sprinkle in sugar, 1 tablespoon at a time, beating well after each addition. Blend vinegar with cornflour and whisk into egg whites with last spoonful of sugar.

3 Spread meringue on circle on baking parchment, building sides up higher than centre. Put in centre of oven, reduce heat to 140°C/275°F/gas 1 and bake for 1 hour or until pale cream in colour.

4 Turn oven off and leave Pavlova to cool completely in oven. When cool, carefully remove from baking sheet and place on serving plate.

5 With sharp knife, peel off skin and thinly slice kiwi fruit.

6 In small bowl, whip double or whipping cream until stiff peaks form.

TO SERVE
Spoon two-thirds of cream into meringue; reserve few kiwi fruit slices; arrange remainder on cream. Top with remaining cream and reserved kiwi fruit.

Thinly sliced kiwi fruit

Softly whipped cream

Mouthwatering 'marshmallow' meringue

DATE AND WALNUT DACQUOISE

8 servings

Can be made day before and kept in refrigerator

120 g/4 oz walnut pieces

150 g/5 oz stoned dates

5 egg whites

225 g/8 oz caster sugar

25 g/ ³/₄ oz cocoa powder

Mocha Butter Cream (see Box, above right)

Icing sugar for sprinkling

1 Set aside a few walnut pieces and a few dates to use for decoration later. Coarsely chop remaining walnuts and cut remaining dates into 1 cm/¹/₂ inch pieces.

2 In large frying pan over medium heat, toast chopped walnuts until golden brown, stirring occasionally; remove pan from heat.

3 Line 2 baking sheets with non-stick baking parchment or foil. Using 23 cm/9 inch round plate or cake tin as guide, mark 1 circle on baking parchment on each baking sheet; set aside.

4 In large bowl, with electric mixer on full speed, beat egg whites until soft peaks form. Gradually sprinkle in caster sugar, 1 tablespoon at a time, beating well after each addition until sugar dissolves completely and egg whites stand in stiff, glossy peaks.

Meringue layers made with chopped dates, walnuts and cocoa are sandwiched together with a rich mocha-flavoured butter cream

5 Preheat oven to 180°C/350°F/gas 4. In small bowl, with spoon, mix chopped dates with about 4 tablespoons meringue mixture to separate pieces. With rubber spatula, gently fold cocoa, date mixture and toasted chopped walnuts into remaining meringue mixture.

6 Inside each circle on baking parchment, spoon half of the meringue mixture; with palette knife, evenly spread meringue to cover entire circle. Place baking sheets with meringue on 2 oven racks; bake for 15 minutes. Switch baking sheets between racks so meringue browns evenly; bake for 15 minutes longer or until meringue layers are crisp on the outside, but still soft and chewy on the inside.

MOCHA BUTTER CREAM

In large bowl, with electric mixer, beat *450 g/1 lb icing sugar, sifted, 90 g/3 oz butter, softened, 45 g/1 ¹/₂ oz cocoa powder* and *5 tablespoons hot black coffee* until blended. Beat until butter cream has an easy spreading consistency, adding more coffee if necessary.

7 Cool meringues on baking sheets on wire racks for 10 minutes. With palette knife, carefully loosen meringues from baking sheets and transfer them to wire racks to cool completely. (If not assembling dessert immediately, meringue layers can be stored, covered, for 1 day.)

8 When meringues are cool, prepare Mocha Butter Cream.

Walnut and date topping – a clue to what is inside this luscious meringue gâteau

9 To assemble cake: place 1 meringue layer, flat side up, on cake plate. Cover evenly with Mocha Butter Cream; spread to 1 cm/ ¹/₂ inch of edge. Top with second meringue layer, flat side down; press down gently. Cover; refrigerate until filling is firm.

TO SERVE
Sift icing sugar over dacquoise; decorate with reserved walnuts and dates. While firm, cut into wedges, then leave to soften for 5 minutes.

MERINGUE SHAPES

MERINGUE SHELLS

 6 shells

Can be made day before and kept in refrigerator

3 egg whites

175 g/6 oz caster sugar

1 Preheat oven to 140°C/275°F/gas 1.

2 Line large baking sheet with non-stick baking parchment or foil.

3 In large bowl, with electric mixer on full speed, beat egg whites until soft peaks form.

4 Add sugar to egg whites 1 tablespoon at a time, beating well after each addition until egg whites stand in stiff, glossy peaks.

5 Spoon meringue into large piping bag fitted with medium star tube. Pipe meringue into six 10 cm/4 inch rounds, about 2.5 cm/1 inch apart, on lined baking sheet.

6 Pipe remaining meringue in decorative star border round edge of each meringue round.

7 Bake meringues for 45 minutes. Turn oven off; leave meringues in oven for 45 minutes longer to dry completely.

8 Cool meringues on baking sheet on wire rack for 10 minutes. With palette knife, carefully loosen and remove meringues from baking sheet to wire rack and leave to cool completely.

9 If not using meringues immediately, store in tightly covered container.

MINIATURE MERINGUE SHELLS

Prepare meringue as for Meringue Shells (above), up to end of step 4. With medium writing tube, pipe into thirty 4 cm/1¹/₂ inch rounds on baking sheet lined with non-stick baking parchment. With teaspoon, shape into nests. Bake in oven for 30 minutes. Turn oven off; leave in oven for 30 minutes longer. Cool as above in step 8. Yield: 30 miniature shells.

MERINGUE MUSHROOMS

1 Preheat oven to 95°C/200°F/gas ¹/₄. Line large baking sheet with non-stick baking parchment or foil. Prepare meringue as in Meringue Shells (left).

2 With large writing tube, pipe meringue on to baking sheet in 24 mounds, 4 cm/1 ¹/₂ inches in diameter, to resemble mushroom caps.

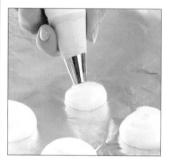

3 Pipe remaining meringue upright on to baking sheet in twenty-four 3 cm/1¹/₄ inch lengths, to resemble stalks.

4 Bake for 1³/₄ hours. Turn oven off; leave meringues in oven for 30 minutes longer. Cool completely on baking sheet on wire rack.

5 Break *60 g/2 oz plain chocolate* into pieces, melt in small bowl over saucepan of gently simmering water, stirring frequently; cool slightly.

6 With tip of small knife, cut small hole in centre of underside of mushroom cap. Place a little melted chocolate in hole; spread underside of cap with chocolate.

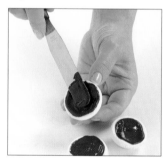

7 Carefully insert pointed end of stalk into chocolate-filled hole in centre of underside of mushroom cap.

8 Repeat with remaining caps and stalks. Leave chocolate to dry and set, about 1 hour. Store in tightly covered container. Before serving, sift *cocoa powder* lightly over tops. Yield: 24 mushrooms.

Meringue Shells filled with ice cream or whipped cream, topped with a variety of different coloured fresh fruits, make glorious table centrepieces

Miniature Meringue Shells and Meringue Mushrooms make mouthwatering bite-sized petits fours

STRAWBERRY AND ALMOND DACQUOISE

🍴 8 servings

⏰ Can be made day before (up to end of step 12) and kept in refrigerator

---

60 g/2 oz slivered almonds

6 egg whites

225 g/8 oz caster sugar

600 g/1 ¼ lb strawberries

Chocolate Butter Cream (see Box, below)

450 ml/ ³/₄ pint double or whipping cream

---

1 In frying pan over medium heat, toast almonds until golden, stirring frequently; cool. In food processor or blender, blend almonds until finely ground; set aside.

2 Line 2 large baking sheets with non-stick baking parchment or foil. Using 20 cm/8 inch round plate or cake tin as guide, mark 2 circles on each lined baking sheet.

3 Preheat oven to 140°C/275°F/gas 1. In large bowl, with electric mixer on full speed, beat egg whites until soft peaks form. Gradually sprinkle in sugar, 1 tablespoon at a time, beating well after each addition until whites stand in stiff, glossy peaks.

4 Into meringue mixture, with wire whisk or rubber spatula, carefully fold ground toasted almonds.

5 Spoon one-quarter of mixture inside each circle on baking parchment or foil; with palette knife, evenly spread meringue to cover entire circle.

6 Place baking sheets with meringue on 2 oven racks; bake for 30 minutes. Switch baking sheets between racks so meringue browns evenly; bake for 30 minutes longer or until golden.

7 Cool meringues on baking sheets on wire racks for 10 minutes. With fish slice, loosen meringues from baking sheets and transfer them to wire racks; cool completely.

8 Hull and thinly slice 150 g/5 oz strawberries. Prepare Chocolate Butter Cream.

9 Place 1 meringue layer on serving plate; spread with one-third of butter cream; top with one-third of sliced strawberries. Make 2 more layers and top with last meringue layer (see Box, right).

10 In medium bowl, whip double or whipping cream until stiff peaks form. Spoon about one-third of whipped cream into piping bag with large star tube; set aside.

11 Spread remaining whipped cream on top and side of gâteau. With cream in piping bag, decorate top edge.

12 Chill dacquoise in refrigerator for 4 hours to soften meringue layers slightly so that they are easier to cut.

13 Cut 16 slices from remaining strawberries; press into cream on side of cake.

14 Top cake with remaining strawberries, hulled and cut in half.

CHOCOLATE BUTTER CREAM

In large bowl, with electric mixer, beat 450 g/1 lb icing sugar, sifted, 90 g/3 oz butter, softened, 3 tablespoons milk or single cream, and 45 g/1 ½ oz cocoa powder until smooth. Add more milk, if necessary, until butter cream has an easy spreading consistency.

ASSEMBLING THE DACQUOISE

Spreading top layer of butter cream: with palette knife, evenly spread third layer of butter cream over third meringue layer.

Topping with strawberries: arrange remaining sliced strawberries over Chocolate Butter Cream.

Topping with meringue: place fourth meringue layer on top to complete.

TO SERVE
After dacquoise has been spread with whipped cream, use a 4-pronged fork to make attractive vertical lines all round side; decorate with strawberry slices just before serving.

Pancakes and Crêpes

Pancakes can be folded, rolled or stacked, with or without a filling, to make a different dessert every time you serve them, or they can be enjoyed just as they are, with a simple sprinkling of caster sugar and a squeeze of lemon. One side is always browner than the other, so have the pale side up when you fold or roll the pancakes, so that the browner, more attractive side is visible.

FREEZING PANCAKES

Pancakes can be prepared and frozen up to 2 months ahead. After stacking pancakes, interleaving them with non-stick baking parchment, allow to cool, then wrap stack tightly in foil; label and freeze. Use within 2 months. To thaw, allow to stand, wrapped, at room temperature for about 2 hours.

PANCAKES

8-10 pancakes

120 g/4 oz plain flour

1 egg, beaten

300 ml/ ½ pint milk and water mixed

1 tablespoon salad oil

Oil for frying

1 Put flour in bowl and make a well in centre. Add egg and gradually stir in half of the milk and water mixture. Using a whisk, blend in flour from sides of bowl. Beat well until mixture is smooth. Stir in remaining liquid and oil.

A handy measuring cup gives you an equal amount of batter every time

2 With pastry brush, brush bottom of 17.5 cm/7 inch pancake pan and 25 cm/10 inch frying pan with oil.

3 Over medium heat, heat both pans.

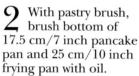

Tilt pan to coat bottom evenly

4 Pour 3-4 tablespoons batter into pancake pan; tilt pan to coat bottom evenly. Cook pancake for 2 minutes or until top is set and underside slightly browned.

5 Using palette knife, work carefully round pancake to loosen it from pan.

6 Invert pancake into hot frying pan. Cook other side for about 30 seconds. While first pancake is cooking, start cooking another pancake in pancake pan.

7 Slide pancake on to non-stick baking parchment. Repeat until all batter is used, stacking pancakes, with non-stick baking parchment between them. Use immediately or wrap in foil and refrigerate or freeze.

CRÊPES SUZETTE

 6 servings

Allow about 1 hour preparation and cooking time

| 12 pancakes (page 44) |
| 1 large orange |
| 60 g/2 oz butter |
| 30 g/1 oz caster sugar |
| 4 tablespoons orange liqueur |

Orange slices and shredded orange zest to decorate

1 Prepare pancakes. (If using frozen pancakes, allow to stand, wrapped, at room temperature for about 2 hours until thawed.)

2 About 30 minutes before serving, grate 1/2 teaspoon zest from orange. Halve orange crossways; squeeze enough juice from orange halves to give 5 tablespoons.

3 Prepare sauce: in large frying pan or chafing dish, over low heat, place grated orange zest, juice, butter and sugar. Heat gently until butter melts.

4 Fold each pancake in half, then fold each one again into quarters.

5 Arrange pancakes in sauce in pan or chafing dish and heat through.

6 In very small saucepan over low heat, gently heat liqueur until warm; remove saucepan from heat. Ignite liqueur with match; pour flaming liqueur over pancakes.

FLAMBÉ

Flambé is the French word for flamed, and generally refers to foods that are bathed in flaming spirits, usually brandy, Cognac or high-proof liqueur. Flaming burns off some of the alcohol, and when the flames die down, the food, now deliciously flavoured, is ready to enjoy. Crêpes Suzette is one of the best-known desserts to use this classic French cooking technique, which is also used in Cherries Jubilee (see recipe below). Here are some tips for success.

• Use a frying pan or chafing dish, preferably a shallow one, to let more oxygen reach the flames and keep them alive longer so they burn off more alcohol.

• Serving dishes should be heatproof; do not use your fine crystal.

• Use wooden matches or long fireplace matches, not book matches, for igniting the spirit.

• Gently warm the spirit before igniting it. Heat it in a very small metal saucepan or ladle, over a low heat – such as a candle – until it is warm but not hot.

• Hold the lighted match over the spirit to ignite the vapours, then slowly pour the flaming spirit over the food. Or, if there isn't much liquid in the frying pan, pour the warm spirit into the pan (don't stir) and light it. Tilt the pan to keep the flames alive as long as possible.

• When the flames die, serve the food at once.

CHERRIES JUBILEE

Just before serving, scoop *vanilla ice cream* into 6 dessert bowls. In large frying pan or in chafing dish at the table, melt *300 g/10 oz redcurrant jelly*; stir until smooth. Add *one 425 g/15 oz can stoned black cherries, drained*; heat until simmering. Pour in *125 ml/4 fl oz brandy*; heat, without stirring, for 1 minute. Light brandy with match. Spoon flaming cherries over ice cream. Makes 6 servings.

TO SERVE
When flames die down, place pancakes on warm dessert plates; decorate with orange slices and shredded orange zest.

SWEET CHEESE BLINIS WITH CHERRY SAUCE

🍴 6 servings

🕐 Allow about 1 hour preparation and cooking time

12 pancakes (page 44)

350 g/12 oz curd cheese

175 g/6 oz full-fat soft cheese, softened

60 g/2 oz caster sugar

$^1/_2$ teaspoon vanilla essence

Cherry Sauce

1 x 425 g/15 oz can stoned black cherries in syrup

60 g/2 oz caster sugar

Here canned black cherries are used to make a simple sauce for pouring over blinis; fresh cherries can be used when they are in season

1 Prepare pancakes. (If using frozen pancakes, allow to stand, wrapped, at room temperature for about 2 hours until thawed.)

2 About 30 minutes before serving, in medium bowl, with electric mixer, beat curd cheese, full-fat soft cheese, sugar and vanilla essence until smooth.

3 Spread about 1 tablespoon of cheese mixture on each pancake.

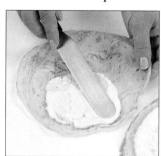

4 Fold one side and then its opposite side slightly towards centre.

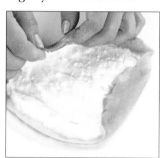

Blinis are rolled up Swiss roll fashion around a sweet cheese filling

5 Roll up pancake, Swiss roll fashion, starting from an unfolded side.

6 Prepare cherry sauce: put cherries and their syrup in a frying pan or skillet; add sugar and bring to the boil, stirring. Simmer for 5 minutes or until syrup has reduced slightly, stirring occasionally.

7 Add filled pancakes to cherry sauce in pan. Over low heat, simmer for 10 minutes to heat through.

TO SERVE
Place 2 pancakes on each plate and spoon over sauce.

PINEAPPLE PANCAKES

🍴 6 servings
⏱ Allow 1 ½ hours
preparation and
cooking time

12 pancakes (page 44)

Vanilla Custard Cream (see Box, right)

1 large pineapple

300 g/10 oz raspberries plus extra for decoration

6 tablespoons icing sugar

6 tablespoons brandy (optional)

1 Prepare pancakes. Prepare Vanilla Custard Cream and refrigerate.

2 About 45 minutes before serving, with sharp knife, cut crown and stalk ends from pineapple; cut off skin. Slice pineapple lengthways in half; remove core from each half. Cut pineapple halves crossways into slices about 5 mm/¼ inch thick; set aside.

3 Over bowl with, back of spoon, press and scrape 300 g/10 oz raspberries firmly against medium-mesh sieve to purée; discard pips left in sieve. Set purée aside.

4 Preheat grill to high. Place 3 pancakes on large baking sheet. On each pancake, spread about 2 tablespoons Vanilla Custard Cream; arrange several slices of pineapple on top of custard cream.

5 Spread about 2 more tablespoons custard cream over pineapple on each pancake; top with another pancake and slice of pineapple. Sift 1 tablespoon icing sugar over each filled pancake.

6 Place baking sheet under hot grill; grill filled pancakes for 6-8 minutes until sugar is caramelized. Remove baking sheet from grill; with fish slice, slide filled pancakes on to large dessert or dinner plates; keep warm. Repeat to make 3 more filled pancakes.

> *TO SERVE*
> *Spoon raspberry purée round warm pancakes. Sprinkle each serving with about 1 tablespoon brandy and, if you like, sprinkle with more icing sugar. Decorate with fresh raspberries.*

VANILLA CUSTARD CREAM

In medium saucepan over medium heat, bring *250 ml/8 fl oz milk* to the boil; remove from heat. In medium bowl, whisk *3 egg yolks*, *½ teaspoon vanilla essence* and *60 g/2 oz caster sugar* until mixture is thick and lemon-coloured; beat in *30 g/1oz plain flour*. Add half of the hot milk, whisking well; pour egg mixture back into remaining milk in pan, stirring constantly. Cook over medium-low heat, stirring, until mixture thickens and boils. Reduce heat to low; cook for 1 minute. Pour into small bowl. To keep skin from forming, press dampened greaseproof paper directly on to surface.

UPSIDE-DOWN APPLE PANCAKE

6 servings

Allow 40 minutes preparation and cooking time

3 large Golden Delicious apples

60 g/2 oz butter

1 teaspoon ground cinnamon

120 g/4 oz caster sugar

50 g/1²/₃ oz plain flour

5 tablespoons milk

¹/₂ teaspoon baking powder

4 eggs, separated

1 Peel and core apples; cut each apple into slices about 3 mm/¹/₈ inch thick.

2 Place large frying pan with all-metal handle over medium-low heat (if handle is not all metal, cover it with heavy-duty foil).

3 Put butter in frying pan (do not use margarine because it separates from sugar during cooking). Melt butter, then stir in cinnamon and 60 g/2 oz sugar; remove pan from heat.

4 In butter mixture in pan, arrange apple slices, overlapping them slightly (see Box, below). Repeat with smaller circle of apple slices in centre.

5 Return pan to low heat; cook for 10 minutes or until apples are tender but still crisp (see Box, below).

6 Meanwhile, preheat oven to 200°C/ 400°F/gas 6. In medium bowl, with fork, beat flour, milk, baking powder and egg yolks until blended; set aside.

If apple slices are arranged carefully in pan before cooking, they will turn out beautifully

7 In large bowl, with electric mixer on full speed, beat egg whites and remaining sugar until soft peaks have formed. With rubber spatula, very gently fold egg whites into egg yolk mixture.

8 Cover apple slices in pan with egg mixture (see Box, below); with rubber spatula, spread mixture evenly.

9 Bake pancake in oven for 10 minutes or until golden brown. Remove pan from oven and carefully invert pancake on to warm platter.

PLACING APPLES AND PANCAKE MIXTURE IN PAN

Arranging apple slices: *round edge of pan, place apple slices in a circle. Do not crowd apple slices — overlap them slightly so they cook evenly.*

Spoon pancake mixture carefully over apple slices or slices will be dislodged and spoil the look of the finished dessert

Testing apple slices: *with prongs of fork, gently pierce apple slices. They are done when easy to pierce.*

Covering apple slices: *with large metal spoon, slowly pour egg mixture over apple slices, taking care not to shift them.*

FRUIT DESSERTS

When eaten by itself at the peak of its freshness and flavour, fruit is truly a 'natural' dessert. But it can also be transformed into a myriad of different and delicious puddings, ranging from simple mixtures such as Gingered Fruit (below) and Festival Fruit Bowl (page 58), to more elaborate preparations like Grape Clusters in Shimmering Lemon Cheese (page 56), and Fresh Fruit Gâteau (page 60). Importing has extended the seasonal availability of many familiar fruits, and given us new and exotic kinds, to add flavour, colour and texture to desserts all year round.

GINGERED FRUIT

🥄 8 servings
⏱ Allow 1 ½ hours preparation and chilling time

2 x 425 g/15 oz cans apricot halves in syrup

1 x 475 g/17 oz can or jar figs in syrup

3 large Red Delicious apples

3 large pears

350 g/12 oz seedless red grapes

350 g/12 oz seedless green grapes

4 tablespoons chopped stem ginger in syrup

2 tablespoons lemon juice

1 Into large bowl, pour apricot halves with their syrup and figs with their syrup.

2 With sharp knife, cut unpeeled apples and pears into bite-sized chunks; discard cores.

3 Add apples and pears to fruit mixture in bowl with grapes, ginger and lemon juice; toss to mix well.

4 Cover and refrigerate for at least 1 hour to blend flavours.

This combination of fresh and canned fruits can be enjoyed all year round

CHERRIES EN GELÉE

🥄 4 servings

🕐 Can be made day before and kept in refrigerator

1 x 425 g/15 oz can stoned black cherries in syrup

1 x 142 g/4 ³/₄ oz packet cherry or blackcurrant jelly

4 tablespoons cream sherry

Snow-White Custard (see Box, right) or 300 ml/ ¹/₂ pint double or whipping cream

1 tablespoon bottled chocolate syrup or sauce

Citrus Curls (page 62) to decorate (optional)

Wisps are made by drawing tip of knife or skewer through piped dots of chocolate syrup on custard or cream

1 Drain syrup from can of cherries into large measuring jug; set cherries aside.

2 Add enough *water* to cherry syrup to make 600 ml/1 pint liquid.

3 Heat liquid in large saucepan; add cubes of jelly and stir until dissolved. Remove pan from heat

4 Stir cream sherry into dissolved jelly and syrup mixture.

For this presentation, each cherry jelly is given individual treatment by being set in a different shaped mould

5 Pour jelly mixture into large bowl; cover and refrigerate until jelly mixture mounds slightly when dropped from a spoon, about 1 hour, stirring occasionally.

6 When jelly mixture is ready, gently stir in cherries. Spoon mixture into 4 individual moulds. Cover and refrigerate until jelly is firm, about 3 hours or overnight.

7 Meanwhile, prepare Snow-White Custard, if using; refrigerate.

SNOW-WHITE CUSTARD

In medium non-stick saucepan, with wire whisk, beat *4 egg yolks* and *60 g/2 oz caster sugar* until evenly blended together. Stir in *450 ml/ ³/₄ pint single cream* and cook over medium-low heat, stirring constantly with wooden spoon, until mixture thickens and coats a spoon well, about 25 minutes (do not boil or mixture will curdle).

Remove saucepan from heat; stir in *¹/₂ teaspoon vanilla essence*. To keep skin from forming as custard cools, press dampened greaseproof paper directly on to surface of hot custard.

8 To serve, turn each jelly out into a large dessert glass or bowl. Spoon custard round jelly (if you are using cream, whip it lightly, then spoon round jelly).

9 With chocolate syrup or sauce in small piping bag with very small writing tube (or paper piping bag with tip cut to make 3 mm/¹/₈ inch hole), make wisps (see Cream Wisps, page 24). If you like, decorate each serving with a Citrus Curl.

Cherries and sherry account for the superb taste of this simple dessert

POACHED PEARS

 12 servings

Allow 4 ½ hours preparation and chilling time

1 x 1 litre/1 ³/4 pint carton cranberry juice drink or diluted blackcurrant cordial

100 g/3 ½ oz caster sugar

1 medium-sized lemon, cut in half

12 medium-sized firm pears

2 tablespoons redcurrant jelly

Mint to decorate

1 In large flameproof casserole, combine fruit juice or cordial, sugar, lemon halves and *450 ml/ ³/4 pint water.*

TO SERVE
Arrange pear halves in deep platter; pour syrup over pears. Decorate with mint leaves.

2 Peel 6 pears, being careful to leave their stalks attached.

3 With sharp knife, cut peeled pears length-ways in half. With tea-spoon, scoop out cores and stringy portions from pear halves.

4 As each pear half is peeled and cored, place it in fruit juice mixture, turning to coat completely to help prevent pears from discolouring.

5 Over high heat, bring pear mixture to the boil. Reduce heat to low; cover and simmer for 10-15 minutes until pears are tender. With slotted spoon, transfer pear halves to large bowl.

6 Repeat same procedure (steps 2 to 5) with remaining 6 pears.

7 After all pears are poached, over high heat, bring fruit juice mixture in casserole to the boil; cook, uncovered, for about 20 minutes or until liquid is reduced to about 350 ml/12 fl oz.

PEARS
William's and Comice are the best varieties of pear for cooking.

If you have a melon baller, you can use it to remove cores from pears easily and without waste, instead of a teaspoon. After scooping out core, run melon baller from core to stalk and blossom end of pear to remove stringy portion.

To prevent peeled or chopped pears from browning if left to stand, sprinkle them with lemon juice.

8 Add redcurrant jelly to hot liquid; stir until dissolved. Pour hot syrup over pear halves in bowl; cool. Cover and refrige-rate until pears are chilled, about 3 hours, turning them occasionally.

Stalks on some pear halves round edge of platter are left on to create interest

Pears have been poached in cranberry juice drink to colour them a delicate rosy pink

PEARS WITH ZABAGLIONE CREAM

  4 servings
Begin about
10 minutes before
serving

2 large pears

125 ml/4 fl oz double or whipping cream

1 tablespoon sweet Marsala

1 teaspoon icing sugar, sifted

Mint to decorate

1 Cut each pear in half lengthways; with teaspoon or melon baller, scoop out core, then run spoon or melon baller from core to stalk and blossom ends of pears to remove stringy portion.

Pears are sliced lengthways, without being cut at stalk end

2 With sharp knife, cut each pear half lengthways into thin slices, almost but not all the way through the stalk end.

3 Place each pear half, cut side down, on dessert plate; spread pear slices open to form fans.

ZABAGLIONE

There are a number of classic dessert recipes using wine and eggs, and Italian Zabaglione is probably the most well known. Its key ingredient, Marsala, is a fortified wine, which means that it contains both wine and brandy, and has a dark, rich flavour similar to sweet, aged sherry.

Traditionally, Zabaglione is made with egg yolks, cooked in a bowl over hot water until thickened, but this method of cooking eggs is no longer recommended. Using double or whipping cream, as in the recipe here, gives a similar delicious taste.

4 In small bowl, whip double or whipping cream with Marsala and sifted icing sugar until soft peaks form.

5 Spoon some zabaglione cream on each plate with pear. Decorate with mint.

POACHED PEACHES IN ROSÉ WINE

6 servings

Can be made day before and kept in refrigerator

---

600 ml/1 pint rosé wine

---

8 lemon balm, geranium or bay leaves, plus extra for decoration

---

About 75 g/2 ½ oz caster sugar

Grated zest of 1 lemon

---

6 large peaches

1 In flameproof casserole into which peaches will fit snugly, mix wine, lemon balm, geranium or bay leaves, sugar, lemon zest and *450 ml/ ³/4 pint water.*

2 Peel peaches (see Box, above right). Add peaches to wine mixture in casserole as soon as they are peeled to prevent discolouring.

PEELING PEACHES

1 Into saucepan of rapidly boiling water, with slotted spoon, dip peaches for about 15 seconds.

2 With slotted spoon, immediately transfer peaches to saucepan or bowl of cold water.

3 Lift peaches out of water; carefully peel off skins with sharp knife.

3 Over high heat, bring peaches and wine mixture to the boil. Reduce heat to low; cover and simmer for 5-10 minutes, shaking pan occasionally.

4 Spoon peaches and wine mixture into large bowl. Cover, then refrigerate for at least 6 hours or overnight. Discard leaves before serving.

Decorate peaches with fresh leaves to echo the flavour of those used in cooking

FRUIT CONTAINERS

Many fruits come 'pre-packaged' in pretty casings which, once freed of their fillings, can be carved and cut for more spectacular servings.

The peel of melons and oranges can be given a scalloped edge, or formed into baskets, with or without a strip over the top for the handle; pineapples can be scooped out, part of their crowns intact, to make attractive 'fruit bowls', filled simply with their own chopped fruit to make easier eating.

Especially eye-catching effects are achieved by using contrasting fruits and shells: red fruits, such as watermelon and raspberries, stand out in green-fleshed melons, while rich green kiwi fruit contrasts well with the amber flesh of papaya in its shell; or for a more delicate effect, fill with mixed pastel-shaded balls of charentais, honeydew and watermelon.

Rock Melon Cup
Cut rock melon crossways in half. Hollow out halves, then fill with balls of charentais, honeydew or Gallia and watermelon. For added colour, sprinkle with a few blueberries, then decorate with a small sprig of mint.

Gallia Bowl
Cut slice off top of Gallia melon; scoop out seeds from centre. Heap centre with watermelon balls and raspberries, allowing them to spill out over top of melon flesh.

Watermelon Basket
Into small round watermelon, make horizontal cut from each end 5 cm/2 inches from top (do not cut through); leave 2.5 cm/1 inch strip in centre. Then make two vertical cuts from top of melon down to horizontal cuts, to create handle. Scoop out melon. If you like, cut scalloped edge round rim of basket. Fill with watermelon, charentais, honeydew or Gallia melon balls, and decorate with sprigs of mint.

Papaya Boat
Slice papaya (pawpaw) lengthways in half. Remove seeds; scoop out flesh and cut into bite-sized chunks. Fill papaya halves with chunks of papaya and honeydew melon. Top with kiwi fruit triangles and decorate with sprig of mint.

Grapefruit Half
Cut grapefruit crossways through centre in zig-zag pattern. Scoop out sections. Fill with clementines in liqueur and raspberries. Decorate with sprig of mint.

Pineapple Boat
Cut pineapple lengthways in half. Cut out core and chunks of flesh. Cut thin slice from underside. Fill shell with kiwi fruit and pineapple; crown with strawberry half.

Filled Fruits
Cut deep 'X' in top of figs, kiwi fruit and strawberries (peel kiwi fruit first). Gently spread fruit apart to make 'petals'; pipe whipped cream into centre of each fruit.

GRAPE CLUSTERS
IN SHIMMERING LEMON CHEESE

🥄 8 servings

🕐 Can be made day before and kept in refrigerator

Mint leaves

2 x 142 g/4³/₄ oz packets lemon jelly

450 g/1 lb full-fat soft cheese

300 ml/¹/₂ pint double cream

Grated zest and juice of 2 large lemons

120 g/4 oz seedless green grapes

350 g/12 oz seedless red grapes

1 Chop enough mint leaves to make 2 teaspoons; set aside.

2 Dissolve 1 packet lemon jelly in *150 ml/ ¹/₄ pint boiling water*. In food processor or blender, work jelly liquid, cheese, cream, lemon zest and lemon juice and chopped mint until smooth. Pour mixture into 20 cm/8 inch springform cake tin; cover and chill until almost set, about 1 hour.

3 Meanwhile, in medium bowl, dissolve remaining packet lemon jelly in *600 ml/1 pint boiling water*. Chill until jelly is cool but not set, about 1 hour.

4 While cheese mixture and jelly are chilling, with sharp knife, carefully cut each green grape and 120 g/4 oz red grapes in half lengthways.

5 With kitchen scissors, cut remaining red grapes into small bunches for decoration; wrap and refrigerate.

6 Make grape clusters on cheese layer in springform tin (see Box, right). Carefully pour enough lemon jelly over grape design just to cover grapes but not so much that they will float.

7 Cover tin and chill in refrigerator until jelly is almost set, about 20 minutes. Leave remaining lemon jelly at room temperature so that it does not set.

8 Pour remaining lemon jelly over grapes (see Box, right). Cover and refrigerate until set, about 3 hours.

9 Turn dessert out of tin (see Box, right).

Layers of cheese and lemon jelly look beautiful topped with clusters of grapes

MOULDING DESSERT

Making grape clusters: arrange green grape halves and red grape halves in 2 clusters on cheese layer in springform tin.

Pouring lemon jelly over grapes: carefully pour remaining lemon jelly over grape design; some grapes may not be submerged in jelly.

Turning out dessert: with palette knife dipped in hot water, gently loosen edge of dessert; remove side of tin.

TO SERVE
*Place dessert on serving
plate; decorate with
reserved grape bunches
and mint leaves.*

FESTIVAL FRUIT BOWL

  8 servings

Can be made day before and kept in refrigerator

---

300 g/10 oz caster sugar

3 tablespoons lemon juice

1 small pineapple

1 small honeydew melon

1 small charentais melon

2 oranges

2 large nectarines or 4 apricots

2 large red plums (optional)

225 g/8 oz seedless green grapes

2 kiwi fruit

---

1 In medium saucepan over medium heat, heat *450 ml/³/₄ pint water* with sugar and lemon juice to boiling point; cook for 15 minutes or until mixture becomes a light syrup. Pour into bowl; cool, then cover and refrigerate until well chilled.

2 Meanwhile, prepare pineapple (see Box, above right).

Festival Fruit Bowl is the perfect summer dessert – you can change the type of fruit according to whatever is freshest and best on the day

3 Cut honeydew and charentais melons into wedges; discard seeds. Cut rind from melon wedges, then cut flesh into bite-sized chunks.

4 With sharp knife, peel oranges, removing all white pith; cut along both sides of each dividing membrane and lift out orange segments from centre.

5 Cut nectarines or apricots and plums (if using) in half and remove stones; slice. Cut grapes in half.

6 In large serving bowl, combine prepared fruit. Pour chilled syrup through sieve over fruit. Cover and refrigerate until well chilled, stirring frequently.

Skin is left on nectarines and plums to provide colour contrast

PREPARING A PINEAPPLE

1 With sharp knife, cut crown and stalk ends from pineapple.

2 Stand pineapple on one cut end; cut off skin in large strips.

3 Cut pineapple from core in large strips; discard core.

4 Cut pineapple strips into bite-sized chunks.

TO SERVE
Peel and slice kiwi fruit. Gently stir kiwi fruit slices into fruit mixture.

SUMMER FRUIT
WITH ALMOND CHANTILLY YOGURT

🍴 8 servings

⏱ Allow about 30 minutes preparation time

Almond Chantilly Yogurt (see Box, right)

4 large kiwi fruit

4 medium-sized plums

2 large peaches

2 medium-sized bananas

1 small charentais melon

120 g/4 oz raspberries

120 g/4 oz blueberries

120 g/4 oz blackberries

Lemon leaves and flaked almonds to decorate

1 Prepare Almond Chantilly Yogurt; spoon into small serving bowl. Cover and chill in refrigerator until ready to serve.

2 About 20 minutes before serving, with sharp knife, peel kiwi fruit; cut each one in half lengthways.

3 Cut each plum and peach in half; discard stones. Peel bananas; cut each in half crossways, then cut each half lengthways into 2 pieces.

4 With sharp knife, cut charentais melon into thin wedges; remove seeds and cut rind from each wedge.

5 Arrange prepared fruit decoratively on large platter. Top with raspberries, blueberries and blackberries.

ALMOND CHANTILLY YOGURT

Whip *300 ml/ ¹/₂ pint double or whipping cream* with *45 g/1 ¹/₂ oz icing sugar, sifted,* and *1 teaspoon almond essence* until stiff peaks form. With rubber spatula or wire whisk, fold in *300 ml/ ¹/₂ pint plain yogurt* until evenly blended.

TO SERVE
Decorate dessert with lemon leaves; decorate Almond Chantilly Yogurt with flaked almonds and serve to spoon over fruit.

FRESH FRUIT GÂTEAU

This spectacular showpiece is an artfully arranged selection of juicy, ripe charentais and honeydew melons, red and blue berries, kiwi fruit and pineapple. It makes a wonderful centrepiece for a summer buffet table, and is ideal for barbecues and other informal events when guests can serve themselves. It can be prepared ahead of time too, as long as it is kept, well wrapped, in the refrigerator until you are ready to serve. The calorie-conscious will find the combination of fruit flavours absolutely delicious when eaten plain, but for those who don't mind throwing caution to the wind, a dollop of Crème Cointreau will make it sweeter.

 8-10 servings
Allow 3 hours preparation and chilling time

1 large charentais melon

1 medium-sized honeydew melon

1 large pineapple

2 large kiwi fruit

350 g/12 oz strawberries

225 g/8 oz blueberries

225 g/8 oz raspberries

Crème Cointreau (see Box, page 61)

Mint sprig to decorate

1 Cut each charentais and honeydew melon lengthways into 4 wedges. With spoon, scoop out seeds. Cut wedges crossways into 2.5 cm/1 inch thick slices; cut rind off each slice. Set aside.

2 Cut crown and skin off pineapple. Cut pineapple lengthways in half; cut crossways into 1 cm/ ½ inch thick slices. Cut out tough core of each slice. Cut about one-quarter of the pineapple slices into bite-sized pieces. Peel kiwi fruit; cut into wedges.

3 On large plate with rim (to catch any fruit juices), arrange half of the nice large honeydew slices round rim. Reserve small honeydew slices.

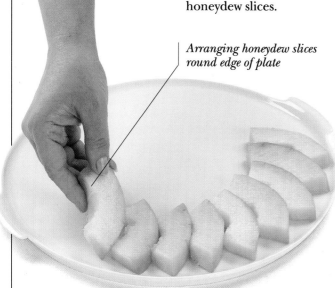

Arranging honeydew slices round edge of plate

ALTERNATIVE FRUIT ARRANGEMENT

Using only four different kinds of fresh fruit, you can create just as eye-catching an arrangement as in the main photograph on page 61. Neat wedges of charentais and honeydew melon can be combined with slices of fresh pineapple, with 'cherry blossoms' providing a pretty finishing touch.

Cherry Blossoms

Fresh mint leaf adds vibrant colour

Cherry is cut lengthways with stalk end left intact to form 'petals'

Four Fruit Gâteau

1 Cut *1 large charentais melon* lengthways into 3 wedges, and cut *1 medium-sized honeydew* lengthways into 4 wedges. With spoon, scoop out seeds. Cut wedges crossways into 2.5 cm/1 inch thick slices, then cut rind off each slice.

2 Cut crown and skin off *1 large pineapple*; reserve crown for decoration. Cut pineapple lengthways in half, then cut crossways into 2.5 cm/1 inch slices. Cut out tough core of each pineapple slice and discard.

3 On large round platter with rim (to catch any fruit juices), arrange large honeydew slices in a ring; fill centre of ring with end pieces; cut pieces to fit, if necessary. Repeat layering with charentais, pineapple and more honeydew slices, filling centre of ring with end fruit pieces as you assemble each layer.

4 Make Cherry Blossoms (page 62) from *450 g/1 lb fresh cherries*; arrange on top of gâteau. Cover tightly and refrigerate for at least 1 hour or until ready to serve.

4 Arrange layers of pineapple slices in centre of plate.

5 Arrange half of the large charentais slices over honeydew slices on rim of plate. Reserve small charentais slices.

6 Repeat with another layer of honeydew and charentais slices. With remaining pineapple and reserved small melon slices, fill in any gaps. Place kiwi fruit wedges on top.

This gâteau isn't a gâteau at all – simply a clever arrangement of fruit in the shape of a cake!

7 Make neat piles of strawberries, blueberries, raspberries and bite-sized pieces of pineapple to cover rest of top of fruit gâteau.

8 Cover gâteau tightly; refrigerate for at least 1 hour or until ready to serve.

9 Meanwhile, prepare Crème Cointreau.

CRÈME COINTREAU
In medium bowl, whip *450 ml/³/₄ pint double or whipping cream* with *60 g/2 oz icing sugar, sifted,* just until soft peaks form. Gradually beat in *4 tablespoons orange liqueur.*

Spoon cream into bowl; cover and refrigerate until ready to serve.

Variegated mint is an unusual decoration for a dessert, but here it looks most effective perched on top of summer fruits

DECORATING WITH FRESH FRUIT

Fruit used for decoration adds little in the way of calories, but much in terms of colour, brightness and a fresh look to a wide range of desserts.

Like all carefully chosen decorations, fruit should be appropriate in size, shape, taste and colour to the food with which it is served.

Choose fruit that is as near perfect as possible, and leave it until the last moment to prepare, to prevent discoloration.

Small strawberries look very attractive left whole, with their stalks and hulls left on, as do cherries with their stalks left on. But cut into fans and blossoms or dipped into sugar, they take on a new dimension. The zest of citrus fruit such as lemons, limes and oranges is readily shaped into curls, julienne and twists, while slices, rounds and chunks of brightly coloured kiwi fruit, warmly shaded nectarine and coolly neutral pineapple can be used to good effect on contrasting bases or combined with berries.

Strawberry Fans
Starting just below hull, thinly slice strawberry lengthways several times, leaving strawberry connected at hull end. Press down gently to fan out slices slightly.

Lemon Cartwheels
With canelle knife, make vertical grooves at regular intervals in peel of whole lemon. With sharp knife, cut fruit crossways into thin slices.

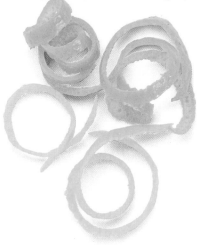

Citrus Curls
Using canelle knife, remove long thin strips of zest from citrus fruit. Coil zest round to create curls. Use curls individually or mix colours together.

Cherry Blossoms
Starting just below stalk end, make 8 cuts lengthways in cherry, leaving cherry connected at stalk end. Press down gently to fan out 'petals' slightly and expose stone. Place cherry on mint leaf.

Lemon Twists
With sharp knife, cut lemon crossways into thin slices. Cut from centre to edge of each slice; twist cut edges in opposite directions.

Frosted Cherries
Wash cherries but do not remove stalks or stones. While still wet, dip bottoms in caster sugar until evenly coated; allow to dry before using.

Nectarine Slices
Cut nectarine (or peach) in half and twist apart; remove stone. Cut each half lengthways into thin slices; sprinkle with lemon juice if not using immediately. Arrange in fan shape; add mint sprig.

FRUIT COMBINATIONS
Eye-catching arrangements of fruit can be used to good effect as decorations on plates and platters when the dessert you are serving is simple. Experiment with different fruits, grouping them together to create dramatic designs and a variety of stunning shapes.

Pineapple and Raspberry Clusters
Cut crown and stalk ends from pineapple. Stand pineapple on one cut end; cut off skin in large strips. Cut pineapple crossways into thin slices and remove core. Cut slice into 4 wedges; arrange as slice. Fill centre with raspberries and mint sprig.

Strawberry Halves
Select firm berries with fresh green hulls and stalks. Cut strawberries lengthways through centres, being careful to leave some of the hull on each half. Arrange cut side up or cut side down, or alternate for a more striking effect.

Honeydew Slices
Cut melon lengthways into wedges. Remove seeds and cut flesh from rind. Cut wedges into thin slices and arrange in fan shape, adding a few redcurrants for contrast.

Kiwi Fruit Slices
With sharp knife, remove fuzzy skin from kiwi fruit, then cut fruit crossways into thin slices. Combine with blueberries for extra effect.

Citrus Julienne
With vegetable peeler, remove zest from citrus fruit in lengthways strips. Lay strips on top of each other; cut into julienne.

SHORTCAKE WITH FRUIT AND CREAM

Whipped cream and strawberries are the usual filling and topping for a traditional American summer shortcake; this deluxe version goes one step further, combining a variety of different coloured fresh fruits with sweetened whipped cream for a more dramatic effect. Of course you don't have to use the fruits suggested here, as long as you are careful to choose ripe, juicy fruits in season and aim for a good contrast of bright colours and interesting shapes and flavours. This fresh, attractive dessert is perfect to serve at an informal gathering with friends, such as at a summer brunch party or al fresco lunch.

 8 servings

Allow 1 hour preparation and cooking time

2 large nectarines

45 g/1 ½ oz caster sugar

30 g/1 oz light soft brown sugar

190 g/6 ½ oz self-raising flour

90 g/3 oz butter

1 teaspoon baking powder

½ beaten egg

85 ml/3 fl oz milk

120 g/4 oz cherries

1 small kiwi fruit

225 g/8 oz blackberries or blueberries

300 ml/ ½ pint double or whipping cream

1 Cut nectarines in half and remove stones; slice. In medium bowl, toss nectarines with 1 tablespoon caster sugar. Cover and refrigerate.

2 Preheat oven to 230°C/450°F/gas 8. Grease 20 cm/8 inch round cake tin.

3 Make crumble topping: in small bowl, with fork, mix brown sugar and 40 g/1 ¼ oz flour. With pastry blender or fingertips, cut or rub 30 g/1 oz butter into flour mixture until consistency of mixture resembles peas. Set aside.

MAKING SHORTCAKE

Spreading mixture: *in greased cake tin, with rubber spatula, evenly spread shortcake mixture.*

Sprinkling topping: *over mixture in tin, evenly sprinkle crumble topping.*

Testing if cooked: *when shortcake is golden, insert cocktail stick in centre; it should come out clean.*

Transferring to rack: *after removing from cake tin, place shortcake, crumble side up, on wire rack to cool.*

Sprinkle crumble topping evenly over shortbread so that it will brown nicely during baking

Handle shortcake gently so crumble topping is not dislodged

4 In large bowl, with fork, mix together baking powder, remaining flour and 1 tablespoon caster sugar.

5 With pastry blender or fingertips, cut or rub remaining butter into flour mixture until consistency of mixture resembles coarse crumbs.

6 In another small bowl, stir beaten egg into milk. Add egg and milk mixture all at once to flour mixture, then stir lightly together with fork until flour mixture is just moistened.

7 Spread shortcake mixture in tin and sprinkle with topping, then bake for 20 minutes or until golden (see Box, page 64). Cover with foil during last 5 minutes of baking if topping is browning too quickly.

8 Carefully remove shortcake from tin; transfer to wire rack (see Box, page 64); cool slightly, about 10 minutes. (Or cool completely to serve later.)

Luscious layers of fresh, juicy fruits, whipped cream and crumbly shortcake are topped with a trio of sweet red cherries

9 Reserve several cherries with stalks for decoration; remove stalks and stones from remaining cherries. Peel kiwi fruit; cut into bite-sized pieces. Gently stir stoned cherries, kiwi fruit and blackberries or blueberries into nectarine mixture.

10 In small bowl, whip double or whipping cream with remaining caster sugar until stiff peaks form.

11 With long serrated knife, carefully split shortcake in half horizontally.

12 Place bottom half of shortcake, cut side up, on dessert plate; top with all but about 60 g/2 oz fruit.

13 Spoon about two-thirds of whipped cream over top of fruit on shortcake.

Spooning whipped cream evenly over fruit so that it spills out over edge when shortcake is placed on top

14 Place top half of shortcake, crumble side up, on cream.

15 Pile reserved fruit in centre of shortcake. Top shortcake with remaining whipped cream and reserved cherries.

WINTER FRUIT COMPOTE

🍴 4 servings
🕐 Allow about
    20 minutes
    preparation time

120 g/4 oz stoned prunes

120 g/4 oz dried apricot halves

125 ml/4 fl oz apple juice or orange juice

2 teaspoons light soft brown sugar

¼ teaspoon ground cinnamon

1 large banana

Whipped Topping (see Box, right)

Dried fruits retain their shape if they are poached gently and not overcooked

1 In medium saucepan over high heat, bring prunes, apricots, apple or orange juice, brown sugar and cinnamon to the boil.

2 Reduce heat to low; cover and simmer for 10 minutes, stirring fruit mixture occasionally.

Stirring banana into dried fruit mixture

3 Meanwhile, peel banana and cut into chunks 2.5 cm/1 inch thick. Prepare Whipped Topping.

4 Remove saucepan from heat. With rubber spatula, gently stir banana chunks into dried fruit mixture.

WHIPPED TOPPING

In small bowl, with electric mixer, beat *4 tablespoons well-chilled evaporated skimmed milk* with *1 tablespoon sifted icing sugar* until stiff peaks form.

Evaporated skimmed milk beats better if partially frozen.

TO SERVE
Spoon warm fruit and Whipped Topping on to 4 dessert plates.

SUMMER FRUIT MÉLANGE

- 6-8 servings
- Allow about 30 minutes preparation time

2 pink grapefruit

175 ml/6 fl oz apple juice

60 g/2 oz caster sugar

$\frac{1}{4}$ teaspoon ground ginger

About 1 kg/2 lb piece watermelon

3-4 large nectarines or peaches

About 450 g/1 lb medium-sized plums

350 g/12 oz strawberries

Fresh mint leaves to decorate

1 Cut grapefruit in half and squeeze out juice.

2 Into large bowl, pour grapefruit juice and apple juice.

3 Add sugar and ginger and stir well to mix.

4 Cut watermelon into bite-sized pieces; discard rind.

5 Cut nectarines or peaches and plums into wedges; discard stones from fruit.

6 Hull strawberries; cut each berry in half lengthways if berries are large.

7 Add fruit to juice mixture in bowl. With rubber spatula, gently toss to mix well.

> **TO SERVE**
> Transfer fruit mélange to large serving bowl; decorate with mint leaves.

CHERRIES GLACÉS

8 servings

Allow 35 minutes preparation, plus freezing time

900 g/2 lb cherries

350 g/12 oz plain chocolate, broken into pieces

300 ml/¹/₂ pint single cream

1 Wash cherries but do not remove stalks or stones; pat cherries dry with kitchen paper.

2 Place cherries in single layer on freezer tray; make sure they do not touch each other.

3 Place cherries in freezer until 15 minutes before serving.

4 Remove cherries from freezer; leave to stand at room temperature to soften slightly. Do not allow cherries to thaw completely.

5 Meanwhile, in heavy medium saucepan over low heat, heat chocolate pieces and single cream, stirring frequently, until chocolate is melted and smooth.

TO SERVE
Arrange cherries in large bowl. Pour chocolate sauce into small bowl. Let each person dip partially frozen cherries into chocolate sauce.

CREAM-FILLED STRAWBERRIES

 6 servings

Allow about 30 minutes preparation time

18 very large strawberries

300 ml/ ¹/₂ pint double cream

3 tablespoons lemon curd (preferably home-made) or lemon cheese

1 Cut stalk ends off strawberries so that strawberries will stand upright when filled. With sharp knife, cut deep 'X' in opposite (pointed) end of each fruit.

2 With fingertips, gently spread each strawberry apart to make 'petals'; set aside.

3 In small bowl, whip double cream until stiff peaks form.

4 Gently fold lemon curd or lemon cheese into whipped cream.

5 Spoon cream mixture into piping bag with large writing tube.

6 Pipe cream mixture into strawberries.

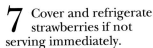

Piping cream mixture into strawberries

7 Cover and refrigerate strawberries if not serving immediately.

ALTERNATIVE FRUIT

When figs are in season, you can fill them with lemon-flavoured whipped cream, in the same way as strawberries.

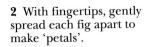
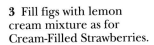

Cream-Filled Figs

1 With sharp knife, cut stalk ends off *12 medium-sized figs*, then cut deep 'X' in top of each fruit.

2 With fingertips, gently spread each fig apart to make 'petals'.

3 Fill figs with lemon cream mixture as for Cream-Filled Strawberries.

Whipped cream is subtly flavoured with lemon curd or lemon cheese and softly piped in swirls into strawberry 'flowers'

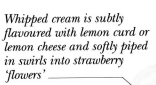

Here the flavours of strawberry and lemon are linked together. For a change, try filling fresh apricots with almond-flavoured cream

PUDDINGS

Of all the different kinds of desserts, puddings are the ones to call 'comfort food'. Look for variety in texture as well as flavour: smooth and custardy, like Hot Lemon Soufflé Puddings, substantial, like Cinnamon Rice Pudding, or sinfully rich, like Magic Chocolate Pudding.

ORANGE 'PUDDING' CUPS

 8 servings
Allow 1 ½ hours preparation and chilling time

| 4 large oranges |
| 300 ml/ ½ pint double cream |
| 175 ml/ 6 fl oz canned custard |
| Orange zest to decorate |

Zig-Zag Cups: *with sharp pointed knife, cut crossways through centre of each orange in sawtooth pattern, so that each orange half has zig-zag edge.*

Personalized Cups: *with canelle knife, carve initials of each guest in orange skin. Carve 2 sets of initials in each orange, then, with sharp knife, cut orange crossways in half.*

Striped Cups: *with canelle knife, cut thin strips from orange skin, working from top to bottom of orange. With sharp knife, cut orange crossways in half.*

1 Prepare orange cups of your choice (see above right). With sharp knife, cut thin slice off base of each half so orange halves stand level. Carefully remove fruit from orange halves; cut fruit into small bite-sized pieces. Set fruit and orange cups aside.

2 In small bowl, whip cream until stiff peaks form. Reserve a few pieces of orange to decorate. With rubber spatula, fold remaining orange pieces and canned custard into cream.

3 Spoon mixture into orange cups; chill for about 1 hour. To serve, decorate with reserved fruit pieces and orange zest.

Serve these eye-catching orange cups for a children's birthday party – children will love the patterns in the orange skins, especially if you make them different from each other as shown here

CINNAMON RICE PUDDING

- 6-8 servings
- Allow 2 hours preparation and cooking time

1.2 litres/2 pints milk

120 g/4 oz short-grain or pudding rice

60 g/2 oz caster sugar

Ground cinnamon

Fresh or Maraschino cherries to decorate

1 In very large saucepan over medium heat, heat milk to simmering; stir in rice. Reduce heat to low; cover and simmer for 45-50 minutes until rice is very tender and mixture is thick, stirring occasionally.

2 Preheat oven to 180°C/350°F/gas 4. Grease large rectangular baking dish; set in large roasting tin.

3 Stir sugar gradually into hot rice mixture.

Sweet fresh cherries nestle together in centre of rice pudding to give a touch of bright colour

4 Place baking dish in tin on oven rack; carefully pour rice mixture into baking dish (mixture will almost fill dish). Fill roasting tin with boiling water to come halfway up sides of baking dish. Bake for 40-45 minutes until knife inserted in centre of pudding comes out clean.

5 Make Cinnamon Lattice on top of pudding (see Box, right).

> **TO SERVE**
> *Decorate pudding with cherries. Serve warm or cool and refrigerate to serve cold later.*

CINNAMON LATTICE

Hold ruler diagonally across 1 corner of dish, about 2.5 cm/1 inch in from edge of rice pudding. Holding cinnamon jar in other hand, evenly shake spice through sprinkler holes along ruler edge. Shake excess spice off ruler. Repeat at 2.5 cm/1 inch intervals.

Repeat in opposite direction to form lattice pattern.

Diamond lattice pattern of ground cinnamon both looks and tastes good

HOT LEMON SOUFFLÉ PUDDINGS

🍴 6 servings

⏲ Allow 1 ³/₄ hours preparation and chilling time

2 medium-sized lemons

2 eggs, separated

150 g/5 oz caster sugar

250 ml/8 fl oz milk

20 g/ ³/₄ oz plain flour

30 g/1 oz butter, melted

1 Preheat oven to 180°C/350°F/gas 4. Grease six 175 ml/6 fl oz mousse pots or ramekins.

2 Finely grate enough zest from lemons to give 1 tablespoon.

3 Squeeze juice from lemons to make 5 tablespoons; set aside.

4 In medium bowl, with electric mixer, beat egg whites on full speed until soft peaks form; gradually sprinkle in 100 g/3 ¹/₂ oz sugar, beating until sugar completely dissolves and whites stand in stiff peaks.

5 In large bowl, using electric mixer, beat egg yolks with remaining sugar until blended; add lemon zest and juice, milk, flour and butter, and beat until well mixed, occasionally scraping bowl with rubber spatula.

6 With wire whisk or with rubber spatula, gently fold beaten egg whites into egg yolk mixture just until mixed.

7 Into prepared mousse pots or ramekins, carefully pour mixture.

8 Set mousse pots in large roasting tin; place on oven rack. Fill tin with boiling water to come halfway up sides of mousse pots. Bake puddings for 40-45 minutes until tops are golden and firm. (Puddings separate into sponge layer on top, sauce layer underneath.)

9 Remove puddings from oven and cool in mousse pots on wire rack.

Individual puddings look really sweet in deep mousse pots, but if you do not have enough pots, make the pudding in 1 large baking dish and bake it for 55-65 minutes

MAGIC CHOCOLATE PUDDING

🍴 6 servings

🕐 Allow 1 1/4 hours preparation and cooking time

175 g/6 oz butter
1 teaspoon vanilla essence
400 g/14 oz caster sugar
65 g/2 1/4 oz cocoa powder
25 g/ 3/4 oz drinking chocolate powder
300 g/10 oz plain flour
5 teaspoons baking powder
450 ml/ 3/4 pint milk
Whipped cream (see Box, below right) or ice cream

1 Preheat oven to 180°C/350°F/gas 4. In large bowl, with electric mixer, beat butter, vanilla and 225 g/8 oz sugar until soft. Sift in 45 g/1 1/2 oz of the cocoa powder, the chocolate powder, flour, baking powder and milk; beat until smooth.

2 Pour mixture into 28 x 20 cm/ 11 x 8 inch baking dish.

3 In small bowl, mix remaining sugar and cocoa; sprinkle over mixture in baking dish.

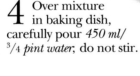

Pouring mixture into baking dish

4 Over mixture in baking dish, carefully pour *450 ml/ 3/4 pint water*; do not stir.

TO SERVE
Serve with whipped cream or ice cream, whichever you prefer.

---

5 Bake for 45-55 minutes. (Mixture separates into sponge layer on top and sauce layer underneath.)

6 Serve immediately or sauce will become absorbed by cake.

WHIPPED CREAM

Indispensable as an ingredient in many dessert dishes, whipped cream can be made from either of two different creams of varying fat content. Double cream contains about 48 per cent fat while whipping cream is slightly lighter, at about 40 per cent fat. When whipped, cream doubles in volume, and it should stay whipped for a few hours before it begins to 'weep'. The following should help ensure a perfect outcome every time.

• Before starting to whip, make sure that cream, bowl and beaters are well chilled.

• Start by whipping slowly at first. This will stabilize cream by incorporating small air bubbles into it.

• Finish whipping more vigorously, until stiff enough. Longer whipping may break cream down into butter and whey.

• If not using whipped cream immediately, cover and refrigerate.

FRENCH BREAD PUDDING

🍴 6 servings

⏱ Allow 1 hour preparation and cooking time

1 x 60 cm/24 inch long loaf French or Italian bread (about 225 g/8 oz)

60-90 g/2-3 oz butter, softened

750 ml/1 ¼ pints single cream

75 g/2 ½ oz caster sugar

4 eggs

Grated zest of 1 lemon

Golden syrup for brushing

Double or whipping cream (optional)

Crusty French bread slices take on a glossy sheen when brushed with golden syrup just before serving

1 Preheat oven to 180°C/350°F/gas 4. Cut bread diagonally into 1 cm/½ inch thick slices, each slice about 12.5 cm/5 inches long. Spread one side of each slice with softened butter.

2 In 25 cm/10 inch round flan dish or baking dish at least 4 cm/1 ½ inches deep, arrange bread slices, buttered side up, to fill dish, overlapping slices if necessary.

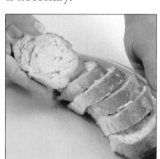

3 Place one end slice of bread in centre. (Save remaining end to make breadcrumbs.)

4 In medium bowl, with wire whisk or fork, beat single cream, sugar, eggs and lemon zest until well mixed.

5 Slowly pour egg mixture over bread slices in dish.

6 With fork, gently press bread slices into egg mixture.

7 Bake for 45-50 minutes until knife inserted in centre of pudding comes out clean. Remove pudding from oven and brush with golden syrup.

Concentric circles of overlapping bread slices accentuate the shape of this continental-style bread pudding

> **TO SERVE**
> *Serve pudding warm, or leave to cool and serve cold later. Serve with double or whipping cream, if you like.*

CAKES
75-130

CAKES

Here is a dazzling assortment of cakes for all occasions, from elegant dinner parties and special holidays to a cosy cup of tea with a friend – try indulgently rich Swiss Chocolate Cheesecake, or Calypso Fruit Cake, so colourful and tasty! Cappuccino Cake with its creamy coffee butter cream icing and Chocolate Buttermilk Gâteau – moist chocolate cake laced with orange liqueur – are as eye-catching as they are delicious. Recipes range from temptingly sumptuous Chocolate Truffle Cake to old-fashioned American Carrot Cake – there is even an ultra-light Angel Cake for the health-conscious dessert lover! In this chapter you will find every kind of cake and gâteau: easy but spectacular Celebration Buffet Cake, made from a packet of sponge cake mix, or the more fancifully decorated Fresh Strawberry Cream Cake, with helpful directions on piping whipped cream. And be sure to use the ideas for using chocolate and flower garnishes to make your luscious cakes even lovelier to look at!

CONTENTS

CAKES AND GÂTEAUX

There's a cake or gâteau in this section for every occasion, every feast day, every season. There are lavish cakes to glorify grand celebrations such as weddings, and simple cakes to accompany a cup of morning coffee or afternoon tea, or bring a family meal to a happy ending. The gâteaux are richer and more elaborate, ideal for dinner parties and other such special occasions. Most of the recipes in this section start 'from scratch', but Celebration Buffet Cake cleverly turns a packet sponge mix into a spectacularly delicious (and deliciously spectacular) treat.

CINNAMON CREAM GÂTEAU

 16 servings

Can be made up to 3 days ahead and kept in refrigerator

175 g/6 oz soft margarine
100 g/3 ½ oz caster sugar
1 tablespoon ground cinnamon
1 egg
215 g/7 ½ oz plain flour
450 ml/ ³/4 pint double or whipping cream
Cocoa powder

1 Preheat oven to 190°C/375°F/gas 5. Tear 9 sheets of non-stick baking parchment, each about 21 cm/8 ½ inches long. On 1 sheet of baking parchment, trace circle, using base of 20 cm/8 inch round cake tin as a guide. Evenly stack all the baking parchment sheets with the marked sheet on top. With kitchen scissors, cut out rounds (see Box, above right).

2 In large bowl, combine margarine, sugar, cinnamon, egg and 150 g/5 oz flour. With electric mixer, beat ingredients until well mixed, constantly scraping bowl with rubber spatula. Continue beating until light and fluffy, about 3 minutes, occasionally scraping bowl. With spoon, stir in remaining flour to make a soft dough.

3 With wet cloth, dampen 1 large or 2 small baking sheets. Place 2 baking parchment rounds on large baking sheet, or 1 on each small baking sheet; with palette knife, spread 4 tablespoons dough in very thin layer on each round (see Box, right).

4 Bake for 6-8 minutes until lightly browned round the edges. Cool on baking sheet on wire rack for 5 minutes; with fish slice, carefully remove biscuit, still on paper, to wire rack to cool completely (see Box, right).

MAKING BISCUIT LAYERS

Cutting baking parchment rounds: *holding stack of baking parchment sheets, with kitchen scissors, cut out nine 20 cm/8 inch rounds, using top marked sheet as guide.*

Spreading dough on baking parchment: *with palette knife, spread very thin, even layer of dough on each baking parchment round.*

Placing rounds on baking sheet: *on dampened large baking sheet, place 2 baking parchment rounds, side by side. (Or place 1 round on 1 small baking sheet.)*

Transferring biscuit to wire rack: *with fish slice, transfer biscuit, on parchment round, to wire rack.*

Peeling off paper: *with fingers, carefully peel baking parchment off each biscuit.*

5 Let baking sheet cool before spreading parchment rounds with more dough. (The more baking sheets you have, the faster you can bake the biscuits.) Repeat until all dough is baked, to make 9 biscuits in all. If not assembling gâteau immediately, stack cooled biscuits carefully on flat plate; cover tightly and store in cool, dry place.

6 Early on day of serving, in medium bowl, whip cream until stiff peaks form.

7 Carefully peel parchment off 1 biscuit (see Box, page 78); place on cake plate. Spread with whipped cream. Repeat layering until all biscuits are used, ending with whipped cream.

8 Sift cocoa over whipped cream. If you like, with dull edge of knife, mark 16 wedges on top of gâteau. Refrigerate for at least 4 hours to let biscuits soften slightly for easier cutting.

GINGER CREAM GÂTEAU

If you like, you can change the flavour of this spectacular-looking gâteau from cinnamon to ginger.

Substitute *1 tablespoon ground ginger* for the ground cinnamon in the biscuit dough, then, for decoration, omit sprinkling whipped cream top with cocoa and instead make decorative pattern of finely chopped *crystallized ginger* on each marked wedge of gâteau.

Cocoa powder is sprinkled liberally over whipped cream on top of gâteau

After being sprinkled with cocoa, top of gâteau is marked into 16 wedges to make it easy to serve

Nine layers of crisp, cinnamon-flavoured 'biscuit' are sandwiched together with luscious whipped cream

DOUBLE CHOCOLATE MOUSSE CAKE

This luscious, rich mousse cake is the best chocolate dessert ever – dark, moist, very chocolatey, and soul satisfying! There is no flour in it; but the cake holds together beautifully when cut into slices for serving. Crystallized violets adorning the cream add an elegant finishing touch to the top of the cake.

- 8-10 servings
- Can be made day before and kept in refrigerator

450 g/1 lb plain chocolate, broken into pieces

450 g/1 lb butter, cut into cubes

200 g/7 oz caster sugar

250 ml/8 fl oz single cream

8 eggs

Chocolate Glaze (see Box, page 81)

300 ml/ 1/2 pint double or whipping cream

Crystallized violets to decorate

1 Preheat oven to 180°C/350°F/gas 4. Grease 23 cm/9 inch springform cake tin.

2 In large heavy saucepan over low heat, heat chocolate, butter, sugar and single cream, stirring frequently, until chocolate melts and mixture is smooth.

3 In large bowl, with wire whisk or fork, beat eggs lightly; slowly beat warm chocolate mixture into eggs until well blended.

4 Pour mixture into springform tin so that it spreads evenly.

5 Bake for about 45 minutes or until skewer inserted in cake 5 cm/2 inches from edge comes out clean. Cool cake completely in tin on wire rack.

Pouring mixture into tin

> **TO SERVE**
> Decorate piped cream round top edge of cake with crystallized violets.

Ridged effect on chocolate glaze is made by swirling spatula over glaze while glaze is still warm

6 When cake is cool, carefully remove side of tin; wrap cake tightly, still on tin base, and refrigerate until it is well chilled, at least 6 hours.

7 Prepare Chocolate Glaze.

8 Line cake plate with strips of greaseproof paper. Unwrap cake; remove from tin base. Place cake on plate and spread with warm glaze (see Box, right). Discard greaseproof paper.

9 In small bowl, whip double or whipping cream until stiff peaks form. Spoon whipped cream into piping bag with medium star tube (see Box, right) and pipe cream round top edge of cake. Refrigerate cake if not serving immediately.

CHOCOLATE GLAZE

In heavy non-stick saucepan over very low heat, heat *175 g/6 oz plain chocolate chips* and *30 g/1 oz butter*, stirring frequently, until chocolate is melted and smooth. (If pan is too thin it will transfer heat too fast and burn chocolate.)

Remove pan from heat; beat in *3 tablespoons milk* and *2 tablespoons golden syrup*.

GLAZING AND DECORATING CAKE

Placing cake on plate: *on cake plate lined with strips of greaseproof paper (to catch glaze as it drips), carefully place well-chilled cake.*

Spreading glaze over cake: *with palette knife, evenly spread warm glaze over top and down side of cake.*

Don't worry if your cake sinks and looks unattractive at this stage; once glazed and decorated, it will look superb

Piping cream: *round top edge of cake, pipe scrolls of whipped cream to make continuous circle.*

Filling piping bag with cream: *into piping bag with medium star tube, spoon whipped cream. Twist end of bag to enclose cream.*

PILGRIM PUMPKIN TORTE

 8 servings

Can be made day before and kept in refrigerator

Nutty Topping (see Box, right)

250 g/9 oz caster sugar

175 g/6 oz butter, softened

225 g/8 oz canned pumpkin or Mashed Cooked Pumpkin (see Box, page 83)

375 g/13 oz self-raising flour

125 ml/4 fl oz plain yogurt

1 tablespoon mixed spice

3 eggs

450 ml/³/4 pint double or whipping cream

Rich tea biscuit crumbs to decorate

1 Prepare Nutty Topping; set aside in tins. Preheat oven to 180°C/350°F/gas 4.

2 In large bowl, with electric mixer, beat sugar and butter for 10 minutes or until light and fluffy, scraping bowl often with rubber spatula. Add pumpkin, flour, yogurt, mixed spice and eggs; beat until well mixed, constantly scraping bowl. Beat mixture for a further 2 minutes, occasionally scraping bowl (mixture will be thick).

*CAKE TINS
If you have only 2 cake tins, make 2 separate batches of both topping and cake mixture. Fill and bake 2 tins with 1 batch of each, cool in tins for 10 minutes, then turn out and bake remaining batch. Mixtures will not spoil when left to stand.

3 Spoon mixture over nutty topping in tins; spread evenly with rubber spatula.

4 Arrange 4 cake tins on 2 oven racks, so tins are not directly on top of one another. Bake for 20 minutes or until skewer inserted in centre of each cake comes out clean, swopping racks and, if necessary, position of tins after 10 minutes.

5 Cool cakes in tins on wire racks for 10 minutes. With palette knife, loosen each cake from edge of tin.

6 Turn cakes out on to wire racks; cool.

7 In medium bowl, whip double or whipping cream until stiff peaks form.

NUTTY TOPPING

175 g/6 oz walnut pieces, finely chopped

125 g/4 oz rich tea biscuits, finely crushed

350 g/12 oz light soft brown sugar

175 g/6 oz butter, melted

1 In large bowl, with spoon, mix walnuts, biscuit crumbs, light brown sugar and butter until well blended.

2 Into each of four 23 cm/9 inch round cake tins*, put one-quarter of topping.

3 With fingers, evenly pat topping to cover bottoms of tins.

8 On cake plate, place 1 cake, nutty topping side up; top with one-quarter of whipped cream and spread evenly.

9 Repeat layering, ending with a cake layer, topping side up. Spoon remaining cream round top edge of cake; sprinkle lightly with biscuit crumbs. Refrigerate if not serving immediately.

USING FRESH PUMPKIN

Fresh pumpkin is in season in October. Look for firm, bright pumpkins, free from blemishes. Store in a cool, dry place and cook within 1 month. Mashed cooked pumpkin can be frozen until you are ready to use it.

Mashed Cooked Pumpkin

With sharp knife, cut pumpkin in half; with spoon, scoop out seeds and fibres. Cut pumpkin into chunks. Place chunks in large saucepan in *2.5 cm/1 inch boiling water*; bring back to the boil.

Reduce heat to low, cover and simmer for 25-30 minutes or until tender. Drain, cool slightly and remove peel. Return pumpkin to saucepan and mash with potato masher. Drain well.

The eight blobs of whipped cream around top edge of cake make it easy to cut cake into slices of equal size

Finely crushed rich tea biscuits are sprinkled over blobs of cream to add texture and flavour

Each of the four layers of cake has two layers of its own – a nutty, crunchy layer on top, and a spicy pumpkin sponge underneath

CHOCOLATE BUTTERMILK GÂTEAU

8-10 servings

Can be made day before and kept in refrigerator

300 g/10 oz caster sugar

150 g/5 oz butter, softened

250 g/9 oz self-raising flour

350 ml/12 fl oz buttermilk

60 g/2 oz cocoa powder

1/2 teaspoon coffee essence

2 eggs

120 g/4 oz plain chocolate flavour cake covering

Vanilla Butter Cream (see Box, above right)

3 tablespoons orange liqueur (optional)

Vanilla-flavoured butter cream is piped in large 'dollops' round edge of cake, in smaller 'dollops' in centre

1 Preheat oven to 180°C/350°F/gas 4. Grease 25 cm/10 inch springform cake tin; line bottom of tin with non-stick baking parchment.

2 In large bowl, with electric mixer, beat sugar and butter for 10 minutes or until light and fluffy, scraping bowl often with rubber spatula. Add flour, buttermilk, cocoa, coffee essence and eggs; beat until well mixed, constantly scraping bowl. Beat for a further 2 minutes, occasionally scraping bowl.

3 Spoon mixture into springform tin, spreading evenly.

4 Bake for 45 minutes or until skewer inserted in centre of cake comes out clean.

5 Cool cake in tin on wire rack for 10 minutes. With palette knife, loosen cake from edge of tin; turn out on to wire rack. Peel off paper. Cool completely.

6 Meanwhile, using plain chocolate flavour cake covering, make Dark Chocolate Curls (page 142).

7 Prepare Vanilla Butter Cream.

8 Place cake on large platter. If using liqueur, with skewer or fork, make holes all over top of cake. Sprinkle liqueur evenly over top of cake.

VANILLA BUTTER CREAM

In large bowl, with electric mixer, beat *450 g/1 lb icing sugar, sifted, 90 g/3 oz butter, softened, 3 tablespoons milk* and *1 1/2 teaspoons vanilla essence* until smooth. Add more milk if necessary until butter cream is smooth, with an easy spreading consistency.

9 Spoon about one-third of butter cream into piping bag with large writing tube; set aside. Cover top and side of cake with remaining butter cream. With butter cream in piping bag, pipe circle of small 'dollops' round top edge of cake, then pipe another circle of smaller 'dollops' 7.5 cm/ 3 inches from edge of cake. Press some chocolate curls on to side of cake; sprinkle remaining choco-late curls in between 2 circles of dollops on top of cake. Refrigerate if not serving immediately.

AUSTRIAN CHOCOLATE CAKE

8 servings

Can be made day before and kept in a cool place

250 g/9 oz plain chocolate, broken into pieces

175 g/6 oz unsalted butter

6 eggs, separated

200 g/7 oz caster sugar

30 g/1 oz self-raising flour

60 g/2 oz plain chocolate flavour cake covering

1 tablespoon icing sugar

Whipped cream (see Box, page 73)

1 Preheat oven to 170°C/325°F/gas 3. Grease and flour 23 cm/ 9 inch springform cake tin.

2 In heavy non-stick saucepan over low heat, heat plain chocolate and butter, stirring often, until melted and smooth. Remove pan from heat.

3 In large bowl, with electric mixer on full speed, beat egg whites until soft peaks form; gradually sprinkle in 60 g/2 oz caster sugar, beating until sugar completely dissolves and whites stand in stiff peaks.

4 In another large bowl, using electric mixer, beat egg yolks and remaining caster sugar until very thick and lemon-coloured, about 5 minutes. Add melted chocolate mixture, beating until well mixed.

5 Add flour to mixture; continue beating until blended, occasionally scraping bowl with rubber spatula.

6 With rubber spatula or wire whisk, gently fold beaten egg whites into chocolate mixture, one-third at a time.

7 Spoon mixture into tin, spreading evenly. Bake for 30-35 minutes (cake will rise and crack on top while baking).

8 Cake is done when mixture appears set and when skewer inserted in centre comes out moist (but centre should not be runny).

9 Cool cake completely in tin on wire rack (cake will fall and top will crack as it cools).

10 Meanwhile, using plain chocolate flavour cake covering, make Dark Chocolate Curls (page 142).

11 With palette knife, loosen cake from side of tin; remove tin side. Place cake on serving plate.

Icing sugar can be sifted over cake as liberally as you like

TO SERVE
Sift icing sugar over top of cake; decorate with chocolate curls. Serve with whipped cream.

Cracks on top of cake are unavoidable, and quite acceptable with this type of very rich continental-style chocolate cake. No-one will notice once they have taken their first ecstatic bite

CAPPUCCINO CAKE

The layers of chocolate cake in this Italian-inspired gâteau are made without flour like a roulade. The cake will rise up in the oven then sink down after baking, giving a light, spongy texture – ideal for a layered cake with a rich filling.

 8 servings
Can be made day before and kept in refrigerator

5 eggs, separated

165 g/5 ¹/₂ oz icing sugar, sifted

45 g/ ³/₄ oz cocoa powder, sifted, plus extra for sprinkling

150 ml/ ¹/₄ pint double or whipping cream

225 g/8 oz full-fat soft cheese, softened

30 g/1 oz plain chocolate, coarsely grated

Coffee Butter Cream (see Box, above right)

Chocolate 'coffee beans' to decorate

COFFEE BUTTER CREAM

In cup, mix *2 tablespoons hot water* and *2 teaspoons instant coffee powder* until coffee dissolves. In large bowl, with electric mixer, beat *225 g/8 oz icing sugar, sifted*, and *225 g/8 oz butter, softened*, for 10 minutes or until fluffy, scraping bowl often. Gradually beat in coffee mixture until smooth, occasionally scraping bowl. If butter cream is made in advance, store until needed in tightly covered container to prevent crust forming on top.

---

1 Preheat oven to 200°C/400°F/gas 6. Grease 33 x 23 cm/13 x 9 inch Swiss roll tin; line bottom with non-stick baking parchment.

2 In large bowl, with electric mixer on full speed, beat egg whites until soft peaks form.

3 Gradually sprinkle in 60 g/2 oz icing sugar, beating until sugar completely dissolves and whites stand in stiff peaks.

4 In another large bowl, using electric mixer, beat egg yolks until very thick and lemon-coloured. Beat in 60 g/2 oz icing sugar and cocoa.

5 With rubber spatula or wire whisk, gently fold beaten egg whites into egg yolk mixture, one-third at a time.

6 Spoon mixture into tin, spreading evenly. Bake for 15 minutes or until top of cake springs back when lightly touched with finger.

7 Sprinkle clean tea towel with cocoa. When cake is done, immediately turn cake out on to towel. Carefully peel baking parchment off cake. If you like, cut off crisp edges. Cool cake completely.

8 While cake is cooling, prepare soft cheese filling: in small bowl, whip double or whipping cream until stiff peaks form.

ASSEMBLING CAKE LAYERS

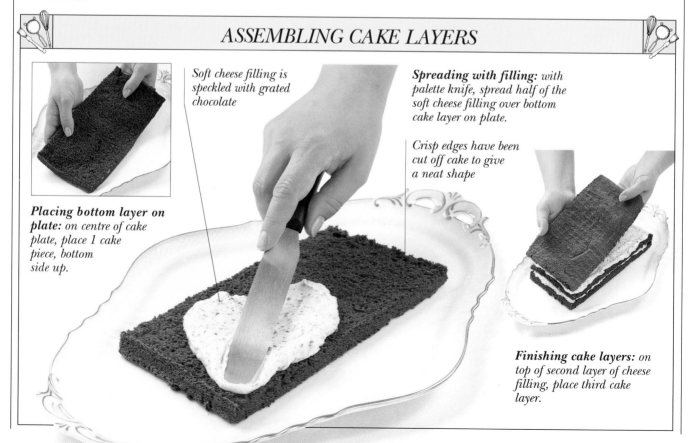

Placing bottom layer on plate: *on centre of cake plate, place 1 cake piece, bottom side up.*

Soft cheese filling is speckled with grated chocolate

Spreading with filling: *with palette knife, spread half of the soft cheese filling over bottom cake layer on plate.*

Crisp edges have been cut off cake to give a neat shape

Finishing cake layers: *on top of second layer of cheese filling, place third cake layer.*

9 In large bowl, with electric mixer, beat remaining icing sugar into full-fat soft cheese. Stir in grated chocolate. With rubber spatula, fold in whipped cream. Chill in refrigerator until ready to use.

10 Prepare Coffee Butter Cream. Spoon one-quarter of the butter cream into piping bag with small star tube.

11 With serrated knife, cut cake crossways into 3 equal pieces.

12 Place 1 cake piece on cake plate and spread with half of the soft cheese filling (see Box, page 86).

13 Repeat layering, finishing with cake layer (see Box, page 86).

14 Spread butter cream on sides and top of cake. Use butter cream in piping bag to pipe lattice top and border. Place a chocolate 'coffee bean' in each lattice diamond. Refrigerate cake if not serving immediately.

Piping butter cream with a small star tube gives lattice and border an attractive ridged effect

A chocolate 'coffee bean' in each 'window' of diamond lattice looks most effective

CHOCOLATE CARAQUE CAKE

The long, thin scrolls on this spectacular chocolate cake are called 'caraque' in French cooking. In this recipe they are made with chocolate cake covering, which is very easy to use.

 8 servings

 Can be made day before and kept in a cool place

150 g/5 oz self-raising flour

150 g/5 oz caster sugar

175 ml/6 fl oz soured cream

120 g/4 oz butter, softened

30 g/1 oz cocoa powder

1/2 teaspoon baking powder

1 egg

175 g/6 oz plain chocolate flavour cake covering

Chocolate Glaze (see Box, above right)

Icing sugar for sifting

1 Grease 23 cm/9 inch round cake tin; line bottom of tin with non-stick baking parchment.

2 Preheat oven to 180°C/350°F/gas 4. In large bowl, with electric mixer, beat first 7 ingredients until blended, occasionally scraping bowl.

3 Spread mixture evenly in tin. Bake for about 30-35 minutes or until skewer inserted in centre comes out clean. Cool in tin on wire rack for 10 minutes. With palette knife, loosen cake from edge of tin; turn out on to wire rack; peel off parchment. Cool completely.

4 Meanwhile, in small bowl over pan of gently simmering water, heat chocolate, stirring often, until melted and smooth. Pour on to 2 large baking sheets, spread evenly and make Chocolate Scrolls (see Box, below).

CHOCOLATE GLAZE

In small heavy saucepan over very low heat, heat *90 g/3 oz plain chocolate, broken into pieces, 45 g/1 1/2 oz butter* and *2 teaspoons golden syrup,* stirring frequently, until melted and smooth. Remove from heat; stir frequently until glaze cools and thickens slightly.

5 Make more Chocolate Scrolls with chocolate cake covering on second baking sheet. (Consistency of cake covering is very important. If it is too soft, it will not curl; if too hard, it will crumble. If too firm, leave it to stand at room temperature for a few minutes until soft enough to work with; if too soft, return to refrigerator.) Refrigerate scrolls until firm.

6 Make Chocolate Glaze.

7 Carefully brush away crumbs from cake. Place cake on wire rack over greaseproof paper.

8 Spoon Chocolate Glaze over top and side of cake (some glaze will drip on to greaseproof paper underneath).

9 Leave cake to stand at room temperature until glaze is firm, about 45 minutes.

10 Transfer cake to plate. Arrange Chocolate Scrolls on top and sift over icing sugar.

CHOCOLATE SCROLLS

Spreading chocolate: with palette knife, spread melted chocolate flavour cake covering over baking sheets to cover evenly. Refrigerate until firm but not brittle, about 10 minutes.

Making scrolls: place 1 chocolate-covered baking sheet on damp cloth on work surface (damp cloth keeps baking sheet from moving while working). Using straight-edged knife or palette knife, push blade across chocolate to form long, thin scrolls.

Transferring scrolls: with cocktail stick, transfer scrolls to another baking sheet.

CHOCOLATE TRUFFLE CAKE

A gâteau for a special occasion, Chocolate Truffle Cake is a deep, three-layer cake filled and piped with a wickedly rich chocolate truffle mixture. The satiny smooth glaze, a luscious combination of cream and chocolate, gives the finished cake a professional look, yet it is remarkably simple to do.

10 servings

Can be made day before and kept in refrigerator

750 g/1 lb 10 oz plain chocolate, broken into pieces

325 g/11 oz butter, softened

3 eggs

400 g/14 oz plain flour

1¹/₄ teaspoons baking powder

400 g/14 oz caster sugar

300 g/10 oz icing sugar, sifted

175 ml/6 fl oz double or whipping cream

Rose to decorate

1 Grease three 23 cm/9 inch round cake tins. Preheat oven to 170°C/325°F/gas 3.

2 In heavy non-stick saucepan over low heat, heat 350 g/12 oz chocolate, 225 g/8 oz butter and *600 ml/1 pint water*, stirring frequently, until melted and smooth. Remove from heat; cool slightly.

3 In large bowl, with wire whisk or fork, beat eggs. Gradually beat warm chocolate mixture into eggs.

4 Sift flour and baking powder together. Add to chocolate mixture with caster sugar; continue beating with wire whisk or fork until smooth and well blended.

5 Pour mixture into cake tins. Bake for 25-30 minutes or until skewer inserted in centre of cakes comes out clean. Cool cakes in tins on wire rack for 10 minutes. Remove cakes from tins; cool completely on wire rack.

6 Meanwhile, prepare truffle mixture: in bowl over pan of gently simmering water, heat 120 g/4 oz chocolate, stirring frequently, until melted; cool slightly. With spoon, stir in icing sugar, remaining butter and 4 tablespoons double or whipping cream until mixture is smooth and well blended.

7 Prepare glaze: in heavy medium saucepan over low heat, heat 225 g/8 oz chocolate and remaining double or whipping cream, stirring frequently, until melted, smooth and slightly thickened; keep warm.

8 Assemble and glaze cake (see Box, below). Refrigerate cake until glaze is set, about 30 minutes.

9 Remove cake to plate. Pipe border with remaining truffle mixture (see Box, below). Grate remaining chocolate; sprinkle round top edge of cake. Place rose in centre.

ASSEMBLING, GLAZING AND DECORATING CAKE

Assembling cake: *with palette knife, spread 1 cake layer with about one-sixth of truffle mixture. Top with second cake layer, pressing down gently but firmly. Spread with another one-sixth of truffle mixture; top with third cake layer.*

Glazing cake: *over assembled cake, pour prepared glaze. With palette knife, spread glaze to cover top and side of cake completely.*

Piping border: *with star tube, pipe border of remaining truffle mixture round bottom of cake.*

CHOCOLATE COCONUT CAKE

This four-layer treat boasts shreds of coconut in the cake mixture, chopped walnuts in the sweet filling, whipped cream to accent the chocolate flavour, and paper-thin, dainty 'ruffles' of slivered fresh coconut to crown the whole. If you cannot obtain buttermilk, use fresh milk soured with a few drops of lemon juice.

 8 servings
Can be made day before and kept in refrigerator

Cocoa powder

90 g/3 oz plain chocolate, broken into pieces

225 g/8 oz self-raising flour

300 g/10 oz caster sugar

300 ml/ ½ pint buttermilk

120 g/4 oz butter, softened

½ teaspoon baking powder

3 eggs

100 g/3 ½ oz shredded or desiccated coconut

Chocolate Walnut Filling (see Box, above right)

300 ml/ ½ pint double or whipping cream

Coconut Ruffles (see Box, page 93) to decorate

CHOCOLATE WALNUT FILLING

In large non-stick saucepan over medium heat, heat *250 ml/8 fl oz evaporated milk, 120 g/4 oz light soft brown sugar, 120 g/4 oz butter, 60 g/2 oz plain chocolate* and *3 egg yolks, lightly beaten,* until chocolate melts and mixture will coat a spoon well, about 10 minutes, stirring often (do not boil or mixture will curdle). Remove from heat and stir in *225 g/8 oz walnut pieces.* Cool slightly until thick enough to spread, stirring occasionally.

1 Preheat oven to 180°C/350°F/gas 4. Grease two 23 cm/9 inch round cake tins; dust bottoms and sides of tins with cocoa.

2 In small bowl over pan of gently simmering water, melt pieces of chocolate, stirring often, until smooth; remove bowl from pan.

3 In large bowl, combine next 6 ingredients; add melted chocolate. With electric mixer, beat until mixed, scraping bowl often with rubber spatula. Continue beating for 2 minutes, occasionally scraping bowl. Stir in coconut.

4 Spread mixture evenly in tins. Bake for 35 minutes or until skewer inserted in centres of cakes comes out clean.

5 Cool cakes in tins on wire racks for 10 minutes. With palette knife, loosen cakes from edges of tins; turn out on to wire racks to cool completely.

6 When cakes are cool, prepare Chocolate Walnut Filling. In small bowl, whip double or whipping cream until stiff peaks form.

7 Cut each cake horizontally into 2 layers; place 1 layer on cake plate and spread with half of the Chocolate Walnut Filling (see Box, page 93).

8 Top with a second cake layer; spread with half of the cream. Top with another cake layer; spread with remaining filling. Top with last cake layer; spread with remaining cream (see Box, page 93).

> *TO SERVE*
> *Decorate top of cake with Coconut Ruffles. Sprinkle some cocoa through sieve over centre. Refrigerate if not serving immediately.*

Four layers of Chocolate Coconut Cake are sandwiched together with alternate layers of Chocolate Walnut Filling and whipped cream

Inner skin is left on edges of coconut to give definition to coconut 'ruffles'

Top layer of whipped cream is spread just over edge of cake to give a gentle, curvy outline

ASSEMBLING CAKE LAYERS

Cutting cake into layers: *with serrated knife, cut each cake in half horizontally to make 4 thin layers in all.*

Starting to assemble cake: *on cake plate, place 1 cake layer, cut side up.*

Spreading with first layer of filling: *on first cake layer, with palette knife, evenly spread half of the Chocolate Walnut Filling.*

Topping with third cake layer: *over cream layer, place cake layer, cut side up.*

Spreading with cream: *on last cake layer, with palette knife, evenly spread remaining whipped cream.*

COCONUT RUFFLES

With skewer and hammer, puncture 'eyes' of fresh coconut. Drain off coconut milk (add to orange juice or other fruit drinks). Open shell by hitting very hard with hammer. Hit firmly all round middle.

With small sharp knife, prise out coconut meat piece by piece.

With vegetable peeler, draw blade along curved edge of coconut piece to make wafer-thin, wide ruffles with attractive edging.

Remaining coconut meat can be peeled and shredded or grated for later use; wrap tightly in foil or place in sealed container and keep in refrigerator; use within 1-2 days.

GRANNY'S CAKE

 8 servings

Can be made day before

400 g/14 oz caster sugar

225 g/8 oz butter, softened

350 g/12 oz self-raising flour

250 ml/8 fl oz milk

1/2 teaspoon baking powder

4 eggs

Icing sugar for sprinkling

Cherries to decorate (optional)

1 Preheat oven to 180°C/350°F/gas 4. Lightly grease and flour 23 cm/9 inch fluted kugelhopf mould or savarin mould.

2 In large bowl, with electric mixer, beat caster sugar and butter for 10 minutes or until light and fluffy, scraping bowl frequently with rubber spatula.

3 Add flour, milk, baking powder and eggs; beat ingredients until well mixed, constantly scraping bowl.

4 Beat mixture for a further 2 minutes, occasionally scraping bowl.

5 Spread mixture evenly in mould.

6 Bake cake in oven for 50-55 minutes or until skewer inserted in centre comes out clean. Cool cake in mould on wire rack for 10 minutes, then turn out on to wire rack to cool completely.

7 Sift icing sugar over cake.

A pretty doiley sets off this cake a treat, especially when the colours tone so well with the serving plate and cherry decoration

A liberal sprinkling of icing sugar adds an attractive decorative touch to a plain and simple cake

> **TO SERVE**
> *If you like, decorate side of cake with cherries.*

ALMOND SCALLOP CAKES

 Makes 8
Allow 2 hours preparation and cooking time

150 g/5 oz blanched almonds

215 g/7 ½ oz self-raising flour

200 g/7 oz caster sugar

2 eggs

150 ml/ ¼ pint milk

2 tablespoons vegetable oil

1 teaspoon almond essence

Strawberries to decorate

1 In small frying pan over medium heat, cook blanched almonds until golden, stirring often; cool. In food processor or blender, finely grind toasted almonds. (If using blender, grind nuts in 2 batches.)

2 Preheat oven to 180°C/350°F/gas 4. Generously grease eight 12.5 cm/5 inch or 125 ml/ 4 fl oz scallop shell-shaped moulds.

These pretty little teacakes are flecked with ground toasted almonds; if you prefer, you can use walnuts or pecans instead

3 In large bowl, mix ground almonds, flour and sugar.

4 In small bowl, beat eggs lightly; stir in next 3 ingredients.

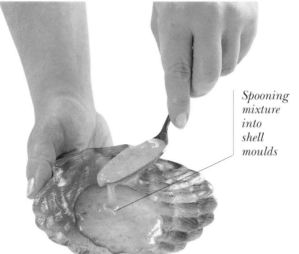

Spooning mixture into shell moulds

Golden-brown edges add to the visual appeal of the dainty scallop shapes

5 Stir liquid mixture into flour mixture just until flour is moistened. Spoon mixture evenly into moulds, leaving 1 cm/ ½ inch border all round moulds.

6 To keep moulds level while baking, arrange them on top of 2 large bun tins, or arrange them on crumpled pieces of foil in baking tray.

7 Bake cakes in oven for 20-25 minutes or until skewer inserted in centres comes out clean.

8 Cool cakes in moulds on wire racks for 5 minutes. Run tip of knife round edges of moulds to loosen cakes; turn cakes out on to wire racks to cool completely. Serve with strawberries.

MOCHA CREAM BUTTERFLY CAKE

16 servings

Can be made day before and kept in refrigerator

225 g/8 oz plain chocolate

8 eggs, separated

200 g/7 oz caster sugar

75 g/2 ½ oz plain flour

Chocolate Butterflies (see Box, right)

1 teaspoon white vegetable shortening

500 ml/16 fl oz double or whipping cream

45 g/1 ½ oz cocoa powder

2 teaspoons instant coffee granules or powder

1 Grate 175 g/6 oz chocolate (or in food processor with knife blade attached, finely grind chocolate). Set aside.

2 In large bowl, with electric mixer on full speed, beat egg whites until stiff peaks form.

3 Preheat oven to 180°C/350°F/gas 4. In another large bowl, using electric mixer, beat egg yolks and half of the sugar until very thick and lemon-coloured, about 5 minutes. Add flour; beat until just mixed, occasionally scraping bowl with rubber spatula. With rubber spatula, stir in grated chocolate. Gently fold beaten egg whites into egg yolk mixture, one-third at a time.

4 Evenly spread mixture in ungreased 25 cm/ 10 inch springform cake tin. Bake in the oven for 40-45 minutes or until top of cake springs back when touched with finger. Invert cake in tin on to rack; cool completely in tin.

CHOCOLATE BUTTERFLIES

Making rectangles: cut baking parchment into five 10 x 6 cm/4 x 2 ½ inch rectangles. Fold each in half crossways to form 5 x 6 cm/ 2 x 2 ½ inch rectangle.

Making tracing of butterfly: with pencil, draw outline of half a butterfly on each folded rectangle using centre-fold for butterfly body (pressure of pencil point will mark bottom half of paper as well). Unfold rectangles and place on clean flat surface, tracing side down. Stick rectangles to work surface about 5 cm/2 inches apart with small pieces of tape.

Piping chocolate butterfly: pipe some chocolate mixture on to a parchment rectangle in thin continuous lines over tracing and along centre-fold to make a butterfly. Repeat with remaining chocolate to make several butterflies. Remove and discard tapes.

Moulding butterflies: with fish slice, carefully lift each piece of parchment and place, chocolate side up, in 6 cm/2 ½ inch hole in deep bun tin or in section of empty egg carton so that parchment is slightly bent on centre-fold. Refrigerate chocolate butterflies for at least 1 hour or until chocolate is set.

Removing parchment: with cool hands, carefully peel off parchment. Keep butterflies refrigerated until ready to use.

5 Meanwhile, prepare Chocolate Butterflies: cut non-stick baking parchment into rectangles and use to make tracings of butterflies (see Box, page 96). In heavy non-stick saucepan over low heat, heat vegetable shortening and remaining chocolate, stirring frequently, until melted and smooth; cool for 10 minutes for easier piping. Spoon chocolate mixture into paper piping bag with tip cut to make 3 mm/⅛ inch hole (or use small piping bag with small writing tube). Pipe butterflies and leave to cool (see Box, page 96).

Chocolate 'butterflies' perched on cake are made by piping melted chocolate over tracings of butterflies on parchment paper

6 When cake is cooled, prepare mocha cream: in large bowl, whip double or whipping cream with cocoa, instant coffee and remaining sugar until stiff peaks form. Spoon one-quarter of the mocha cream into piping bag with medium star tube; set aside.

7 With palette knife, loosen cake from side of tin; remove tin side. Loosen cake from tin base; remove tin base. With serrated knife, cut cake horizontally into 3 layers.

8 Place bottom cake layer, cut side up, on cake plate; spread with about one-quarter of the mocha cream in bowl. Repeat layering, ending with third cake layer, cut side down.

9 Spread top of cake with thin layer of mocha cream; use remaining mocha cream to ice side of cake. Use mocha cream in piping bag to pipe pretty design on top of cake. Refrigerate cake if not serving immediately.

10 To serve, decorate cake with chocolate butterflies.

Mocha cream is piped with star tube to give this spiral effect on top of cake

DECORATING WITH CHOCOLATE

A chocolate butterfly perched on top of a simple dessert will delight the sophisticated dinner party guest as much as it will enchant children at a birthday party. Like the majority of chocolate decorations, butterflies require no special skill, but they do need time for the chocolate to harden. All chocolate decorations except curls can be made with real chocolate; for making curls, use plain chocolate flavour cake covering, which is more manageable.

To melt chocolate: break it into pieces and place in a small bowl over a pan of gently simmering water. Heat for about 5 minutes or until melted and smooth, stirring often with rubber spatula. If using for piping, leave to cool first.

Chocolate Dipped Fruits
Small fruits like grapes, cherries and strawberries dipped in melted chocolate look very pretty arranged round edge of a cake or dessert, or grouped together in clusters in centre.

Chocolate Leaves
A variety of leaves is brushed with different kinds of melted chocolate to make interesting shapes and colours. Grouping chocolate leaves together in centre of dessert or cake to make a flower shape is especially effective.

Chocolate Cups
Miniature paper or foil cake cases are used as moulds for melted chocolate, then peeled off when chocolate is firm. Filled with piped whipped cream, icing or pieces of fruit, they look good on the edge of plates and platters.

NON-TOXIC LEAVES
These non-toxic leaves are safe for making chocolate leaves: gardenia, grape, lemon, magnolia, nasturtium, rose, violet.

Do not use the following leaves in contact with chocolate or other foods: amaryllis, azalea, caladium, daffodil, delphinium, dieffenbachia, English ivy, hydrangea, jonquil, larkspur, laurel, lily of the valley, mistletoe, narcissus, oleander, poinsettia, rhododendron.

Wash non-toxic leaves in warm, soapy water; rinse and dry well before use.

Lacy Lattice
Melted chocolate piped free-hand in lattice design on non-stick baking parchment is refrigerated until firm, then carefully lifted off.

Chocolate Heart
Heart shape is cut out of melted and chilled plain chocolate with a biscuit cutter, then piped with melted white chocolate. Hole is punched with fine skewer for ribbon to be threaded through.

Chocolate Scrolls
Elegant curls are made by pushing knife or palette knife across surface of melted and cooled plain chocolate flavour cake covering.

Chocolate Ruffles
These are made like Chocolate Scrolls (left), but knife or palette knife is pushed only halfway across surface of melted and cooled plain chocolate flavour cake covering.

Dainty Daisy
Melted plain chocolate is piped over daisy design on non-stick baking parchment, then left to set before being flooded with melted white chocolate. Daisy is refrigerated until firm, then lifted off parchment.

Simple Curls
These can be made quickly by warming bar of milky white chocolate or plain chocolate flavour cake covering in your hands, then drawing a vegetable peeler along it to produce short, plump shapes.

Fleur-de-Lis
Shape of fleur-de-lis is drawn on non-stick baking parchment, then melted chocolate piped over. Decoration is refrigerated until firm before being carefully lifted off and placed on dessert.

Marbled Triangles
Melted plain and white chocolates are swirled together to make marbled design, then refrigerated until firm. Triangles are then stamped out with small cutter.

CHOCOLATE DIPPED FRUIT

CHOCOLATE CURLS

CHOCOLATE BUTTERFLIES

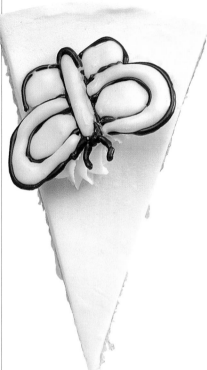

Cherries dipped in melted plain and white chocolates

Chocolate Scrolls (see Box, page 88), together with white Chocolate Curls

Two-Tone Butterfly made with piped melted plain and white chocolates

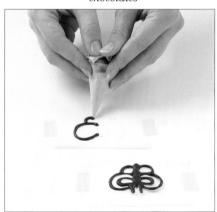

1 *Rinse fruit under cold running water but do not remove stalks; pat completely dry with kitchen paper; set fruit aside. (For dipping, fruit should be at room temperature.)*

2 *Melt chocolate in small bowl over pan of gently simmering water (page 98); leave to cool slightly.*

3 *With fingers, hold stalk of 1 fruit at a time and dip it into chocolate, leaving part of fruit uncovered.*

4 *Shake off excess chocolate; place fruit on non-stick baking gâchment. Leave to stand until chocolate is set, about 10 minutes; remove from parchment.*

1 *Hold bar or piece of milky white or Swiss white chocolate or plain chocolate flavour cake covering between palms of hands to soften chocolate slightly.*

2 *Slowly and firmly draw blade of vegetable peeler across wide side of chocolate for wide curls, thin side for thin curls.*

3 *Use cocktail stick to transfer curls, to avoid breaking them.*

This technique is also shown, with dark chocolate, on page 142.

1 *With pencil, draw butterflies on rectangles of baking parchment. Place rectangles on clean flat surface, pencil-side down; tape to work surface.*

2 *Spoon melted plain chocolate (page 98) into paper piping bag with tip cut to make 3 mm/^{1}/$_8$ inch hole (or small piping bag with small writing tube).*

3 *Pipe melted plain chocolate on to non-stick baking parchment rectangle in thin continuous lines over butterfly outline. Refrigerate until set.*

4 *Spoon melted white chocolate into clean paper piping bag; pipe inside outline. Refrigerate until firm, 1 hour.*

CHOCOLATE TRIANGLES

CHOCOLATE SQUIGGLES

CHOCOLATE LEAVES

Plain and white chocolate triangles

Plain chocolate squiggles

Chocolate leaves in different colours and shapes

1 Tape sheet of non-stick baking parchment to clean work surface.

2 With palette knife, spread melted chocolate (page 98) on sheet of non-stick baking parchment. Refrigerate until chocolate is set.

3 With small decorative cutter, cut out chocolate shapes. Refrigerate shapes until firm.

1 Spoon melted chocolate (page 98) into paper piping bag with tip cut to 3 mm/ ¹/₈ inch hole .

2 On to non-stick baking parchment rectangles, pipe melted chocolate in free-hand squiggle designs.

3 Refrigerate chocolate squiggles until they are firm.

4 With palette knife, carefully lift chocolate squiggles off baking parchment.

1 Rinse leaves of your choice (see Box, page 98); pat dry with kitchen paper.

2 With pastry brush, small painting brush or small palette knife, spread layer of melted chocolate (page 98) on underside of leaves (using underside will give a more distinctive leaf design).

3 Refrigerate chocolate-coated leaves until chocolate is firm, about 30 minutes.

4 With cool hands, carefully peel leaves away from chocolate.

WALNUT CREAM GÂTEAU

🍴 10 servings

⏱ Can be made day before and kept in refrigerator

450 g/1 lb walnut pieces

50 g/1 ²/₃ oz self-raising flour

¹/₂ teaspoon baking powder

5 eggs, separated

150 g/5 oz caster sugar

2 tablespoons corn oil

600 ml/1 pint double or whipping cream

30 g/1 oz icing sugar, sifted

1 In food processor or blender, finely grind three-quarters of walnuts with flour and baking powder. (If using blender, blend ingredients in batches.)

2 Preheat oven to 180°C/350°F/gas 4. Grease two 23 cm/9 inch round cake tins; line bottoms of tins with non-stick baking parchment.

3 In large bowl, with electric mixer on full speed, beat egg whites until soft peaks form; gradually sprinkle in one-third of caster sugar, beating until sugar completely dissolves and whites stand in stiff peaks.

4 In another large bowl, with electric mixer, beat egg yolks, corn oil and remaining caster sugar until very thick and lemon-coloured, about 5 minutes. With rubber spatula or wire whisk, gently fold nut mixture and beaten egg whites into egg yolk mixture just until blended.

5 Spoon mixture into tins, spreading evenly. Bake for 20-25 minutes or until tops of cakes spring back when lightly touched with finger. Immediately loosen edges of cakes from sides of tins; turn out cakes on to wire racks and peel off baking parchment. Cool completely.

6 In large bowl, whip double or whipping cream with icing sugar until stiff peaks form. Spoon about one-quarter of whipped cream into piping bag with large star tube; reserve for decoration. Chop remaining walnuts for decoration.

7 With serrated knife, cut each cake in half horizontally to make 4 thin layers in all.

8 Place 1 cake layer on cake plate; spread with one-quarter of whipped cream.

9 Repeat layering, ending with a cake layer. Spread remaining one-quarter of whipped cream on side of cake.

10 Reserve 30 g/1 oz chopped walnuts; press remaining chopped walnuts into cream on side of cake. Pipe whipped cream in piping bag on top of cake in parallel lines.

11 Sprinkle reserved chopped walnuts in between lines of cream on top of cake.

12 Refrigerate cake if not serving immediately.

Parallel lines of piped whipped cream are separated by chopped walnuts

CHOCOLATE MARSHMALLOW CAKE

 8-10 servings
Can be made day
before

350 g/12 oz soft margarine

90 g/3 oz walnut pieces,
finely chopped

60 g/2 oz rich tea biscuits,
finely crushed

165 g/5 ¹/₂ oz light soft
brown sugar

215 g/7 ¹/₂ oz self-raising
flour

200 g/7 oz caster sugar

30 g/1 oz cocoa powder

¹/₄ teaspoon baking powder

4 eggs

100 g/3 ¹/₂ oz shredded or
desiccated coconut

75 g/2 ¹/₂ oz miniature
marshmallows or
ordinary marshmallows,
halved

Chocolate Glaze (see Box,
below)

Chocolate Curls (see Box,
page 104) to decorate

Squiggly chocolate
curls are a simple
way to dress up a
plain glazed cake

CHOCOLATE GLAZE
In small bowl over
saucepan of gently
simmering water, heat
225 g/8 oz plain chocolate,
broken into pieces,
45 g/1 ¹/₂ oz butter and
3 tablespoons water,
stirring frequently, until
melted and smooth.
Remove bowl from pan
of water. Let chocolate
mixture cool to room
temperature, then sift in
3 tablespoons icing sugar,
beating with a spoon
until glaze has a thick
spreading consistency.

1 Preheat oven to
180°C/350°F/gas 4.
Grease two 23 cm/9 inch
round cake tins; line
bottoms with non-stick
baking parchment.

2 In medium saucepan
over low heat, heat
120 g/4 oz margarine until
melted. Remove from
heat; stir in walnuts,
biscuit crumbs and brown
sugar. Divide mixture
equally between cake tins
and pat to cover bottoms
of tins evenly.

3 In large bowl, with
electric mixer, beat
flour, caster sugar, cocoa,
baking powder, eggs,
coconut and remaining
margarine until blended,
constantly scraping bowl
with rubber spatula.
Continue to beat for
1 minute.

4 Spoon mixture into
tins, spreading evenly.
Bake for 30 minutes or
until skewer inserted in
centre comes out clean.
Immediately, with palette
knife, loosen cakes from
edges of tins; turn out on
to wire racks and carefully
peel off parchment.

5 While still hot, carefully place 1 cake,
crumb mixture side up, on
cake plate; top with
marshmallows.

6 Immediately place
second cake, crumb
mixture side up, on top of
marshmallows so marsh-
mallows will melt.

7 Insert long metal or
wooden skewer in
centre of cake to keep top
layer from sliding off.

8 Cool cake, then
refrigerate until
completely cold and
marshmallows are set.

9 When cake is
completely cold,
prepare Chocolate Glaze.

10 Remove skewer
from cake.
Spread glaze over top and
side of cake. Decorate with
chocolate curls. Allow
glaze to set before serving.

SWISS CHOCOLATE TORTE

This prettily piped and decorated chocolate cake has soured cream in the cake batter, an ingredient that is often used in Swiss, German and Austrian cakes to add moistness. If you would like to intensify the orange flavour of the cake, substitute tiny pieces of candied orange for the crystallized violets in the decoration.

8-10 servings

Can be made day before and kept in refrigerator

120 g/4 oz plain chocolate, broken into pieces

2 eggs, separated

300 g/10 oz caster sugar

120 g/4 oz butter, softened

340 g/11 ¹/₂ oz self-raising flour

125 ml/4 fl oz soured cream

2 teaspoons orange-flower water for culinary use

175 g/6 oz plain chocolate flavour cake covering

Chocolate Cream (see Box, page 105)

300 ml/ ¹/₂ pint double or whipping cream

Crystallized violets to decorate

1 Grease and flour 25 cm/10 inch springform cake tin.

2 In small non-stick saucepan over very low heat, heat pieces of chocolate, stirring often, until melted and smooth. Remove saucepan from heat.

3 In medium bowl, with electric mixer on full speed, beat egg whites until stiff peaks form.

4 Preheat oven to 180°C/350°F/gas 4.

5 In large bowl, using electric mixer, beat egg yolks, 250 g/9 oz sugar and butter until light and fluffy, about 5 minutes, occasionally scraping bowl with rubber spatula.

6 Add melted chocolate, flour, soured cream, orange-flower water, and *250 ml/8 fl oz water*; beat until well mixed, constantly scraping bowl. Beat for a further 2 minutes, occasionally scraping bowl.

7 With rubber spatula or wire whisk, gently fold beaten egg whites into chocolate mixture.

8 Spoon mixture into tin, spreading evenly. Bake for 45 minutes or until cake springs back when lightly touched with finger. Cool cake in tin on wire rack for 10 minutes.

9 With palette knife, loosen cake from edge of tin; carefully remove side of tin, leaving cake on tin base. Cool completely on wire rack.

10 Meanwhile, break chocolate flavour cake covering into pieces; place in small bowl over saucepan of gently simmering water. Heat chocolate flavour cake covering gently, stirring frequently, until melted and smooth; use to make Chocolate Curls (see Box, below).

11 Prepare Chocolate Cream.

12 Remove cake from tin base. With serrated knife, cut cake horizontally into 2 layers. Place 1 cake layer on cake plate; spread with one-third of the chocolate cream. Top with second cake layer.

CHOCOLATE CURLS

Making chocolate block: *into foil-lined 15 x 8 cm/6 x 3 ¹/₄ inch loaf tin, pour melted chocolate flavour cake covering. Cool, then refrigerate until set, about 2 hours.*

Unmoulding chocolate block: *remove chocolate block from tin; carefully peel off foil.*

Grating chocolate curls: *using coarse side of grater, grate along 1 long side of chocolate block to make long, thin curls (if chocolate appears too brittle to curl, leave to stand at room temperature for 30 minutes to soften slightly).*

13 Spread remaining chocolate cream over top and side of cake. Carefully press chocolate curls on to side of cake.

14 In small bowl, whip double or whipping cream with remaining sugar until stiff peaks form. Spoon whipped cream into piping bag with large star tube; use to pipe border and lattice design on top of cake. Decorate with crystallized violets.

CHOCOLATE CREAM

In non-stick saucepan over medium heat, bring *350 ml/ 12 fl oz double or whipping cream, 225 g/8 oz plain chocolate, broken into pieces,* and *60 g/2 oz butter* to the boil, stirring constantly until mixture is smooth. Pour mixture into large bowl; leave to cool completely at room temperature. With electric mixer, beat chocolate mixture until light and fluffy.

To achieve this looped scroll effect with piped whipped cream, double the scrolls back on themselves while piping

Crystallized violets are placed at the intersections of the whipped cream lattice

MANHATTAN ROULADE

10 servings
Can be made day before and kept in refrigerator

6 eggs, separated

215 g/7 ¹/₂ oz caster sugar

120 g/4 oz self-raising flour

45 g/1 ¹/₂ oz cocoa powder plus extra for sifting

White Chocolate Butter Cream (see Box, right)

White and dark Chocolate Curls (pages 100 and 142) to decorate

1 Grease two 33 x 23 cm/13 x 9 inch Swiss roll tins; line tins with non-stick baking parchment.

2 In large bowl, with electric mixer on full speed, beat egg whites until soft peaks form; gradually sprinkle in 75 g/2 ¹/₂ oz sugar, beating until sugar completely dissolves and whites stand in stiff peaks.

3 Preheat oven to 190°C/375°F/gas 5. In another large bowl, using electric mixer, beat egg yolks and remaining sugar until very thick and lemon-coloured. Add flour and 45 g/1 ¹/₂ oz cocoa; beat until well mixed, occasionally scraping bowl with rubber spatula. With rubber spatula or wire whisk, gently fold beaten egg whites into egg yolk and sugar mixture, one-third at a time.

WHITE CHOCOLATE BUTTER CREAM

In small heavy saucepan over medium heat, heat *3 tablespoons milk* until tiny bubbles form round edge of pan; remove saucepan from heat.

With wire whisk, beat in *60 g/2 oz white chocolate, chopped*; mix until chocolate melts. Stir in *4 tablespoons coffee liqueur*. Cool, then refrigerate until cold, about 30 minutes, stirring occasionally.

In large bowl, place *120 g/4 oz icing sugar, sifted*, and *175 g/6 oz butter, softened* (do not use margarine; butter cream will separate).

With electric mixer, beat for 10 minutes or until light and fluffy, scraping bowl often with rubber spatula.

Gradually beat white chocolate mixture into butter cream until smooth, occasionally scraping bowl with spatula.

4 Spoon mixture into tins, spreading evenly. Bake for 8-10 minutes or until tops of cakes spring back when lightly touched with finger.

5 Sift cocoa over 2 clean tea towels. When cakes are done, immediately turn cakes out on to towels.

6 Carefully peel baking parchment off cakes. If you like, cut off crisp edges. Starting at a narrow end of each cake, roll cakes with towels, Swiss roll fashion. Place cake rolls, seam-side down, on wire racks; leave to cool completely.

MAKING ROULADE

Spreading first cake with butter cream: with palette knife, spread top of 1 cake evenly with about one-third of the butter cream.

Joining cakes: along narrow end of second cake, place a narrow end of filled cake roll.

Rolling cakes together: roll second cake round first cake roll.

7 Meanwhile, prepare White Chocolate Butter Cream.

8 Unroll 1 cooled cake; spread with about one-third of the butter cream (see Box, page 106). Starting at same narrow end, roll cake without towel. Unroll second cake; spread with another third of the butter cream. Join cakes and roll together (see Box, page 106).

9 Place roulade on serving plate; spread remaining butter cream over roulade. Decorate with chocolate curls. Refrigerate cake if not serving immediately.

CUTTING ROULADE

It is important to slice roulade cleanly, so that filling is seen at its best. For perfect results, dip long serrated knife in hot water before slicing. Wipe blade with kitchen paper after cutting each slice and dip again in water.

Two contrasting colours of chocolate curls look striking when mixed together on top of roulade

Layers of roulade are extra thin and dainty because cake mixture is baked in two separate Swiss roll tins and cakes are joined together at the rolling stage

HAZELNUT AND CREAM SWISS ROLL

12 servings

Can be made day before and kept in refrigerator

4 eggs, separated

120 g/4 oz icing sugar plus extra for sprinkling

120 g/4 oz self-raising flour

300 ml/ ¹/₂ pint double cream

120 g/4 oz hazelnut kernels

1 tablespoon liquid honey

1 Grease 33 x 23 cm/ 13 x 9 inch Swiss roll tin; line tin with non-stick baking parchment.

2 In large bowl, with electric mixer on full speed, beat egg whites until soft peaks form; gradually sift in 60 g/2 oz icing sugar, beating until sugar completely dissolves and whites stand in stiff peaks.

3 Preheat oven to 190°C/375°F/gas 5.

4 In another large bowl, using electric mixer, beat egg yolks and 60 g/ 2 oz sifted icing sugar until very thick and lemon-coloured. Add flour; beat until well mixed, constantly scraping bowl with rubber spatula.

5 With rubber spatula or wire whisk, gently fold beaten egg whites into egg yolk mixture, one-third at a time.

6 Spoon mixture into tin, spreading evenly. Bake for 12-15 minutes or until cake springs back when lightly touched with finger.

MAKING SWISS ROLL

1 Sift icing sugar over clean tea towel. When cake is done, immediately turn out on to towel.

2 With fingers, carefully peel non-stick baking parchment off cake. If you like, cut off crisp edges.

3 Starting at a narrow end, roll cake with towel. Place roll, seam-side down, on wire rack; leave to cool completely.

---

7 Make Swiss roll (see Box, above).

8 While Swiss roll is cooling, whip double cream until stiff peaks form.

9 In small frying pan over medium heat, cook hazelnuts until golden, stirring frequently; cool.

10 Coarsely chop 12 toasted hazelnuts and reserve for decoration; finely chop remaining toasted hazelnuts to use in filling.

11 Fold finely chopped hazelnuts and honey into half of the whipped double cream.

12 Unroll cooled Swiss roll; spread top of cake evenly with whipped cream, honey and hazelnut mixture.

13 Starting at same narrow end, roll cake without towel and then place on platter.

ALTERNATIVE FILLING

The whipped cream, hazelnut and honey filling in the main recipe on this page is very quick and easy to do. If you have more time and would like a richer flavour, try the following Maple Cream Filling.

Maple Cream Filling
In medium saucepan, place *2 tablespoons plain flour*; with wire whisk or spoon, slowly stir in *150 ml/ ¹/₄ pint milk* and *5 tablespoons maple syrup* until smooth.

Cook over medium heat, stirring constantly, until mixture boils; boil for 1 minute until thick. Remove saucepan from heat.

In cup, with fork, beat *2 egg yolks* lightly; stir in small amount of hot maple mixture. Slowly pour egg mixture back

into remaining maple mixture in pan, stirring rapidly with spoon to prevent lumping; cook over low heat, stirring constantly, until mixture thickens and coats back of spoon well, about 5 minutes (do not boil or mixture may curdle).

Remove saucepan from heat and pour filling into bowl. To keep skin from forming on top of filling as it cools, press a sheet of dampened greaseproof paper directly on to surface of hot filling.

---

14 Spoon remaining whipped cream into piping bag with large star tube; pipe whipped cream on Swiss roll to make attractive design. Refrigerate roll if not serving immediately.

TO SERVE
Just before serving, sprinkle reserved coarsely chopped hazelnuts over whipped cream on top of cake.

FRESH STRAWBERRY CREAM CAKE

8-10 servings

Can be made day
before and kept in
refrigerator

175 g/6 oz soft margarine

175 g/6 oz caster sugar

3 eggs, beaten

175 g/6 oz self-raising
flour

1 ½ teaspoons baking
powder

700 g/1 ½ lb strawberries

750 ml/1 ¼ pints double
or whipping cream

4 tablespoons strawberry
jam

1 Grease two 18 cm/
7 inch round cake tins
and line with non-stick
baking parchment.

2 Preheat oven to
180°C/350°F/gas 4.

3 In large bowl, place
margarine, sugar,
eggs, flour and baking
powder. With electric
mixer, beat well until all
ingredients are thoroughly
blended.

4 Spoon cake mixture
into prepared cake
tins, spreading evenly.

5 Bake for 25 minutes
or until skewer
inserted in centres of
cakes comes out clean.

6 Cool cakes in tins
on wire racks for
10 minutes.

7 With palette knife,
loosen cakes from
edges of tins; turn out on
to wire racks to cool
completely.

8 Hull half of the
strawberries and cut
each in half; set aside.

9 With serrated knife,
cut each cake in half
horizontally to make
4 thin layers in all.

10 In large bowl,
whip double or
whipping cream until stiff
peaks have formed.

Strawberries are at their
prettiest when hulls and stalks
are left on for decoration

Gentle waves of whipped
cream are piped with large
star tube on top and side
of cake

PIPING WHIPPED CREAM

Double or whipping cream can be whipped to double its volume and will stay stiff for several hours. For perfect results, chill bowl, beater and cream before beating. Whip until stiff peaks form, but be careful not to overwhip as this causes cream to become granular and it will then turn to butter. Refrigerate whipped cream if not using immediately. After piping design on to cake, refrigerate until ready to serve. Here we show you how, with piping bag and star tube, you can make a wide range of different shapes and designs.

Adaptor and tube

Piping bag fitted with adaptor and tube

11 Place 1 cake layer on plate; spread with whipped cream. Arrange half of the strawberry halves on top of cream.

12 Top strawberries with second cake layer, pressing down gently but firmly; spread strawberry jam over cake.

13 Top strawberry jam with third cake layer; repeat with whipped cream and strawberry halves. Top with remaining cake layer.

14 Cover top and side of cake with one-third of remaining whipped cream. Spoon rest of whipped cream into piping bag with large star tube; use to decorate top and side of cake.

15 Arrange 3 whole strawberries on top of cake. Cut remaining strawberries in half; use to decorate side of cake. Refrigerate cake if not serving immediately.

ALTERNATIVE FILLING

The simple Victoria sandwich cake on these two pages has a classic filling of jam and whipped cream. For a change, try the following filling.

Raspberry Custard Filling
Sprinkle *225 g/8 oz frozen raspberries* with *60 g/2 oz caster sugar*; thaw, then drain, reserving *125 ml/ 4 fl oz juice.* In saucepan, mix *1 tablespoon powdered gelatine, 4 teaspoons caster sugar* and *4 teaspoons plain flour.* Beat *2 egg yolks* with *250 ml/8 fl oz milk* and raspberry juice; stir into gelatine mixture. Set aside for 1 minute. Cook over low heat, stirring, until mixture thickens and coats a spoon well. Remove from heat; stir in raspberries. Cool, then cover and refrigerate until mixture mounds slightly, stirring occasionally. Whip *150 ml/ 1/4 pint double or whipping cream*; fold into custard. Refrigerate until firm enough tô spread, about 20 minutes.

CELEBRATION BUFFET CAKE

8-10 servings

Can be made day before and kept in refrigerator

450 g/1 lb plain chocolate, broken into pieces

350 ml/12 fl oz double or whipping cream

125 ml/4 fl oz cream liqueur

2 x 225 g/8 oz packets sponge cake mix

30 g/1 oz cocoa powder

Strawberries to decorate

1 Place chocolate in large bowl. In medium saucepan over medium heat, heat double or whipping cream and cream liqueur until tiny bubbles form round edge of pan; pour hot cream mixture into bowl with chocolate. With electric mixer, beat until chocolate melts and mixture is smooth. Cover and refrigerate chocolate ganache until thickened.

2 Preheat oven to 180°C/350°F/gas 4. Line two 33 x 23 cm/ 13 x 9 inch Swiss roll tins with non-stick baking parchment.

3 Prepare sponge mixture according to packet instructions. Spoon half of the mixture into 1 Swiss roll tin and spread evenly. Sift three-quarters of the cocoa into remaining mixture; stir well. Spread in second tin.

4 Bake cakes for 10 minutes or until skewer inserted in centre comes out clean. Cool in tins on wire racks for 10 minutes. With palette knife, loosen cakes; turn out on to wire racks, peel off parchment and cool.

5 With serrated knife, using cardboard strip as guide, cut each cake in half lengthways, to make 4 equal strips in all.

6 With electric mixer, beat chilled chocolate ganache until thick and with an easy spreading consistency.

7 Place 1 white cake strip on large baking sheet; spread with 5 tablespoons chocolate ganache. Top with 1 chocolate cake strip; spread with 5 tablespoons chocolate ganache.

8 Repeat layering, ending with chocolate cake strip. Set aside remaining ganache.

9 Cover cake and place in freezer until chocolate ganache filling is firm, about 1 hour.

10 Assemble and ice cake (see Box, right). Sift remaining cocoa powder over cake.

11 Transfer cake to serving plate; refrigerate if not serving immediately.

12 To serve, decorate cake with whole fresh strawberries.

ASSEMBLING CAKE

Cutting cake diagonally: *place frozen cake on work surface with long side parallel to edge. With long serrated knife, slice cake in half diagonally from upper rear corner to lower front corner, to make 2 long triangles. Place 1 cake half on foil-covered cardboard strip, cut side facing out.*

Spreading first cake half with chocolate ganache: *on uncut side of cake half on foil-covered cardboard strip, with palette knife, evenly spread 5 tablespoons chocolate ganache.*

Joining cake halves: *place second cake half, cut side facing outwards, alongside first cake half. Gently press 2 halves together to form 1 large triangle.*

Icing cake: *spread sloping sides of triangle cake with remaining chocolate ganache.*

No-one will believe
that this dramatic-looking
triangle cake is quick and easy
to make – with a sponge mix
from a packet!

CARROT CAKE

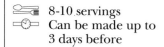 8-10 servings
Can be made up to
3 days before

450 g/1 lb self-raising flour

500 g/1 lb 2 oz caster
sugar

¹/₂ teaspoon baking powder

1 tablespoon ground
cinnamon

4 eggs

350 ml/12 fl oz vegetable
oil

3 medium-sized carrots,
peeled and grated

225 g/8 oz walnut pieces,
chopped

250 ml/8 fl oz apple sauce

150 g/5 oz icing sugar

*Glacé icing should be just
runny enough to drizzle
down side of cake*

1 Preheat oven to
170°C/325°F/gas 3.
Grease 25 cm/10 inch
bundt or kugelhopf
mould; dust lightly with
flour.

2 In large bowl, with
spoon, combine
flour, caster sugar,
baking powder and
ground cinnamon.

3 In medium bowl, with
fork, beat eggs lightly;
stir in oil. Stir egg mixture,
grated carrots, walnuts and
apple sauce into flour
mixture just until flour is
moistened.

4 Spoon mixture into
mould, spreading
evenly. Bake for 1 hour
20 minutes or until skewer
inserted in centre of cake
comes out clean.

5 Cool cake in mould
on wire rack for
10 minutes.

CREAMY CHEESE ICING

In large bowl, place
*350 g/12 oz full-fat soft
cheese, softened, 120 g/
4 oz butter, softened,* and
1 tablespoon lemon juice.
With electric mixer,
beat ingredients until
smooth. Gradually add
*625 g/1 lb 6 oz icing
sugar, sifted,* beating
constantly until
smooth; icing should
have an easy spreading
consistency.

6 With palette knife,
loosen cake from edge
of mould; turn out on to
wire rack and leave to cool.

7 Prepare icing: in small
bowl, with spoon, mix
sifted icing sugar with
5 teaspoons water until
smooth; icing should
have an easy spreading
consistency.

8 Place cake on plate.
With palette knife,
spread icing on cake.

ALTERNATIVE SHAPE

For a different look, you can bake two layers of
carrot cake mixture, then sandwich the layers
together with icing and spread icing over the
whole cake.

Carrot Sandwich Cake

In step 4, spoon mixture
into 2 greased and floured
23 cm/9 inch round cake
tins; bake for 40-45
minutes or until skewer
inserted in centres of
cakes comes out clean.
Cool cakes in tins on wire
racks for 10 minutes; turn
out on to wire racks to
cool completely. Make
Creamy Cheese Icing (see

Box, above left). Place
1 cake, rounded side
down, on serving plate.
With palette knife, spread
cake evenly with 250 ml/
8 fl oz icing. Place second
cake, rounded side up, on
top of first cake. With
palette knife, spread top
and side of cake with
remaining icing, swirling
to make attractive design.

CHOCOLATE CREAM CAKE

16 servings

Can be made day before and kept in refrigerator

225 g/8 oz plain chocolate
6 eggs, separated
75 g/2 ¹/₂ oz caster sugar
50 g/1 ²/₃ oz plain flour
120 g/4 oz flaked blanched almonds
Chocolate Cream Filling (see Box, right)
25 g/ ³/₄ oz cocoa powder

1 Preheat oven to 180°C/350°F/gas 4. Grease 25 cm/10 inch springform cake tin.

2 Grate half of the chocolate; set aside.

3 In large bowl, with electric mixer on full speed, beat egg whites until stiff peaks form.

4 In another large bowl, using electric mixer, beat egg yolks and sugar until very thick and lemon-coloured. Add flour; beat until well mixed, occasionally scraping bowl with rubber spatula. With spatula, stir in grated chocolate. With spatula or wire whisk, gently fold beaten egg whites into egg yolk mixture, one-third at a time.

5 Spoon mixture into tin, spreading evenly. Bake for 25 minutes or until skewer inserted in centre of cake comes out clean. Cool cake in tin on wire rack for 5 minutes. With palette knife, loosen cake from edge of tin; remove tin side. Loosen cake from tin base; slide on to wire rack to cool completely.

6 In frying pan over medium heat, cook almonds until golden, stirring frequently; cool.

7 Prepare Chocolate Cream Filling. Spoon a small quantity of filling into piping bag with small star tube; set aside for decoration. Spoon another small quantity of filling into small bowl; reserve to cover side of cake later.

8 Break remaining chocolate into pieces; place in bowl over saucepan of gently simmering water. Add *2 tablespoons water* to chocolate and heat, stirring frequently, until melted and smooth. Remove from heat.

9 With serrated knife, cut cake horizontally into 2 layers. Spread top cake layer with melted chocolate; leave to stand until chocolate sets slightly, about 10 minutes.

> CHOCOLATE CREAM FILLING
>
> In large bowl, with electric mixer, beat *750 ml/1 ¹/₄ pints double cream, 60 g/2 oz cocoa powder, sifted,* and *150 g/5 oz caster sugar* until stiff peaks form.

10 Meanwhile, place bottom cake layer, cut-side up, on cake plate; spread with filling remaining in large bowl.

11 Cut top cake layer into 16 wedges. Place wedges on top of filling-covered cake layer. Use filling in small bowl to cover side of cake. Pat toasted almonds on to side of cake. Sift cocoa over top of cake. With knife, mark wedges to show servings. Use filling in piping bag to pipe rosette on top of each wedge. Refrigerate cake if not serving immediately.

Chocolate cream filling is piped in rosette shapes on each portion of cake

Cake is marked into serving portions after being sifted with cocoa powder

Toasted flaked almonds add crunch to this rich and creamy cake

CANNOLI CAKE

 8-10 servings

 Can be made day before and kept in refrigerator

6 eggs, separated

200 g/7 oz caster sugar

120 g/4 oz self-raising flour

2 large oranges

2 tablespoons orange liqueur (optional)

900 g/2 lb ricotta cheese

200 g/7 oz full-fat soft cheese, softened

120 g/4 oz icing sugar, sifted

100 g/3 ½ oz plain chocolate chips

Vanilla Cream Icing (see Box, page 117)

1 Preheat oven to 190°C/375°F/gas 5. Line base of 23 cm/9 inch springform cake tin with non-stick baking parchment.

2 In large bowl, with electric mixer on full speed, beat egg whites until soft peaks form; gradually sprinkle in half of the caster sugar, beating until sugar completely dissolves and whites stand in stiff peaks.

3 In another large bowl, using electric mixer, beat egg yolks, flour, remaining caster sugar and *2 tablespoons water* until blended. With rubber spatula, gently fold beaten egg whites into egg yolk mixture, one-third at a time.

4 Spoon mixture into cake tin. Bake for 30-35 minutes or until cake is golden and top springs back when lightly touched with finger.

MAKING FEATHER DESIGN

Piping circles on cake: *using greaseproof paper piping bag with tip cut to make 3 mm/⅛ inch hole, pipe melted chocolate on top of cake in concentric circles, starting in centre and moving to edge of cake.*

Drawing spokes towards centre: *before chocolate hardens, with tip of cocktail stick or small knife, quickly draw lines in spoke fashion, about 4 cm/1 ½ inches apart round edge of cake; alternate direction of each spoke, first from edge to centre of cake, then from centre to edge.*

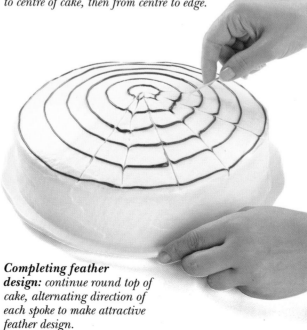

Completing feather design: *continue round top of cake, alternating direction of each spoke to make attractive feather design.*

5 Invert cake in tin on to wire rack; cool completely in tin.

6 From oranges, grate 2 teaspoons zest and squeeze 5 tablespoons juice (if not using liqueur, increase orange juice to 8 tablespoons). Stir liqueur into juice; set aside.

7 In large bowl, with electric mixer, beat ricotta cheese, soft cheese, grated orange zest and icing sugar until smooth. Stir in 45 g/1 ½ oz chocolate chips.

PAPER PIPING BAG

Cut square of grease-proof paper; fold in half into triangle. Lay triangle on flat surface so wide side is at top. Fold left-hand corner down to centre point. Take right-hand corner; wrap it completely round folded left-hand corner, forming cone. Both corners meet at centre point of original triangle.

Fold in these ends twice to hold together.

Fill cone-shaped paper piping bag two-thirds full; fold top over.

8 With palette knife, loosen cake from edge of tin; remove tin side. Loosen cake from tin base; remove tin base. With serrated knife, cut cake horizontally into 2 layers. Brush orange juice mixture evenly over cut side of both layers.

9 Place bottom cake layer, cut side up, on cake plate. Spoon ricotta cheese filling on centre of cake layer. Spread some filling out to edge, leaving centre rounded to achieve a dome effect.

10 Cut a wedge out of remaining cake layer; place cake layer over the filling and replace wedge. (Cutting wedge will allow cake layer to bend, without cracking, to fit over dome shape.)

11 Prepare Vanilla Cream Icing; spread all over top and down side of cake.

12 In small bowl over pan of gently simmering water, heat remaining chocolate chips, stirring frequently, until melted and smooth.

13 Into paper piping bag (see Box, page 116), spoon melted chocolate. With melted chocolate, make feather design on top of cake (see Box, page 116).

14 Refrigerate cake until filling is firm so that cutting is easy, about 3 hours.

Melted chocolate is feathered to give a spider's web effect

Dome-shaped ricotta filling is flavoured with orange; chocolate chips are the surprise ingredient

VANILLA CREAM ICING

In medium bowl, with electric mixer, beat *45 g/1 1/2 oz butter, softened, 3 tablespoons milk, 200 g/7 oz icing sugar, sifted,* and *3/4 teaspoon vanilla essence* until smooth; add more milk if necessary until mixture has an easy spreading consistency. Whip *450 ml/3/4 pint double* or *whipping cream* until stiff peaks form; fold icing sugar mixture into whipped cream.

EDIBLE FLOWERS FOR DECORATING

Many of the flowers that add colour and freshness to the table as the centrepiece can be used to decorate desserts.

When choosing flowers to use with or on foods, keep two important points in mind. First, be sure the ones you want to use are non-toxic. If in doubt, check with the Royal Horticultural Society, or a good reference book. All of the flowers shown in this picture are non-toxic and safe to use with foods.

Next, use flowers that have been grown without the help of pesticides and other chemical sprays. Flowers from the florist have usually been sprayed. Flowers from a home garden, grown without insecticides, are best.

Flowers from a garden should be picked early in the day. Rinse blossoms, leaves and stalks briefly in cool water and shake dry. Keep flowers in water in the refrigerator and use them as soon as you can, as they tend to wilt quickly.

Use flowers in many ways – as buds or open flower heads, with or without the stalk and/or leaves; or pull off individual petals and sprinkle them over the dessert.

Carnation

Pansy

Viola

Borage

Chrysanthemum

Variegated Geranium

Cornflower

Pink Geranium

Gypsophila

Lavender

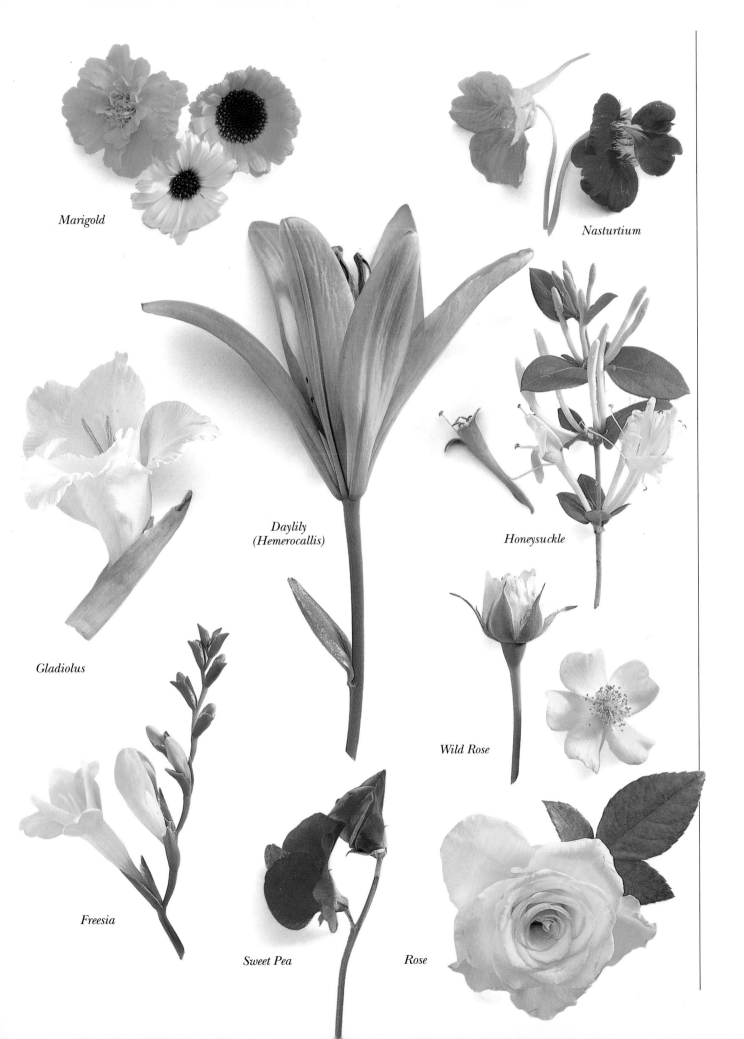

Marigold

Nasturtium

Honeysuckle

Daylily
(Hemerocallis)

Gladiolus

Wild Rose

Freesia

Sweet Pea

Rose

AMERICAN ANGEL CAKE

16 servings
Allow 3 hours preparation and cooking time

150 g/5 oz icing sugar, sifted

120 g/4 oz plain flour

385 ml/13 ¹/₂ fl oz egg whites (12-14 egg whites)

3 tablespoons instant coffee granules or powder

1 ¹/₂ teaspoons cream of tartar

250 g/9 oz caster sugar

Coffee Icing (see Box, above right)

75 g/2 ¹/₂ oz roasted or toasted almonds, coarsely chopped

1 Preheat oven to 190°C/375°F/gas 5. In small bowl, with fork, stir sifted icing sugar and flour; set aside.

2 In large bowl, with electric mixer on full speed, beat egg whites with instant coffee and cream of tartar until soft peaks form. Gradually sprinkle in caster sugar, 2 tablespoons at a time, beating until sugar completely dissolves and whites stand in stiff peaks. With rubber spatula or wire whisk, fold in flour mixture just until flour disappears.

3 Pour mixture into ungreased 25 cm/ 10 inch angel cake tin or 3.5 litre/6 pint ring mould. Bake cake for 35-40 minutes or until top springs back when lightly touched with finger. Invert cake in tin or mould on to funnel or bottle; cool completely in tin or mould.

4 With palette knife, carefully loosen cake from tin or mould, then place on cake plate.

5 Prepare Coffee Icing; spread icing on top of cake. Sprinkle chopped almonds on icing.

COFFEE ICING

In small bowl, stir
1 tablespoon instant coffee granules or *powder* with
2 tablespoons very hot water until coffee dissolves. Stir in
175 g/6 oz icing sugar, sifted, until smooth.

Coarsely chopped toasted almonds and coffee icing add crunch and flavour to this light-as-air cake, but if you omit them the cake will be very low in calories

CHEESECAKES

Cheesecakes are the ideal party dessert! On the dessert table they catch the eye because they are handsome to look at and sizeable enough to please a large group. They are smooth and creamy in texture, deliciously rich and satisfying to eat; and the different flavours make it easy to fit cheesecake into menus for any occasion. All of these cheesecake recipes can be prepared in advance; they can also be made up to a month ahead and frozen. Make as directed and cool completely, then wrap closely in freezer foil and freeze. Thaw, wrapped, for several hours or overnight in the refrigerator, then add any fruit or decoration just before serving.

PECAN CHEESECAKE

 12 servings
Can be made day before and kept in refrigerator

Pastry

150 g/5 oz plain flour
90 g/3 oz butter or block margarine, softened
45 g/1 ¹/₂ oz caster sugar
1 egg yolk

Filling

135 g/4 ¹/₂ oz pecan or walnut halves
3 ¹/₂ x 200 g/7 oz packages full-fat soft cheese, softened
100 g/3 ¹/₂ oz caster sugar
4 eggs
4 tablespoons golden syrup
15 g/ ¹/₂ oz plain flour
Extra pecans or walnuts to decorate (optional)

1 First prepare pastry dough: in small bowl, with electric mixer, beat flour, butter or margarine, sugar and egg yolk just until mixed. Shape dough into 2 balls; wrap and refrigerate for 1 hour.

2 Preheat oven to 200°C/400°F/gas 6. Press one ball of dough on to bottom of 25 cm/10 inch springform cake tin; keep remaining dough refrigerated.

3 Bake pastry base for 8 minutes or until golden; cool in tin on wire rack. Turn oven temperature down to 180°C/350°F/gas 4.

4 While pastry base is cooling, prepare filling: reserve 30 g/1 oz pecan or walnut halves for decoration; chop remaining nuts. In large bowl, with electric mixer, beat soft cheese just until smooth; slowly beat in sugar, scraping bowl often with rubber spatula. Add eggs, golden syrup and flour; beat for 2 minutes, occasionally scraping bowl. Stir in chopped nuts.

5 Press remaining dough round side of tin to within 1-2.5 cm/ ¹/₂-1 inch of top. Pour cheese mixture into tin.

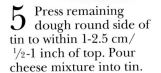

6 Bake cheesecake for 40-45 minutes; cover loosely with foil after 10 minutes, making sure it does not touch filling. Turn oven off; leave cheesecake in oven for 30 minutes. Remove cheesecake from oven; cool completely in tin on wire rack. Cover and refrigerate for at least 3 hours or until well chilled.

7 When cheesecake is firm, with palette knife, loosen tin side from cheesecake and remove; loosen cake from tin base; slide on to plate.

8 Just before serving, arrange reserved nuts on top of cheesecake, using a little extra golden syrup to help them stick. If you like, arrange extra nuts round edge of plate.

Pecan nuts make a pretty pattern round edge of cheesecake and plate

Stirring chopped pecans into cream cheese mixture

CHOCOLATE CHEESECAKE

10-12 servings
Can be made day
before and kept in
refrigerator

Pastry

300 g/10 oz plain flour
60 g/2 oz caster sugar
1/2 teaspoon baking powder
150 g/5 oz butter or block margarine
2 egg yolks
2 tablespoons milk

Filling

225 g/8 oz plain chocolate, broken into pieces
3 1/2 x 200 g/7 oz packages full-fat soft cheese, softened
300 g/10 oz caster sugar
450 ml/ 3/4 pint soured cream
3 eggs
Icing sugar for sprinkling

1 First prepare pastry dough: in medium bowl, with fork, stir flour, sugar and baking powder. With pastry blender or fingertips, cut or rub butter or margarine into flour mixture until mixture resembles coarse crumbs.

2 With fork, stir in egg yolks and milk. With hand, mix just until dough holds together. On lightly floured surface, knead dough until smooth, about 2 minutes. Shape dough into 2 balls; wrap and refrigerate for 1 hour.

3 Preheat oven to 190°C/375°F/gas 5. Lightly grease bottom of 23 cm/ 9 inch springform cake tin.

4 Press one ball of dough on to bottom of tin; keep remaining dough refrigerated. Bake pastry base 15-20 minutes until golden; cool in tin on wire rack. Turn oven temperature down to 170°C/325°F/gas 3.

5 While pastry base is cooling, prepare filling: place pieces of chocolate in bowl over saucepan of gently simmering water and heat, stirring frequently, until melted and smooth. Remove saucepan from heat; leave chocolate to cool to room temperature.

6 In large bowl, with electric mixer, beat soft cheese just until smooth; slowly beat in caster sugar, scraping bowl often with rubber spatula. Add soured cream and eggs; beat for 1 minute, occasionally scraping bowl. Stir melted chocolate into cheese mixture. Pour chocolate and cheese mixture into tin.

7 Divide remaining dough into 10 pieces. On lightly floured surface, with hand, roll each piece into 23 cm/9 inch log.

8 Place 5 pastry logs, 4 cm/1 1/2 inches apart, across top of cheesecake filling.

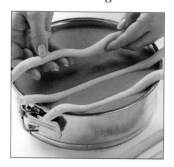

TO SERVE
Sprinkle lattice with sifted icing sugar.

Pastry 'logs' arranged diagonally on top of cheesecake make an attractive diamond lattice

9 Lay remaining pastry logs diagonally across first pastry logs to form lattice top. Trim ends of logs even with side of tin.

10 Bake cheesecake for 50-60 minutes, covering tin loosely with foil after 45 minutes if pastry begins to brown too much. Turn oven off; leave cheesecake in oven for 50 minutes. Remove cheesecake from oven; cool completely in tin on wire rack. Cover and refrigerate for at least 4 hours or until well chilled.

11 When cheesecake is firm, with palette knife, loosen tin side from cheesecake and remove; loosen cake from tin base; slide on to plate.

GERMAN CHEESECAKE

 12 servings
Can be made day before and kept in refrigerator

Pastry

185 g/6 ¹/₂ oz plain flour

120 g/4 oz butter or block margarine, softened

60 g/2 oz caster sugar

1 egg yolk

Grated zest of 1 large lemon

Filling

6 x 200 g/7 oz packages full-fat soft cheese, softened

350 g/12 oz caster sugar

5 eggs

4 tablespoons milk

25 g/³/₄ oz plain flour

2 egg yolks

Grated zest of 1 large lemon

Strawberries and kiwi fruit brushed with melted and sieved raspberry jam (optional)

1 First prepare pastry dough: in medium bowl, with electric mixer, beat flour, butter or margarine, sugar, egg yolk and grated lemon zest until well mixed. Shape dough into ball; wrap and refrigerate for 1 hour.

2 Preheat oven to 200°C/400°F/gas 6. Press one-third of pastry dough on to bottom of 25 cm/10 inch spring-form cake tin; keep remaining dough refrigerated.

3 Bake pastry base for 8 minutes or until golden; cool in tin on wire rack. Turn oven temperature up to 230°C/450°F/gas 8.

4 While pastry base is cooling, prepare filling: in large bowl, with electric mixer, beat soft cheese just until smooth; slowly beat in sugar, scraping bowl often with rubber spatula. Add eggs, milk, flour, egg yolks and lemon zest; beat for 5 minutes, occasionally scraping bowl.

5 Press remaining pastry dough round side of tin to within 1 cm/¹/₂ inch of top. Pour in cheese mixture.

Pouring cheese mixture into tin

ALTERNATIVE TOPPING

Instead of the strawberry and kiwi fruit topping shown in the main picture below, you might like to try this delicious Black Cherry Topping.

Black Cherry Topping
Drain 150 ml/¹/₄ pint juice from *1 x 425 g/15 oz can stoned black cherries* into small saucepan. Blend in *1 rounded teaspoon arrow-root.* Slowly bring to the boil, stirring until thickened. Add cherries and mix lightly; spoon over cheesecake and leave to cool completely. Chill before serving

6 Bake cheesecake for 12 minutes. Turn oven down to 150°C/300°F/gas 2; bake for a further 45 minutes. Turn oven off; leave cheesecake in oven for 30 minutes.

7 Remove cheesecake from oven; cool completely in tin on wire rack.

8 Cover cheesecake and refrigerate for at least 4 hours or until well chilled.

9 When cheesecake is firm, with palette knife, loosen tin side from cheesecake and remove; loosen cake from tin base; slide on to serving plate.

10 If you like, arrange fruit on top of cheesecake and brush with melted and sieved jam.

LEMON CHEESECAKE

 6-8 servings
Make day before and keep in refrigerator

175 g/6 oz digestive biscuits

60 g/2 oz butter

25 g/1 oz demerara sugar

350 g/12 oz full-fat soft cheese

Grated zest and juice of 3 large lemons

1 x 400 g/14 oz can sweetened condensed milk

150 ml/¼ pint double cream

150 ml/¼ pint soured cream

Fresh seasonal fruit to decorate

1 Place digestive biscuits in polythene bag; with rolling pin, roll biscuits until they are crushed to fine crumbs.

2 Melt butter in small saucepan, add sugar and biscuit crumbs and stir well to mix.

Garland of redcurrants, blueberries and strawberries looks very pretty on top of cheesecake

3 Turn biscuit mixture into 20 cm/8 inch springform cake tin and press firmly on to bottom with back of metal spoon.

4 In medium bowl, with electric mixer, beat soft cheese just until smooth; add lemon zest and juice and condensed milk and beat until well combined.

5 In another medium bowl, whip double cream until soft peaks form. Fold whipped cream into cheese mixture.

6 Slowly pour cheese mixture into springform cake tin so that it evenly covers biscuit crust in bottom of tin.

7 Smooth surface of cheese filling; cover and leave in refrigerator overnight, until well chilled and set.

8 Loosen tin side from cheesecake; remove. Loosen cheesecake from base; slide on to plate.

9 With palette knife, spread soured cream over top of cheesecake.

10 Decorate top of cheesecake with seasonal fresh fruit.

SWISS CHOCOLATE CHEESECAKE

12 servings

Can be made day before and kept in refrigerator

---

315 g/10 ½ oz crisp plain chocolate biscuits

200 g/7 oz butter, softened

450 g/1 lb Swiss white chocolate, broken into pieces

4 ½ x 200 g/7 oz packages full-fat soft cheese, softened

60 g/2 oz caster sugar

4 eggs

White Chocolate Curls (page 100) and cocoa powder to decorate

3 Preheat oven to 170°C/325°F/gas 3. Place pieces of chocolate in bowl over pan of gently simmering water and heat, stirring frequently, until melted and smooth. If necessary, with wire whisk, beat chocolate until smooth. Remove from heat; leave chocolate to cool to room temperature.

4 In large bowl, with electric mixer, beat soft cheese and remaining butter just until smooth; slowly beat in sugar, scraping bowl often with rubber spatula. Add melted white chocolate and eggs; beat just until smooth.

5 Pour cheese mixture into biscuit crust. Bake cheesecake for 1 hour; cool in tin on wire rack. Cover and refrigerate for at least 4 hours or until well chilled.

6 When cheesecake is firm, with palette knife, loosen tin side from cheesecake and remove. Loosen cake from tin base; slide on to plate.

7 Pile chocolate curls on top of cheesecake; sift cocoa over chocolate curls.

White chocolate curls look fabulous on slices of white cheesecake, especially with dark cocoa powder dusted over them

1 Place chocolate biscuits, in batches, in polythene bag; with rolling pin, roll biscuits into fine crumbs. Or, in food processor or blender, blend biscuits, in batches if necessary, until fine crumbs form.

2 Lightly grease 25 cm/10 inch springform cake tin. Mix biscuit crumbs and 90 g/ 3 oz butter in tin; press mixture on to bottom and up side of cake tin to within 1 cm/½ inch of top of tin. Set aside.

Serve Swiss Chocolate Cheesecake on dark plates to create a dramatic colour contrast

COFFEE CHEESECAKE

10-12 servings
Can be made day
before and kept in
refrigerator

315 g/10 ½ oz almond
macaroons

90 g/3 oz butter, softened

175 g/6 oz plain chocolate,
broken into pieces

4 ½ x 200 g/7 oz packages
full-fat soft cheese,
softened

135 g/4 ½ oz caster sugar

3 eggs

5 tablespoons milk

2 teaspoons instant coffee
powder

Icing sugar, Chocolate
Leaves (page 101) and
fresh raspberries to
decorate

TO SERVE
*Sift icing sugar over top
of cheesecake, then
arrange chocolate leaves
and raspberries in centre.*

1 Place almond maca-
roons, in batches, in
polythene bag and, with
rolling pin, roll macaroons
into fine crumbs. Or, in
food processor or blender,
blend almond macaroons,
in batches, until fine
crumbs form.

2 In 23 cm/9 inch
springform cake tin,
with hand, mix macaroon
crumbs and butter; press
mixture on to bottom and
up side of cake tin
to within 1 cm/
½ inch of top
of tin. Set aside.

3 Preheat oven to
170°C/325°F/
gas 3. Place pieces of
chocolate in bowl
over pan of gently
simmering water
and heat, stirring
frequently, until
melted and smooth.
Remove from heat.

4 In large bowl, with
electric mixer, beat
soft cheese just until
smooth; slowly beat in
sugar, scraping bowl often
with rubber spatula. Add
melted chocolate, eggs,
milk and instant coffee
powder; beat mixture for
3 minutes, occasionally
scraping bowl.

5 Pour chocolate and
cheese mixture into
biscuit crust.

6 Gently shake tin so
cheesecake mixture
levels out. Bake cheese-
cake for 1 hour. Cool in
tin on wire rack. Cover
and refrigerate for 4 hours
or until well chilled.

7 When cheesecake is
firm, with palette
knife, loosen tin side from
cheesecake and remove;
loosen cheesecake from
tin base; slide cheesecake
on to serving plate.

MELTING CHOCOLATE

Great care must be taken when melting chocolate to
prevent it from burning. Overheated chocolate
scorches easily and becomes bitter, so melt all forms
slowly, using gentle heat. You can use any of these ways.

• Break chocolate into
pieces; place in bowl and
set over saucepan of
gently simmering water.

• Or place in small non-
stick heavy saucepan;
melt over low heat – if
pan is too thin, it will
transfer heat too fast and
burn chocolate.

• Or, for small amounts,
leave chocolate in
original foil wrapper;
set in warm spot on
top of cooker.

• To speed melting, break
up chocolate into smaller
pieces; stir frequently.

• If melting chocolate in
double boiler or bowl over
pan of water, do not boil
water to speed melting.
Any moisture getting into
chocolate will thicken or
curdle chocolate.

• If chocolate thickens or
curdles, add white vege-
table fat (not butter or
margarine) a little at a
time and stir until of
desired consistency.

TORTA RICOTTA

 12 servings

Can be made day before and kept in refrigerator

Pastry

300 g/10 oz plain flour

175 g/6 oz butter or block margarine, softened

60 g/2 oz caster sugar

2 tablespoons dry Marsala wine

2 egg yolks

Filling

900 g/2 lb ricotta cheese

200 g/7 oz caster sugar

250 ml/8 fl oz double or whipping cream

50 g/1 ²/₃ oz plain flour

6 eggs

Grated zest of 2 medium-sized oranges

Grated zest of 2 medium-sized lemons

Icing sugar for sprinkling

Orange twists to decorate

1 First prepare pastry dough: in large bowl, with electric mixer, beat flour, butter or margarine, sugar, Marsala and egg yolks just until mixed. Shape dough into a ball. Wrap tightly and refrigerate for 1 hour.

2 Preheat oven to 180°C/350°F/gas 4.

3 Into 25 cm/10 inch springform cake tin, press three-quarters of dough on to bottom and up side of tin to within 2 cm/³/₄ inch of top; keep remaining dough refrigerated.

4 Bake pastry case for 15 minutes or until golden; cool in tin on wire rack.

5 While pastry base is cooling, prepare filling: press ricotta through fine sieve into large bowl. With electric mixer, beat ricotta just until smooth; slowly beat in caster sugar, scraping bowl often with rubber spatula. Add double or whipping cream, flour, eggs and orange and lemon zest; beat until well blended, occasionally scraping bowl. Pour mixture into tin.

6 On lightly floured surface, with floured rolling pin, roll out remaining dough into 25 x 12.5 cm/10 x 5 inch rectangle. Cut dough lengthways into ten 1 cm/¹/₂ inch wide strips. Place 5 strips about 2.5 cm/1 inch apart across filling. Arrange remaining strips at right angles to make a lattice. Trim ends of strips even with pastry case.

7 Bake cheesecake for 1 ¹/₄ hours. Turn oven off; leave cheesecake in oven for 1 hour. Remove cheesecake from oven; cool completely in tin on wire rack. Cover and refrigerate for at least 4 hours or until chilled.

8 When cheesecake is firm, with palette knife, loosen tin side from cheesecake and remove; loosen cake from tin base; slide on to plate.

9 Sprinkle cheesecake with sifted icing sugar. Arrange orange twists round cake.

RICOTTA CHEESE

Ricotta cheese is a pure white, creamy, satiny-smooth cheese with a fine, slightly moist texture and very bland, sweetish flavour. Its nearest 'relative' is curd cheese, but ricotta is creamier.

• Cheesecake made of ricotta – Torta Ricotta – is one of the great classic dishes of Italy. For another Italian-inspired dessert using ricotta, see Cannoli Cake (pages 116-117).

• Ricotta is made from the whey left from the making of other cheeses. It is uncured, and so should be used within a few days of purchase.

FRUIT CAKES

A beautifully decorated fruit cake makes a perfect centrepiece for any celebration, and a delicious dessert to crown a feast or to accompany mulled wine or cider, coffee or tea. Follow the storage tips below if you want to enjoy your fruit cake even after the celebrations are over.

AMERICAN FESTIVAL FRUIT CAKE

- Makes one 25 cm/ 10 inch cake
- Make day before or up to 1 month ahead

450 g/1 lb red glacé cherries

120 g/4 oz green glacé cherries

350 g/12 oz stoned prunes

300 g/10 oz stoned dates

120 ml/4 fl oz cream sherry

700 g/1 ½ lb mixed nuts

175 g/6 oz shelled pecans or walnut pieces

215 g/7 ½ oz self-raising flour

200 g/7 oz caster sugar

6 eggs, lightly beaten

1 In very large bowl mix first 5 ingredients; leave to stand for 15 minutes or until almost all liquid is absorbed, stirring often.

2 Meanwhile, brush 25 cm/10 inch angel cake tin or 3.5 litre/6 pint ring mould generously with oil and line with foil, smoothing it out as much as possible so cake does not have wrinkles on side and bottom; grease foil.

3 Preheat oven to 150°C/300°F/gas 2. Stir mixed nuts and pecans or walnuts into fruit mixture in bowl. Remove 225 g/8 oz fruit and nut mixture; set aside. Stir flour and sugar into remaining fruit and nut mixture in large bowl until well coated. Stir in eggs until well mixed.

4 Spoon mixture into tin or mould, spreading evenly. Sprinkle reserved fruit and nut mixture on top. Cover tin or mould loosely with foil. Bake for 2 hours.

5 Remove foil and bake for 30 minutes longer or until knife inserted in cake comes out clean.

6 Cool cake in tin or mould on wire rack for 30 minutes; remove from tin or mould and carefully peel off foil. Cool cake completely on rack.

7 Wrap fruit cake tightly; refrigerate overnight so cake will be firm and easy to slice.

TO STORE FRUIT CAKE

Keep cake, wrapped tightly, in airtight container in a cool place or refrigerator. If you like, sprinkle cake first with wine or brandy.

Alternatively, wrap cake with cloth soaked in brandy or wine, then overwrap with foil. Re-soak cloth weekly.

Top of cake is studded with an abundance of colourful fruit and nuts

CALYPSO FRUIT CAKE

- Makes one 25 cm/ 10 inch cake
- Make day before or up to 1 month ahead

350 ml/12 fl oz dry red wine

90 g/3 oz stoned prunes

120 g/4 oz raisins

100 g/3 1/2 oz candied citron, diced

300 g/10 oz caster sugar

225 g/8 oz butter or margarine, softened

425 g/15 oz self-raising flour

1 teaspoon ground cinnamon

3 eggs

1 teaspoon grated lime zest

Lime Glaze (see Box, above right)

100 g/3 1/2 oz mixed glacé fruit, chopped

1 tablespoon golden syrup

1 Bring first 4 ingredients to the boil in medium saucepan over high heat. Remove saucepan from heat; leave to soften for 30 minutes.

2 Process fruit mixture in food processor or blender, in 2 batches if necessary, until smooth; set aside.

3 Preheat oven to 170°C/325°F/gas 3.

4 Grease 25 cm/10 inch kugelhopf mould or savarin mould.

5 In large bowl, with electric mixer, beat sugar and butter or margarine for 10 minutes or until light and fluffy, scraping bowl often with rubber spatula.

6 To butter and sugar mixture, add flour, cinnamon, eggs and fruit mixture; beat until well mixed, constantly scraping bowl. Continue beating for 1 minute, occasionally scraping bowl. Stir in grated lime zest.

LIME GLAZE
In medium bowl, with spoon, stir *175 g/6 oz icing sugar, sifted, 4 teaspoons hot water, 2 teaspoons lime juice* and *1/2 teaspoon grated lime zest* until smooth.

7 Spoon mixture into mould, spreading evenly. Bake for 1 hour or until skewer inserted in centre of cake comes out clean. Cool cake in mould on wire rack for about 10 minutes; remove cake from mould. Cool cake completely on rack.

8 To serve, prepare Lime Glaze. Spoon glaze over cake.

9 In small bowl, stir mixed glacé fruit with golden syrup.

10 As quickly as possible, before glaze sets, arrange glacé fruit in garland on top of cake; leave to set before serving.

Calypso Fruit Cake is drizzled with a lime glaze and decorated with glacé fruit

SPICED MINCEMEAT CAKE

Makes one 25 cm/
10 inch cake

Make day before
or up to 1 month
ahead

| 300 g/10 oz stoned dates |
| 225 g/8 oz dried figs, sliced |
| 175 g/6 oz pecan or walnut halves |
| 120 g/4 oz green glacé cherries |
| 120 g/4 oz red glacé cherries |
| 600 g/1 1/4 lb self-raising flour |
| 325 g/11 oz light soft brown sugar |
| 200 g/7 oz caster sugar |
| 225 g/8 oz soft margarine |
| 6 eggs |
| 1/2 teaspoon ground cinnamon |
| 1/2 teaspoon grated nutmeg |
| 1/2 teaspoon ground allspice |
| 2 x 400 g/14 oz jars mincemeat |
| 2 tablespoons golden syrup |

To give cake a party look, tie a satin ribbon round its waist

1 Reserve 75 g/2 1/2 oz dates, 120 g/4 oz figs, 45 g/1 1/2 oz pecans or walnuts and 60 g/2 oz each green and red glacé cherries. Dice remaining dates and cherries. In bowl, combine diced dates and cherries with remaining figs and pecans or walnuts; coat with 150 g/5 oz flour.

Stirring flour into fruit and nut mixture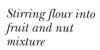

2 Preheat oven to 150°C/300°F/gas 2. Grease 25 cm/10 inch loose-bottomed angel cake tin or springform cake tin with funnel base.

3 In large bowl, using electric mixer, beat brown sugar, caster sugar and soft margarine for 10 minutes or until light and fluffy, scraping bowl often with rubber spatula. Add eggs, cinnamon, nutmeg and allspice; beat until well mixed, constantly scraping bowl. With spoon, stir in mincemeat, fruit mixture and remaining flour.

4 Spoon cake mixture into cake tin, spreading evenly with spoon so mixture is level.

5 Bake for 2 hours or until skewer inserted in cake comes out clean and cake pulls away slightly from side of tin.

6 Cool cake in tin on wire rack for 30 minutes; remove cake from tin and cool completely on wire rack.

7 When cake is cool, prepare topping: in medium saucepan over medium heat, heat reserved fruit and nuts with golden syrup for 5 minutes, stirring; arrange on cake.

8 Let fruit and nut topping cool and set.

9 Wrap fruit cake tightly; refrigerate overnight so cake will be firm and easy to slice.

PIES, TARTS, PASTRIES AND HOT FRUIT PUDDINGS

131-198

Pies, Tarts, Pastries and Hot Fruit Puddings

In this chapter, pastry – timeless and simple – can be used in so many different and exciting ways! Just start with the basic recipes and a variety of fillings, and you'll end up with time-honoured favourites like Apple Pie, Cherry Pie and Strawberry and Rhubarb Pie that your family will love. Make the most of summer and autumn harvests by trying Midsummer Fruit Pie, Ascot Fruit Tart and Individual Peach Cobblers – fruit desserts with a special touch. There are classic pastries from around the world like Baklava and Apple Strudel, comforting hot fruit puddings like Banana Brown Betty and Apple Cobbler that are so quick to make, and magnificent recipes like Swan Choux Puffs and Paris-Brest to add the crowning touch to an elegant meal.

CONTENTS

SWEET PIES

Sweet pies can be as simple and homely or as elaborate and elegant as you wish. Much of their success depends on the pastry, which should enhance, not compete with, the flavour of the filling and be crisp and tender, never soggy. For variety, try a plain top crust one time, a lattice top the next. For biscuit crust pies, try different fillings and toppings. Be creative!

SHORTCRUST PASTRY FOR DOUBLE CRUST PIE

300 g/10 oz plain flour
1 teaspoon salt (optional)
175 g/6 oz butter or block margarine
3-4 tablespoons cold water

1 Make dough as for Shortcrust Pastry for Pie Shell (see Box, right), steps 1 to 3.

2 Divide dough into 2 pieces, 1 slightly larger than the other.

3 On lightly floured surface, with floured rolling pin, roll out larger piece of dough into round about 3 mm/ ⅛ inch thick and 4 cm/1 ½ inches larger all round than upside-down shallow 20-23 cm/8-9 inch pie dish.

4 Roll dough round gently on to rolling pin; transfer to pie dish and unroll. Gently ease dough into bottom and up side of pie dish to line evenly; trim dough edge and fill according to individual recipe instructions.

5 For top crust, roll out smaller piece of dough as for bottom crust; with sharp knife, cut few slashes or design in centre of round; centre top crust over filling in bottom crust.

6 Make Decorative Pastry Edge (pages 136-137); bake pie according to recipe.

MAKING PASTRY IN FOOD PROCESSOR

To save time, pastry dough can be made in the food processor, with excellent results. This is especially helpful if you are catering for a crowd and have a large number of pies to make.

1 In food processor with knife blade attached, combine flour and butter or margarine. Process for 1-2 seconds until mixture forms fine crumbs.

2 Add cold water; process for 1-2 seconds until dough forms on blades.

3 Remove dough from bowl; with hands, shape dough into ball.

SHORTCRUST PASTRY FOR PIE SHELL

200 g/7 oz plain flour
1 teaspoon salt (optional)
120 g/4 oz butter or block margarine
2-3 tablespoons cold water

1 In medium bowl, stir flour and salt, if using.

2 With pastry blender or with fingertips, cut or rub butter or margarine into flour mixture until mixture resembles coarse crumbs.

3 Sprinkle cold water, a tablespoon at a time, into mixture. Mix lightly with fork after each addition, until dough is just moist enough to hold together.

4 In same bowl, with lightly floured hands, shape dough into smooth ball.

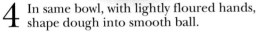

5 On floured surface, with floured rolling pin, roll out dough into round about 3 mm/ ⅛ inch thick.

6 Roll from centre to edge of dough to keep dough circular. Add more flour if dough begins to stick to work surface. Push sides in by hand if necessary and lift rolling pin slightly near edges to avoid making them too thin.

7 Cut dough round 4 cm/1 ½ inches larger all round than upside-down 20-23 cm/ 8-9 inch pie dish.

8 Roll dough round gently on to rolling pin; transfer to pie dish and unroll.

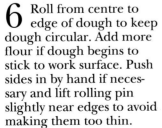

9 Gently ease dough into bottom and up side of pie dish to line evenly.

10 Make Decorative Pastry Edge (pages 136-137); fill and bake pie according to recipe.

BAKING BLIND

Many pie shells are filled with an uncooked mixture, so you will need to bake the pie shell blind first. A crisp baked pastry shell that is to be filled with a chilled mixture should be thoroughly cooled before the filling is added.

1 Preheat oven to 220°C/425°F/gas 7. Line dish with dough.

2 With fork, prick dough liberally.

3 Line dough with foil and spread evenly with dried or baking beans.

4 Bake for 15 minutes or until golden.

5 Remove foil and beans, prick again and bake for a further 3-4 minutes.

6 Cool on wire rack.

DECORATIVE PASTRY EDGES

These eye-catching edges that finish off a pie so beautifully are not hard to make. Choose from Fluted, Sharp Fluted and Ruffled Edges for either pie shells or double crust pies; Leaf, Plaited and Heart Edges are suitable for pie shells only.

Pie Shells

1 Line pie dish with dough (page 135); trim dough edge with kitchen scissors, leaving about 2.5 cm/1 inch overhang all round rim of dish.

2 Fold overhang under, then bring up over rim of pie dish.

3 Make decorative edge of your choice, then bake pie as directed in recipe.

Double Crust Pies

1 Trim edge of top crust with kitchen scissors, leaving about 2.5 cm/1 inch overhang all round rim of pie dish. Fold overhang under, then bring up over rim of pie dish.

2 Make decorative edge of your choice, then bake pie as directed in recipe.

FLUTED EDGE

Canadian Peach Pie (page 158) with Fluted Edge

1 Pinch to form stand-up edge. Place index finger on inside edge of dough and, with index finger and thumb of other hand, pinch dough to make flute.

2 Repeat round edge of dough, leaving 5 mm/¼ inch space between each flute.

SHARP FLUTED EDGE

Old English Apple Pie (page 145) with Sharp Fluted Edge

1 Pinch to form stand-up edge. Place pointed edge of small star or diamond shaped biscuit cutter on inside edge of dough and, with index finger and thumb of other hand, pinch dough to make sharp flute.

2 Repeat round edge of dough, leaving 5 mm/¼ inch space between each flute.

LEAF OR HEART EDGE

*Pecan Pie (page 148)
with Leaf Edge*

1 Prepare Shortcrust Pastry for Double Crust Pie (page 134); use larger piece of dough to line pie dish.

2 Roll out remaining dough until it is 3 mm/ 1/8 inch thick. With sharp knife or small biscuit cutter, cut out shapes (leaves or hearts).

3 Press each shape on to lightly moistened pie shell edge, overlapping shapes slightly or varying angles.

RUFFLED EDGE

*Cherry Pie (page 156)
with Ruffled Edge*

1 Pinch to form stand-up edge. Place index finger under outside edge of dough and, with index finger and thumb of other hand, pinch dough to form ruffle.

2 Repeat round edge of dough, leaving 5 mm/ 1/4 inch space between ruffles.

PLAITED EDGE

*Pumpkin Pie (page 149)
with Plaited Edge*

1 Prepare Shortcrust Pastry for Double Crust Pie (page 134); use larger piece of dough to line pie dish.

2 Roll out remaining dough until it is about 3 mm/ 1/8 inch thick; cut into strips that are 5 mm/ 1/4 inch wide.

3 Gently plait strips together and press on to lightly moistened pie shell edge. Join ends of plait together to cover edge completely.

HARVEST PEAR AND PINEAPPLE PIE

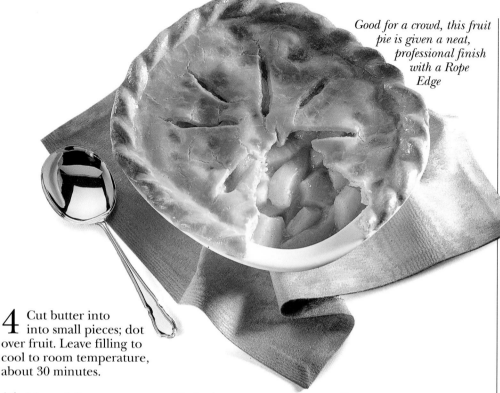

Good for a crowd, this fruit pie is given a neat, professional finish with a Rope Edge

🍴 10 servings
🕐 Allow 2 hours preparation and cooking time

Filling

2 x 820 g/29 oz cans pear halves

2 x 400 g/14 oz cans pineapple pieces in juice

1 rounded tablespoon cornflour

$^1/_2$ teaspoon grated nutmeg

$^1/_2$ teaspoon ground cinnamon

45 g/1 $^1/_2$ oz butter

Pastry

225 g/8 oz plain flour

$^1/_2$ teaspoon salt (optional)

120 g/4 oz butter or block margarine

1 egg yolk, lightly beaten

1 Drain pears, reserving 400 ml/14 fl oz juice; thinly slice pear halves. Drain pineapple.

2 In large saucepan, mix cornflour, nutmeg, cinnamon and reserved pear juice. Cook over medium heat, stirring constantly, until mixture thickens and boils. Remove saucepan from heat; stir in pear slices and pineapple pieces.

3 Into 23 cm/9 inch square baking dish, pour fruit mixture.

Pouring fruit mixture into baking dish

4 Cut butter into into small pieces; dot over fruit. Leave filling to cool to room temperature, about 30 minutes.

5 Meanwhile, prepare pastry dough: in bowl, mix flour with salt, if using. With pastry blender or with fingertips, cut or rub butter or margarine into flour until mixture resembles coarse crumbs. Sprinkle *3 tablespoons cold water*, a tablespoon at a time, into mixture, mixing lightly with fork after each addition until dough is moist enough to hold together. Shape dough into a ball.

6 Preheat oven to 220°C/425°F/gas 7. On floured surface, with floured rolling pin, roll out dough 3 mm/$^1/_8$ inch thick to fit dish, leaving 2.5 cm/1 inch overhang; place over filling.

7 Turn overhang under to make stand-up edge. Make Rope Edge (see Box, right).

8 Cut a few slashes in crust to allow steam to escape during baking. Brush crust lightly with egg yolk.

9 Bake pie for 25-30 minutes until filling is bubbly and pastry is golden brown. Cool pie on wire rack for 15 minutes before serving, or cool completely to serve cold later.

ROPE EDGE

Press thumb into edge of crust at an angle, then pinch dough between thumb and knuckle of index finger. Place thumb in groove that has been left by index finger.

Repeat all round edge of crust to create twisted rope effect.

CHOCOLATE CHIFFON PIE

 8 servings
Make day before and refrigerate

175 g/6 oz rich tea biscuits

120 g/4 oz butter, softened

60 g/2 oz plain chocolate, broken into pieces

2 1/2 x 200 g/7 oz packages full-fat soft cheese, softened

1 x 400 g/14 oz can sweetened condensed milk

Candied Orange Zest (see Box, right)

1 Preheat oven to 190°C/375°F/gas 5. Place biscuits, in batches, in polythene bag and with rolling pin, roll biscuits into fine crumbs. Or, in food processor or blender, blend biscuits, in batches, until fine crumbs form.

2 In shallow 20-23 cm/ 8-9 inch pie dish, mix biscuit crumbs with butter; press mixture on to bottom and up side of pie dish.

3 Bake crust for 8 minutes or until golden; cool on wire rack.

4 Place pieces of chocolate in bowl over pan of gently simmering water and heat, stirring often, until melted and smooth.

5 In large bowl, with electric mixer, beat soft cheese and condensed milk until blended; beat in melted chocolate until smooth.

6 Pour chocolate mixture into biscuit crust. Cover and keep in refrigerator overnight.

7 The next day, prepare Candied Orange Zest and arrange on top of pie.

CANDIED ORANGE ZEST

With vegetable peeler, thinly pare zest from *2 medium-sized oranges* in long pieces; cut zest into 3 mm/1/8 inch-wide matchstick strips. In medium saucepan over high heat, bring orange zest, *125 ml/ 4 fl oz water* and *60 g/ 2 oz caster sugar* to the boil. Reduce heat to medium and cook for 10-15 minutes until orange zest is limp and translucent. Place *30 g/ 1 oz caster sugar* in small bowl. Drain orange zest; place in bowl of sugar and toss to coat.

Once orange zest is evenly coated in sugar, spread it out on a baking sheet to dry.

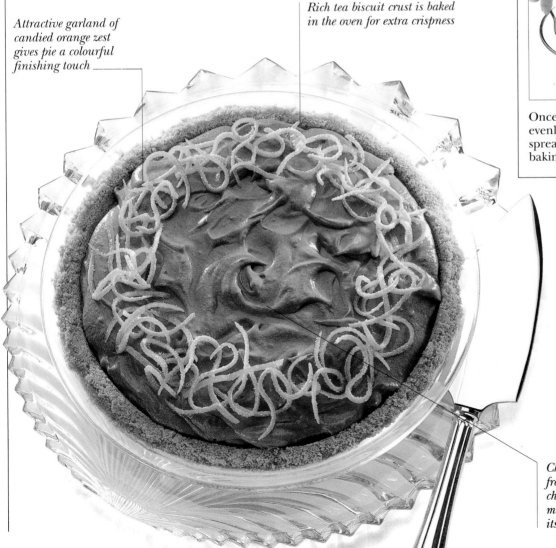

Attractive garland of candied orange zest gives pie a colourful finishing touch

Rich tea biscuit crust is baked in the oven for extra crispness

Chiffon filling made from chocolate, soft cheese and condensed milk is simplicity itself to make

STRAWBERRY AND RHUBARB PIE

Strawberries and rhubarb go together really well, both in terms of colour and flavour – and they're in season at the same time, making them the perfect combination for this luscious-tasting pie.

 8-10 servings

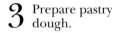 Allow 3 hours preparation and cooking time

Filling

450 g/1 lb strawberries

450 g/1 lb rhubarb (trimmed weight)

175 g/6 oz caster sugar

45 g/1 ½ oz plain flour

15 g/ ½ oz butter

Pastry

Shortcrust Pastry for Double Crust Pie (page 134)

1 tablespoon milk

1 Remove hulls from strawberries and cut each strawberry in half. Cut rhubarb stalks crossways into 1 cm/ ½ inch-thick pieces.

2 In large bowl, with rubber spatula, gently toss halved strawberries, rhubarb pieces, sugar and flour.

3 Prepare pastry dough.

4 On lightly floured surface, with floured rolling pin, roll out two-thirds of dough into 40 cm/16 inch round.

5 Gently ease dough into bottom and up side of 20-23 cm/8-9 inch pie dish that is at least 4 cm/1 ½ inches deep, to line evenly; trim dough edge, leaving 4 cm/ 1 ½ inch overhang.

6 Into pie shell, spoon strawberry and rhubarb mixture.

7 Cut butter into small pieces and dot evenly over strawberry and rhubarb mixture.

8 Preheat oven to 220°C/425°F/gas 7.

9 Roll out remaining dough into a 26.5 cm/ 10 ½ inch round. With fluted pastry wheel or knife, cut into ten 2 cm/ ¾ inch wide strips.

10 Place 5 strips over filling; do not seal ends.

11 With remaining 5 strips, make Diamond Lattice (see Box, page 141).

12 Trim ends of strips; moisten edge of pie shell with water; press ends of strips to pie shell to seal. Bring overhang up over strips; pinch edges to seal; make Ruffled or other Decorative Pastry Edge (pages 136-137). Brush lattice with milk.

13 Bake pie for 45-50 minutes or until fruit mixture bubbles and pastry is golden. After 30 minutes, cover pie loosely with foil if pastry is browning too quickly.

14 Leave pie to stand for 1 hour to allow juices to set slightly; serve warm or cold.

Tossing strawberry and rhubarb mixture

ALTERNATIVE TO LATTICE

A quick and easy alternative pastry topping to the Diamond Lattice in the main picture (page 141) is this Cartwheel, in which the pastry strips are placed over the filling like the spokes of a wheel.

Cartwheel

1 With fluted pastry wheel or knife, cut dough into twelve 1 cm/ ½ inch strips.

2 Arrange 6 strips over filling in 'V' shapes.

3 Use more strips to make smaller 'V' shapes inside larger ones.

4 If you like, cut out small shapes from dough trimmings and place in centre of pie.

DIAMOND LATTICE

Taking pastry strips back: *fold back every other strip three-quarters of its length.*

Placing central cross strip: *arrange 1 strip diagonally across centre of filling to start forming diamond shape, then take folded part of strips over central strip.*

Folding back alternate strips: *fold back strips that were not folded back before.*

Placing second cross strip: *arrange another cross strip, parallel to central strip, 2.5 cm/1 inch away.*

Replacing folded part of strips: *take folded part of strips over second diagonal cross strip. Continue folding back alternate strips and placing cross strips diagonally across filling to weave diamond pattern.*

Crinkled edges on pastry lattice are made by cutting out strips with a pastry wheel

Luscious filling of fresh strawberries and rhubarb can be seen through 'windows' of diamond lattice

BRANDY ALEXANDER PIE

🍴 8-10 servings

🕐 Can be made day before and kept in refrigerator

225 g/8 oz plain dark crisp chocolate biscuits

175 g/6 oz butter, softened

225 g/8 oz icing sugar, sifted

120 g/4 oz plain chocolate, melted

3 tablespoons brandy

150 ml/¼ pint double or whipping cream

Dark Chocolate Curls (see Box, right) to decorate

This superbly rich 'marquise' filling is made from butter, sugar, chocolate, whipped cream - and brandy!

1 Place chocolate biscuits, in batches, in polythene bag; with rolling pin, roll biscuits into fine crumbs. Or, in food processor or blender, blend biscuits, in batches if necessary, until fine crumbs form.

2 In bowl, mix together biscuit crumbs and 60 g/2 oz butter. Press biscuit crumb mixture on to bottom and up side of shallow 20-23 cm/8-9 inch pie dish or ceramic flan dish.

3 In food processor, work icing sugar and remaining butter until creamy and smooth. Add melted chocolate and brandy to creamed sugar and butter mixture and work again in food processor until thick and smooth.

4 In small bowl, whip double or whipping cream until soft peaks form. With wire whisk or rubber spatula, gently fold whipped cream into chocolate mixture. Spoon mixture into biscuit crust.

5 Decorate pie with chocolate curls. Refrigerate for at least 1 hour before serving.

DARK CHOCOLATE CURLS

With heat of your hand, slightly warm *60 g/2 oz plain chocolate flavour cake covering* to soften.

With vegetable peeler, slowly and firmly draw blade along smooth surface of cake covering to make curls.

Use wide side of cake covering for wide curls, thin side for thin curls. Transfer curls with cocktail stick.

If you like, you can use white chocolate instead of plain chocolate flavour cake covering (see page 100).

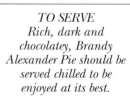

TO SERVE
Rich, dark and chocolatey, Brandy Alexander Pie should be served chilled to be enjoyed at its best.

BLUEBERRY PIE

10 servings
Allow 3 hours preparation and cooking time

Pastry

300 g/10 oz plain flour
³/4 teaspoon salt (optional)
175 g/6 oz butter or block margarine
1 egg
2 teaspoons caster sugar

Filling

700 g/1 ¹/2 lb fresh or frozen (thawed) blueberries
100 g/3 ¹/2 oz caster sugar
1 teaspoon grated lemon zest
15 g/ ¹/2 oz butter

1 First prepare pastry dough: in large bowl, with fork, stir flour with salt, if using. With pastry blender or fingertips, cut or rub butter or margarine into flour mixture until mixture resembles coarse crumbs. In cup, beat egg lightly. Add egg to flour mixture, mixing lightly with fork until dough will hold together, adding a little *cold water* if necessary. With hands, shape dough into 2 balls, 1 slightly larger than the other.

2 On lightly floured surface, with floured rolling pin, roll out larger ball of dough into round about 4 cm/1 ¹/2 inches larger all round than upside-down shallow 20-23 cm/8-9 inch pie dish. Ease dough into pie dish to line evenly.

3 If using frozen blueberries, they should be drained. In large bowl, with rubber spatula, gently toss blueberries with caster sugar and grated lemon zest.

4 Spoon blueberry mixture into pie shell. Cut butter into small pieces; dot on top of blueberry mixture.

5 Preheat oven to 220°C/425°F/gas 7. Roll out remaining dough as before. Moisten edge of pie shell with water; place top crust over filling.

6 Trim dough edge, leaving about 4 cm/1 ¹/2 inch overhang. Fold overhang under; make Sharp Fluted or other Decorative Pastry Edge (pages 136-137).

7 With sharp knife, cut 10 cm/4 inch 'X' in centre of top crust.

8 Fold back points of 'X' to make square opening in centre of pie.

9 Sprinkle top of pie with 2 teaspoons caster sugar.

10 Bake pie for 40 minutes or until filling begins to bubble and pastry is golden. If pastry browns too quickly, cover edge loosely with foil. Cool pie on wire rack before serving. Serve warm or cold.

BANANA CREAM PIE

 8 servings

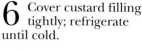 Allow 4 hours preparation and cooking time

100 g/3 ¹/₂ oz shredded or desiccated coconut

60 g/2 oz quick-cooking porridge oats, uncooked

75 g/2 ¹/₂ oz butter, softened

750 ml/1 ¹/₄ pints milk

45 g/1 ¹/₂ oz cornflour

100 g/3 ¹/₂ oz caster sugar

3 egg yolks

3 large bananas

150 ml/ ¹/₄ pint double or whipping cream

Toasted flaked almonds to decorate

1 Preheat oven to 150°C/300°F/gas 2. In shallow 20-23 cm/ 8-9 inch pie dish, mix coconut, porridge oats and 45 g/1 ¹/₂ oz butter. Pat coconut mixture on to bottom and up side of pie dish to line evenly.

2 Bake pie shell for 15 minutes or until golden; cool on wire rack.

3 In medium saucepan, combine milk, cornflour, sugar and remaining butter. Cook over medium-low heat, stirring constantly, until mixture boils and thickens; boil for 1 minute longer.

4 Remove saucepan from heat; stir in egg yolks.

5 Peel 2 bananas and cut into slices 5 mm/ ¹/₄ inch thick. Line cooled pie shell with sliced bananas; pour custard filling over bananas.

6 Cover custard filling tightly; refrigerate until cold.

7 In small bowl, whip double or whipping cream until stiff peaks form.

8 With palette knife, evenly spread whipped cream over custard filling.

9 Cover and refrigerate pie until ready to serve.

TO SERVE
Slice remaining banana.
Decorate pie with banana
slices and toasted almonds.

Coconut and porridge oat crust provides a crisp and crunchy contrast to soft and creamy banana filling

OLD ENGLISH APPLE PIE

 8 servings

Allow 2 hours preparation and cooking time

Filling

8 medium-sized Bramley apples

2 teaspoons lemon juice

1 tablespoon cornflour

100 g/3 1/2 oz caster sugar

15 g/ 1/2 oz butter

Pastry

Shortcrust Pastry for Double Crust Pie (page 134)

Milk for glazing

1 tablespoon caster sugar

7 slices processed cheese (optional)

1 Peel and core apples; cut into thin slices. In large bowl, with rubber spatula, lightly toss apple slices, lemon juice, corn-flour and sugar; set aside.

2 Prepare pastry dough. Divide into 2 pieces, 1 slightly larger. On lightly floured surface, with floured rolling pin, roll out larger piece of dough into round about 4 cm/ 1 1/2 inches larger all round than upside-down shallow 20-23 cm/8-9 inch pie dish. Ease dough into pie dish to line evenly; trim dough edge, leaving 2.5 cm/1 inch overhang. Reserve dough trimmings.

Pastry crust is sprinkled with sugar before baking to give finished pie a frosted top

3 Spoon apple mixture into pie shell. Cut butter into small pieces; dot over apple filling.

4 Preheat oven to 220°C/425°F/gas 7. Roll out remaining dough as before; place over filling. Trim dough edge, leaving 2.5 cm/1 inch overhang. Fold overhang under; make Sharp Fluted or other Decorative Pastry Edge (pages 136-137).

Cheese and apples make good partners; here cheese leaves are placed under pastry leaves to look – and taste – good

5 Reroll dough trim-mings. With floured leaf-shaped biscuit cutter or knife, cut 7 leaves, rerolling dough if neces-sary. Arrange leaves on top of pie. Lightly brush top of pie with milk.

6 With tip of knife, cut hole in top crust to allow steam to escape during baking.

7 Evenly sprinkle caster sugar over pie. Set pie dish on baking sheet and bake for 45 minutes or until pastry is golden and apples are tender.

8 Transfer pie to wire rack; cool slightly. If using cheese slices, cut each slice into leaf shape using biscuit cutter or knife. Gently tuck cheese leaves under pastry leaves, taking care not to break pastry.

CUSTARD PEACH PIE

 8 servings

Allow 3 hours preparation and cooking time

Pastry

Shortcrust Pastry for Pie Shell (see Box, page 134)

Filling

5 medium-sized peaches (about 700 g/1 $1/2$ lb)

150 ml/ $1/4$ pint soured cream

3 egg yolks

200 g/7 oz caster sugar

30 g/1 oz plain flour

Streusel Topping

60 g/2 oz butter

75 g/2 $1/2$ oz plain flour

60 g/2 oz caster sugar

$1/2$ teaspoon ground cinnamon

1 Prepare pastry dough.

2 Preheat oven to 220°C/425°F/gas 7. On lightly floured surface, with floured rolling pin, roll out dough into round about 4 cm/1 $1/2$ inches larger all round than upside-down shallow 20-23 cm/8-9 inch pie dish; ease dough into pie dish to line evenly.

3 Trim dough edge, leaving 2.5 cm/1 inch overhang. Fold overhang under; make Fluted or other Decorative Pastry Edge (pages 136-137).

4 Peel 4 peaches (see Box, page 53); cut peaches into 5 mm/ $1/4$ inch-thick slices with sharp knife.

5 In pie shell, arrange peach slices in concentric circles, overlapping them slightly.

6 In medium bowl, beat soured cream, egg yolks, sugar and flour just until blended; pour slowly over peaches in pie dish, taking care not to dislodge them.

7 Bake pie for 30 minutes, or just until custard mixture is beginning to set.

8 Meanwhile, prepare streusel topping: in small bowl, rub together butter, flour and sugar until mixture resembles coarse crumbs. Stir in ground cinnamon.

STREUSEL TOPPING

Streusel is a crisp topping of flour, butter and sugar, often mixed with spices such as cinnamon, nutmeg and cloves, which is sprinkled on breads, cakes and puddings before baking. The topping is of German origin, and is very similar to crumble toppings for fruit.

9 After pie has baked for 30 minutes, evenly sprinkle streusel topping over peaches and custard.

Sprinkling streusel topping over peaches and custard

10 Bake for 15 minutes longer or until streusel is golden and knife inserted in centre of pie comes out clean.

11 If pastry browns too quickly, cover edge loosely with foil.

12 Cool pie on wire rack for 1 hour; serve warm, or cool completely to serve cold later.

At end of baking time, insert tip of knife into centre of pie; if custard is set, tip of knife will come out clean

TO SERVE
Cut remaining peach
into 5 mm/¼ inch thick
slices; use to decorate
centre of pie.

PECAN PIE

 8 servings

Allow 4 hours preparation and cooking time

Pastry

Shortcrust Pastry for Double Crust Pie (page 134)

Filling

4 eggs

250 ml/8 fl oz golden syrup

60 g/2 oz light soft brown sugar

60 g/2 oz caster sugar

30 g/1 oz butter, melted

90 g/3 oz shelled pecans or walnuts, chopped

Honey Pecan Topping (see Box, above right)

1 Prepare pastry dough. Divide dough into 2 pieces, 1 slightly larger.

2 Preheat oven to 180°C/350°F/gas 4. On lightly floured surface, with floured rolling pin, roll out larger piece of dough into round about 4 cm/1 ½ inches larger all round than upside-down shallow 20-23 cm/8-9 inch pie dish.

3 Ease dough into pie dish to line evenly; trim dough edge, leaving 1 cm/½ inch overhang. Fold overhang under. Make Leaf or other Decorative Pastry Edge (pages 136-137) with remaining dough.

Spreading Honey Pecan Topping over pie filling

4 In medium bowl, beat eggs lightly; stir in golden syrup, brown sugar, caster sugar and butter; stir in chopped pecans or walnuts. Spoon into pie shell; bake pie for 40 minutes.

5 Meanwhile, prepare Honey Pecan Topping.

6 When pie has baked for 40 minutes, remove from oven; spread topping over filling.

HONEY PECAN TOPPING

In medium saucepan over medium heat, combine *75 g/2 ½ oz light soft brown sugar, 3 tablespoons honey* and *45 g/1 ½ oz butter;* cook for 2-3 minutes, stirring constantly, until sugar dissolves. Stir in *150 g/5 oz shelled pecan* or *walnut halves.* Remove saucepan from heat.

7 Return pie to oven and bake for 10-15 minutes longer until topping is bubbly and golden brown. Cover edge of pastry with foil, if necessary, to prevent overbrowning.

8 Cool pie on wire rack before serving.

Golden-brown leaf edge accents the autumnal look of this popular American pie

Pecan Pie, perfect for a winter party

PUMPKIN PIE

8 servings

Allow 3 hours preparation and cooking time

Pastry

Shortcrust Pastry for Double Crust Pie (page 134)

Filling

450 g/1 lb canned pumpkin or Mashed Cooked Pumpkin (page 83)

1 x 400 g/14 oz can evaporated milk

2 eggs

165 g/5 ½ oz light soft brown sugar

1 ½ teaspoons ground cinnamon

½ teaspoon ground ginger

½ teaspoon grated nutmeg

Walnut Crunch Topping (see Box, below)

150 ml/ ¼ pint double or whipping cream to decorate

Chopped walnuts, brown sugar and butter make up this topping, a deliciously crunchy contrast to the soft texture of the pumpkin filling underneath

1 Prepare pastry dough. Divide dough into 2 pieces, 1 slightly larger than the other.

2 Preheat oven to 200°C/400°F/gas 6. On lightly floured surface, with floured rolling pin, roll out larger piece of dough to round about 4 cm/1 ½ inches larger all round than upside-down shallow 20-23 cm/8-9 inch pie dish.

3 Line pie dish with dough; trim edge, leaving 1 cm/ ½ inch overhang. Fold overhang under. With remaining dough, make Plaited or other Decorative Pastry Edge (pages 136-137).

4 In large bowl, with electric mixer, beat pumpkin and next 6 ingredients.

5 Place pie dish on oven rack; pour filling into pie shell. Bake pie for 40 minutes or until knife inserted 2.5 cm/1 inch from edge comes out clean.

6 Cool pie on wire rack for about 1 ½ hours.

7 When pie is cool, preheat grill to high. Prepare Walnut Crunch Topping; spoon evenly over pie. Place pie about 15 cm/6 inches below source of heat and grill for 3 minutes or until topping is golden and sugar dissolves. Cool pie again on wire rack.

8 In small bowl, whip double or whipping cream until stiff peaks form. Decorate pie with cream.

Piped swirls of cream complement the plaited edge of this traditional American Thanksgiving pie

WALNUT CRUNCH TOPPING

In small saucepan over low heat, melt *60 g/2 oz butter.* Stir in *120 g/4 oz walnut pieces, chopped,* and *165 g/5 ½ oz light soft brown sugar* until well mixed; cook for a few minutes until butter is absorbed.

LEMON MERINGUE PIE

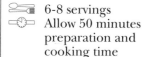

6-8 servings

Allow 50 minutes preparation and cooking time

Crumb Crust

175 g/6 oz digestive biscuits	
75 g/2 ½ oz butter	
45 g/1 ½ oz demerara sugar	

Lemon Filling

Grated zest and juice of 2 large lemons	
45 g/1 ½ oz cornflour	
2 egg yolks	
75 g/2 ½ oz caster sugar	

Topping

3 egg whites	
120 g/4 oz caster sugar	

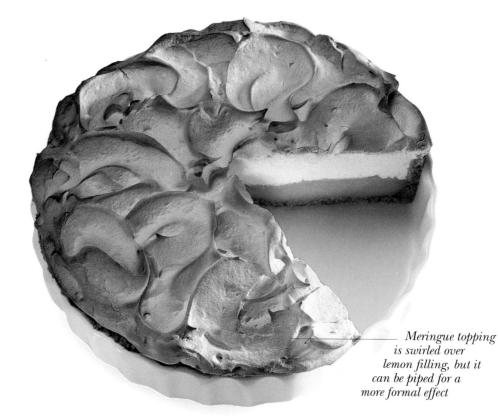

Meringue topping is swirled over lemon filling, but it can be piped for a more formal effect

1 Make crumb crust: place digestive biscuits in polythene bag; with rolling pin, roll biscuits into fine crumbs.

2 Melt butter in small saucepan over gentle heat, add sugar and biscuit crumbs and mix well.

3 Turn biscuit mixture into deepish 23 cm/ 9 inch flan dish; with back of metal spoon, press mixture on to bottom and up side of dish.

4 Make lemon filling: put lemon zest and juice in bowl with cornflour; blend to a smooth paste.

5 In medium saucepan, bring *300 ml/ ½ pint water* to the boil; pour on to cornflour mixture. Return cornflour mixture to pan, bring to the boil and simmer for 3 minutes until thick, stirring.

Pressing crushed biscuit mixture on to bottom and up side of flan dish

6 Remove saucepan from heat; add egg yolks and caster sugar. Return to heat; cook for 1 minute, to thicken sauce. Cool slightly, then spoon into biscuit crust.

7 Preheat oven to 170°C/325°F/ gas 3.

8 Make topping: in large bowl, with electric mixer on full speed, beat egg whites until soft peaks form. Add caster sugar, 1 table-spoon at a time, beating well after each addition until sugar dissolves completely and egg whites stand in stiff, glossy peaks.

9 Spoon topping over lemon filling, taking care to spread it right to edge of crust, leaving no spaces.

10 Bake pie for about 30 minutes or until meringue is golden brown. Serve warm or cold.

WALNUT FUDGE PIE

🥄 8-10 servings
⏱ Allow 4 hours preparation and cooking time

225 g/8 oz walnut pieces

Shortcrust Pastry for Double Crust Pie (page 134)

60 g/2 oz butter

60 g/2 oz plain chocolate, broken into pieces

200 g/7 oz caster sugar

5 tablespoons milk

4 tablespoons bottled chocolate syrup

4 eggs

Vanilla ice cream (optional)

TO SERVE
If you like, top each serving of pie with a scoop of vanilla ice cream.

---

1 Preheat oven to 180°C/350°F/gas 4. Place walnuts in baking tray; toast in oven for about 10 minutes or until golden brown, shaking tray occasionally. Set aside to cool. Do not turn oven off.

2 Meanwhile, prepare pastry dough. Divide into 2 pieces, 1 slightly larger than the other.

3 On lightly floured surface, with floured rolling pin, roll out larger piece of dough into round about 4 cm/1 ½ inches larger all round than upside-down shallow 20-23 cm/8-9 inch pie dish.

4 Ease dough into pie dish to line evenly; trim dough edge, leaving 1 cm/½ inch overhang. Fold overhang under.

5 In medium saucepan over low heat, heat butter and chocolate, stirring often, until melted and smooth. Remove saucepan from heat. With wire whisk, beat in sugar, milk, chocolate syrup and 3 eggs until blended. Stir in toasted walnuts. Pour walnut mixture into pie shell.

6 Roll out remaining dough 3 mm/⅛ inch thick. With different sized heart-shaped pastry cutters, cut out hearts for decorating edge of pie shell and top of pie.

7 Place hearts on edge of pie and on filling to make pretty design.

8 In cup, with fork, lightly beat remaining egg. Brush egg lightly over edge of pie shell.

9 Brush hearts in centre and on edge with beaten egg.

10 Bake pie for 1 hour or until knife inserted in centre of pie comes out clean. Cool pie on wire rack. Serve warm or cold.

Placing heart shapes over filling

MIDSUMMER FRUIT PIE

 8-10 servings

Allow 4 hours preparation and cooking time

Almond Pastry

225 g/8 oz plain flour
1 tablespoon caster sugar
1/2 teaspoon salt (optional)
120 g/4 oz butter
2 tablespoons finely chopped blanched almonds

Fruit Filling

300 g/10 oz fresh or frozen (thawed) blueberries or blackcurrants
30 g/1 oz caster sugar
1 tablespoon cornflour
1 tablespoon lemon juice
1 tablespoon grated lemon zest
30 g/1 oz butter

White Chocolate Filling

215 g/7 1/2 oz white chocolate, broken into pieces
15 g/ 1/2 oz butter
30 g/1 oz blanched almonds, toasted and coarsely chopped
150 ml/ 1/4 pint double or whipping cream

Cream Layer

300 ml/ 1/2 pint double or whipping cream
30 g/1 oz icing sugar

1 Prepare pastry dough: in large bowl, with fork, stir flour, sugar and salt, if using. With pastry blender or fingertips, cut or rub butter into flour mixture until mixture resembles coarse crumbs. Stir in almonds. Sprinkle *3 tablespoons cold water*, a tablespoon at a time, into mixture, mixing lightly with fork after each addition until dough is just moist enough to hold together. With hands, shape dough into ball.

2 Preheat oven to 220°C/425°F/gas 7.

3 On lightly floured surface, with floured rolling pin, roll out dough into round about 4 cm/ 1 1/2 inches larger all round than upside-down shallow 20-23 cm/8-9 inch pie dish.

4 Ease dough into pie dish to line evenly. Trim dough edge, leaving 1 cm/ 1/2 inch overhang; reserve dough trimmings. Fold overhang under.

5 At regular intervals round edge of dough, cut out narrow sections, about 1 cm/1/2 inch long.

Cutting out sections from edge of dough

6 Place 1 thumb on inside edge of each section of dough, and, with index finger and thumb of other hand, pinch dough and press upwards to make rounded 'petal' shape.

7 Prick bottom and side of pie shell liberally with fork to prevent puffing and shrinkage during baking.

8 Line pastry with foil; spread evenly with dried or baking beans.

9 Bake blind for 15 minutes or until pastry is golden; remove foil and beans, prick bottom again and bake for further 3-4 minutes. Cool on wire rack.

10 Roll out dough trimmings. With small biscuit cutters or knife, cut out a few flowers and leaves for decoration. Bake pastry shapes on ungreased baking sheet for about 10 minutes or until golden; cool.

11 Prepare fruit filling; if using frozen fruit, it should be drained. In medium saucepan, mix sugar, cornflour, lemon juice and lemon zest; add half of the fruit. Cook over low heat, mashing fruit with spoon and stirring, until mixture boils and thickens. Remove pan from heat; stir in butter and remaining fruit, reserving a few blueberries for decoration. Cool.

12 For white chocolate filling: place pieces of chocolate, butter and *2 tablespoons water* in bowl over saucepan of gently simmering water and heat, stirring often, until melted and smooth. Remove saucepan from heat; cool completely. Stir in chopped toasted almonds. In small bowl, whip double or whipping cream until stiff peaks form. Stir a few spoonfuls of whipped cream into chocolate mixture to lighten, then with wire whisk or rubber spatula, gently fold in remaining cream.

13 For cream layer: in same bowl, whip double or whipping cream with sifted icing sugar until stiff peaks form.

14 In cooled pie shell, with spoon, evenly spread fruit filling.

15 Top fruit filling with white chocolate filling. Spread with whipped cream mixture, reserving 1 tablespoon for decoration.

BLUEBERRIES

Big, sweet, succulent blueberries are purplish-blue in colour with a powdery bloom – the 'aristocrats' of soft fruit. They come in many varieties, cultivated and wild, and can be found at most good supermarkets and greengrocers.

• Blueberries are traditionally a summer fruit, at their best from June to September.

• Just before using blueberries, remove any stalks and discard any bruised, soft or damaged berries; rinse blueberries gently in cold water, drain well and dry on kitchen paper.

• To freeze blueberries, overwrap berries in containers as bought; freeze. Or place them in a single layer in a baking tray, freeze until firm, then transfer to freezer container; use within 12 months.

• When using frozen blueberries, thaw only if recipe tells you to do so.

16 Decorate pie with pastry flowers, reserved whipped cream and blueberries, and pastry leaves.

Arranging blueberries and pastry flowers and leaves on whipped cream topping

Here's a pie with a hidden secret – the whipped cream topping hides a white chocolate filling and a luscious layer of sweet summer berries

PARISIENNE APPLE PIES

6 servings

Allow 2 hours preparation and cooking time

Pastry

375 g/13 oz plain flour

225 g/8 oz unsalted butter, softened

75 g/2 ¹/₂ oz caster sugar

2 egg yolks, lightly beaten

1 tablespoon milk

Filling

8 large Golden Delicious apples

100 g/3 ¹/₂ oz caster sugar plus extra for sprinkling

60 g/2 oz unsalted butter

1 Prepare pastry dough: in large bowl, with fingertips, quickly mix flour, butter and sugar until mixture resembles coarse crumbs. Add egg yolks and milk; mix until dough will hold together.

2 Shape two-thirds of dough into ball; wrap and set aside. On non-stick baking parchment, with rolling pin, roll out remaining one-third of dough 3 mm/¹/₈ inch thick. With 6 x 4 cm/ 2 ¹/₂ x 1 ¹/₂ inch leaf-shaped biscuit cutter, cut out 36 leaves. With cocktail stick, press 'vein' into each leaf; place on baking sheet and refrigerate.

3 Divide larger ball of dough into 6 equal pieces. Press one piece of dough on to bottom and up side of each of six 10-11 cm/4-4 ¹/₂ inch loose-bottomed tartlet tins; refrigerate.

4 Prepare filling: peel and core apples; cut into 5 mm/¹/₄ inch thick slices. In large frying pan over medium-high heat, heat sugar and butter until butter melts, stirring occasionally (do not use margarine because it separates from sugar during cooking). Sugar will not be completely dissolved.

5 Arrange apple slices on top of sugar mixture; heat to boiling (do not stir). Cook for about 20 minutes, depending on juiciness of apples, until sugar mixture is caramel-coloured; stir to mix apples with caramelized sugar. (Apples should still be slightly crunchy.) Remove pan from heat.

6 Preheat oven to 200°C/400°F/gas 6. Spoon apple mixture into tartlet shells. Arrange 6 dough leaves on top of each pie, leaving some of filling uncovered. Arrange apple pies in baking tray for easier handling. Bake pies for 25-30 minutes until pastry is golden (cover leaves with foil after 15 minutes, if necessary, to prevent overbrowning).

7 Cool pies on wire rack for 10 minutes; lightly sprinkle with caster sugar. Serve warm, or cool completely to serve cold later. Remove sides and bases of tins before serving.

Parisienne Apple Pies are lightly dusted with caster sugar just before serving, to give pastry leaves a frosted look

Pies are baked in fluted, loose-bottomed tartlet tins so they can be removed from tins before serving; this way they look their best for serving

KEY LIME PIE

6-8 servings

Can be made day before and kept in refrigerator

---

135 g/4 ¹/₂ oz digestive biscuits, finely crushed

---

60 g/2 oz caster sugar

---

75 g/2 ¹/₂ oz butter, softened

---

1 x 400 g/14 oz can sweetened condensed milk

---

125 ml/4 fl oz freshly squeezed lime juice (3-4 limes)

---

2 teaspoons grated lime zest

---

2 eggs, separated

Green food colouring (optional)

---

300 ml/ ¹/₂ pint double or whipping cream

Lime decoration of your choice (see Box, above right)

---

1 Preheat oven to 170°C/325°F/gas 3. In shallow 20-23 cm/ 8-9 inch pie dish, mix biscuit crumbs, sugar and butter; press mixture on to bottom and up side of pie dish, making small rim.

2 In medium bowl, with wire whisk or fork, stir sweetened condensed milk with lime juice, grated lime zest and egg yolks until mixture thickens. If liked, add sufficient green food colouring to tint mixture pale green.

3 In small bowl, with electric mixer on full speed, beat egg whites until stiff peaks form. With rubber spatula or wire whisk, gently fold egg whites into lime mixture.

4 Into biscuit crust, pour lime filling; smooth top. Bake pie for 15-20 minutes until lime filling is just firm.

5 Cool pie in pie dish on wire rack, then refrigerate until well chilled, about 3 hours.

6 In small bowl, whip double or whipping cream until stiff peaks form. Pipe border of whipped cream round edge of filling, or spread cream completely over top of pie and swirl to make attractive design.

TO SERVE
Top cream with Lime Kites or other lime decoration of your choice.

LIME DECORATIONS

The contrasting greens of lime peel and flesh make this a good choice for decorating desserts, and a welcome change from the more usual orange and lemon decorations.

Lime Cones
With sharp knife, cut lime crossways into thin slices. Make 1 cut from centre to edge of each slice, then curl slice round from centre to form cone shape.

Lime Kites and Bow-Ties
With sharp knife, cut lime crossways into thin slices, then cut each slice into quarters. Use singly, or place 2 kites together as shown above to make bow-tie shape.

CHERRY PIE

8 servings
Allow 4 hours
preparation and
cooking time

Filling

2 x 425 g/15 oz cans
  stoned cherries in juice

75 g/2 ½ oz light soft
  brown sugar

60 g/2 oz caster sugar

30 g/1 oz cornflour

15 g/ ½ oz butter

1 teaspoon almond essence

Pastry

Shortcrust Pastry for
  Double Crust Pie
  (page 134)

Milk for glazing

2 teaspoons caster sugar

1 Drain juice from
canned cherries;
reserve 250 ml/8 fl oz
juice.

2 In medium saucepan,
combine brown sugar,
caster sugar, cornflour and
reserved cherry juice.
Cook over low heat,
stirring constantly, until
mixture boils and thick-
ens; boil for 1 minute
longer. Remove pan from
heat; stir in butter and
almond essence. Fold
in cherries.

3 Prepare pastry dough.
Divide dough into
2 pieces, 1 slightly larger
than the other.

4 Preheat oven to
220°C/425°F/gas 7.
On lightly floured surface,
with floured rolling pin,
roll out larger piece of
dough into round about
4 cm/1 ½ inches larger all
round than upside-down
shallow 20-23 cm/8-9 inch
pie dish; ease dough into
pie dish to line evenly.
Trim dough edge even
with rim of pie dish;
reserve dough trimmings.

5 Spoon filling into
pie shell. Roll out
remaining dough as
before. With leaf-shaped
biscuit cutter, cut out
leaves in top crust; reserve
cut out shapes. Place top
crust over filling. Trim
edge of top crust, leaving
1 cm/½ inch overhang;
reserve dough trimmings.
Fold overhang under;
make Ruffled or other
Decorative Pastry Edge
(pages 136-137).

6 With reserved dough
trimmings, make
'berries' (see Box, right).
Score veins on reserved cut
out leaves and arrange
with berries on top crust.
Brush top crust with milk
and sprinkle with sugar.
Bake pie for 15 minutes.
Turn oven to 180°C/
350°F/gas 4; bake for
25 minutes longer or until
pastry is golden brown.

7 Cool pie in pie dish
on wire rack before
serving.

PASTRY LEAVES AND BERRIES

Pastry 'leaves' can be
made by cutting out
shapes from top crust
of pie with biscuit cutter
as in the recipe here
for Cherry Pie, or by
rolling out pastry dough
trimmings, then cutting
pastry dough into leaf
shapes with sharp knife
or biscuit cutter. After
making leaf shapes,
score 'veins' on surface
of leaf shapes with tip of
sharp knife.

Between fingertips of
both hands, roll dough
trimmings into 'berry'
shapes. Arrange leaves
and berries together,
twisting leaves at base to
give a more realistic
look.

To decorate a large pie
for a special occasion,
group lots of berries
together to make a
cluster of grapes; for a
Christmas pie, create a
seasonal look by deco-
rating top or edge of pie
with pastry holly leaves
and berries.

CHOCOLATE CREAM PIE

8 servings

Can be made day before and kept in refrigerator

120 g/4 oz rich tea biscuits

120 g/4 oz butter, softened

50 g/1 ²/₃ oz cornflour

100 g/3 ¹/₂ oz plus
  1 teaspoon caster sugar

450 ml/ ³/₄ pint milk

90 g/3 oz plain chocolate,
  broken into pieces

2 egg yolks

¹/₂ teaspoon vanilla essence

30 g/1 oz walnut pieces

150 ml/ ¹/₄ pint double or
  whipping cream

1 Preheat oven to 190°C/375°F/gas 5. Place biscuits, in batches, in polythene bag and with rolling pin, roll biscuits into fine crumbs. Or in food processor or blender, blend biscuits, in batches if necessary, until fine crumbs form.

2 In shallow 20-23 cm/ 8-9 inch pie dish, mix biscuit crumbs and 90 g/3 oz softened butter; press mixture on to bottom and up side of pie dish, making small rim.

3 Bake biscuit crust for 8 minutes; cool on wire rack.

4 While crust is cooling, prepare filling: in large non-stick saucepan, mix cornflour and 100 g/3 ¹/₂ oz sugar. Stir in milk and chocolate. Cook over medium heat, stirring constantly, until chocolate melts and mixture thickens and boils; boil for 1 minute longer. Immediately remove saucepan from heat.

5 In cup, with fork, beat egg yolks; stir in small amount of hot chocolate mixture. Slowly pour egg mixture back into remaining chocolate mixture in pan, stirring rapidly to prevent lumping. Cook, stirring constantly, until mixture thickens and coats a spoon well (do not boil or mixture will curdle). Stir in vanilla essence and remaining butter until blended.

6 Into biscuit crust, pour chocolate filling; smooth top with rubber spatula.

Pouring chocolate filling into baked biscuit crust

7 To keep skin from forming as filling cools, press dampened greaseproof paper directly on to surface of hot filling. Refrigerate pie for at least 3 hours or until well chilled.

8 Meanwhile, in small saucepan over medium heat, cook walnuts until toasted, stirring frequently; cool. Chop walnuts.

9 In small bowl, whip double or whipping cream with remaining 1 teaspoon sugar until soft peaks form.

10 Discard greaseproof paper from filling. Spoon or pipe whipped cream on to filling and swirl to make attractive design.

TO SERVE
Sprinkle top of pie with toasted chopped walnuts.

CANADIAN PEACH PIE

 8 servings
Allow 3 hours preparation and cooking time

Filling

| 14 large peaches |
| 30 g/1 oz cornflour |
| 2 tablespoons lemon juice |
| 1 teaspoon ground cinnamon |
| 200 g/7 oz caster sugar |
| 15 g/ 1/2 oz butter |

Pastry

| 175 g/6 oz plain flour |
| 1/2 teaspoon salt (optional) |
| 1 teaspoon caster sugar |
| 90 g/3 oz butter |
| 1 egg yolk, beaten |

1 Prepare filling: peel peaches (see Box, page 53). With sharp knife, cut peeled peaches into thick slices.

2 In bowl, gently toss peaches, cornflour, lemon juice, cinnamon and sugar. Set aside.

3 Prepare pastry dough: in medium bowl, with fork, stir flour, salt (if using) and sugar. With pastry blender or finger-tips, cut or rub butter into flour mixture until mixture resembles coarse crumbs. Sprinkle *2-3 tablespoons cold water*, a tablespoon at a time, into mixture, mixing lightly with fork after each addition until dough is just moist enough to hold together. With hands, shape dough into ball.

4 Spoon peach mixture into deep 20-23 cm/ 8-9 inch pie dish. Cut butter into small pieces; dot on top of peach mixture.

5 Preheat oven to 220°C/425°F/gas 7. Roll out dough into 28-32 cm/11-12 1/2 inch round. Cut a few small slashes in centre of round to allow steam to escape during baking.

6 Place dough round over peach filling; trim dough edge, leaving 2.5 cm/1 inch overhang. Fold overhang under; make Fluted or other Decorative Pastry Edge (pages 136-137).

7 Reroll dough trimmings; cut out a few leaves. Arrange leaves on top of pie. Brush all over with beaten egg yolk.

8 Because peaches vary in juiciness, place sheet of foil underneath pie dish; crimp edges to form rim to catch any drips during baking. Bake pie for 50 minutes or until pastry is golden and peaches are tender. If pastry begins to brown too much, cover loosely with foil.

9 Slightly cool pie on wire rack; serve warm. Or cool pie completely to serve cold later.

Slashes are made in top crust before baking. This lets steam from fruit escape and helps keep pastry dry and crisp

Deep-dish pies with juicy fruit fillings need only a top crust as here; pastry on bottom of dish would be soggy from the juice of the fruits

TARTS AND FLANS

Tarts and flans – crisp, rich and sweet pastry filled with creamy custards, juicy fresh fruits, fine chocolate and crunchy nuts – make the most delectable of desserts. In this collection of recipes you will find old favourites as well as new and exciting ideas, each one of them as good to look at as it is to eat, and you don't have to be a pastry chef to make them!

TART OR FLAN SHELL

| 175 g/6 oz plain flour |
| 1 tablespoon caster sugar |
| ¼ teaspoon salt (optional) |
| 120 g/4 oz cold butter |
| 2-3 tablespoons cold water |

1 In medium bowl, with fork, stir flour with sugar and salt, if using. With pastry blender or with fingertips, cut or rub butter into flour mixture until mixture resembles coarse crumbs.

2 Sprinkle cold water, a tablespoon at a time, into mixture, mixing lightly with fork after each addition, until dough just holds together. With hands, shape dough into ball. Wrap and refrigerate for 1 hour.

3 Preheat oven to 220°C/425°F/gas 7. On lightly floured surface, with floured rolling pin, roll out dough into round about 2.5 cm/1 inch larger all round than 23-25 cm/9-10 inch loose-bottomed tart or flan tin.

4 Ease dough into tin to line evenly; press dough on to bottom and up side of tin.

5 Roll rolling-pin across top of tin to trim off excess dough; reserve trimmings for decoration.

6 With fork, prick dough liberally to prevent puffing and shrinkage during baking.

7 Line shell with foil; fill with dried or baking beans. Bake shell for 10 minutes. Remove foil and beans; again prick dough. Bake shell for 10-15 minutes longer until golden brown.

8 If pastry puffs up, gently press it to tin with spoon.

9 Cool tart or flan shell in tin on wire rack.

TARTLET SHELLS

1 In bowl, with fork, stir *75 g/2 ½ oz plain flour, 1 teaspoon caster sugar* and *¼ teaspoon salt (optional)*. With pastry blender or fingertips, cut or rub *60 g/2 oz cold butter* into flour mixture until mixture resembles coarse crumbs. Sprinkle *4-5 teaspoons cold water*, a teaspoon at a time, into mixture, mixing lightly with fork after each addition until dough is just moist enough to hold together. With hands, shape dough into ball. Wrap and refrigerate for 1 hour.

2 Preheat oven to 190°C/375°F/gas 5. On lightly floured surface, with floured rolling pin, roll out half of the dough 3 mm/⅛ inch thick. With floured 7.5 cm/3 inch round pastry cutter, cut out as many rounds as possible. Repeat with remaining dough and trimmings to make 18 rounds.

3 Press each round of dough on to bottom and up side of eighteen 6 cm/2 ½ inch round tartlet tins (2 cm/¾ inch deep).

4 With fork, prick tartlet shells in many places to prevent puffing and shrinkage during baking. Place tartlet tins in baking tray for easy handling. Bake for 12-15 minutes until lightly browned.

5 Cool tartlet shells in tins on wire racks for 10 minutes. With knife, gently loosen tartlet shells from sides of tins; remove from tins and cool completely on wire racks.

6 If not using tartlet shells immediately, store them in airtight container.

WICKED TRUFFLE TARTS

Makes 18
Can be made day
before and kept in
refrigerator

350 g/12 oz plain chocolate, broken into pieces
300 ml/½ pint double cream
90 g/3 oz butter
2 tablespoons orange liqueur or brandy
18 Tartlet Shells (see Box, page 159)
Shredded orange zest to decorate

These dainty little tartlet shells are home-made, but if you are short of time, you can buy ready-made tartlet shells

1 In non-stick saucepan over low heat, heat pieces of chocolate, double cream and butter, stirring frequently, until melted and smooth. Remove saucepan from heat; stir in liqueur or brandy.

2 Refrigerate chocolate mixture for about 2 ½ hours or until very thick and an easy piping consistency, stirring occasionally.

3 Meanwhile, prepare and bake Tartlet Shells as directed; cool on wire rack.

ALTERNATIVE FILLING

For a change, use white rather than plain chocolate to make the truffle filling for these elegant tartlets.

White Truffle Tartlets
In step 1, substitute *350 g/12 oz white chocolate* for the plain chocolate, and *2 teaspoons vanilla essence* for the orange liqueur or brandy. For decoration, use chocolate 'coffee beans', grated chocolate, Chocolate Curls (page 100), or a cluster of raspberries.

4 Spoon chocolate mixture into large piping bag fitted with large star tube; pipe into shells.

5 Serve tartlets while truffle mixture is velvety soft, or refrigerate filled tartlets for several hours so truffle mixture has firmer consistency. Decorate with orange zest before serving.

PLUM AND ALMOND FLAN

 8 servings

Allow 3 hours preparation and cooking time

Cinnamon Shortbread

| 175 g/6 oz plain flour |
| 120 g/4 oz butter, softened |
| 60 g/2 oz caster sugar |
| ½ teaspoon ground cinnamon |

Filling

| 700 g/1 ½ lb Victoria plums |
| 100 g/3 ½ oz caster sugar |
| 1 tablespoon cornflour |
| ½ teaspoon ground cinnamon |
| ¼ teaspoon almond essence |
| 30 g/1 oz slivered blanched almonds |

Whipped cream for serving (optional)

1 Prepare cinnamon shortbread dough: in medium bowl, combine flour, butter, sugar and cinnamon. With fingertips, mix until dough just holds together.

2 Press shortbread on to bottom and up side of 20 cm/8 inch loose-bottomed tart or flan tin.

3 Preheat oven to 190°C/375°F/gas 5. Prepare filling: cut each plum in half and remove stone; slice plums.

Sprinkling almonds over plums

Flan case is rich and buttery, more like shortbread than pastry

4 In large bowl, toss plums, sugar, cornflour, cinnamon and almond essence.

5 Arrange plum slices, closely overlapping, to form concentric circles in shortbread shell.

PLUMS

These plump, fragrant fruits are in season from the beginning of May until the end of October, but are at their plentiful best in August.

• Plums come in a wide range of sizes, shapes and colours, with skin ranging from bright yellow-green to reddish-purple to purplish-black, depending on variety.

• It doesn't matter which variety of plum you choose for cooking – all types of plum can be used interchangeably in recipes, including damsons and greengages.

• A perfect plum is richly coloured and firm, with a slight softening at stalk end.

• Five or six plums weigh 450 g/1 lb.

• Store ripe plums in refrigerator, for 3-5 days.

• Plums can be frozen – halve and remove stones, then freeze plums in small quantities in freezer bags.

6 Evenly sprinkle slivered almonds over plum slices.

7 Bake in the oven for 45 minutes or until pastry is golden and plums are tender. Cool flan in tin on wire rack.

8 Carefully remove side of tin. Transfer flan to serving plate.

9 Serve Plum and Almond Flan cut into wedges, with whipped cream if you like.

ASCOT FRUIT TART

8 servings

Allow 3 ½ hours preparation and cooking time

Coconut Pastry

150 g/5 oz plain flour
75 g/2 ½ oz shredded or desiccated coconut
90 g/3 oz butter
30 g/1 oz caster sugar
1 egg yolk

Lemon Custard Filling

1 large lemon
90 g/3 oz butter
60 g/2 oz caster sugar
1 tablespoon cornflour
4 egg yolks
300 ml/ ½ pint double or whipping cream

Fruit Topping

350 g/12 oz raspberries
225 g/8 oz blueberries

1 Prepare coconut pastry dough: in medium bowl, combine flour, coconut, butter, sugar and egg yolk. With fingertips, mix together just until blended.

2 Press dough on to bottom and up side of 25 cm/10 inch loose-bottomed tart or flan tin. With fork, prick pastry shell in many places to prevent puffing and shrinkage during baking.

3 Preheat oven to 180°C/350°F/gas 4. Line pastry shell with foil and spread evenly with dried or baking beans; bake for 10 minutes. Remove beans and foil; again prick dough. Bake for 10-15 minutes longer until golden (if pastry puffs up, press it to tin with spoon). Cool pastry shell in tin on wire rack.

4 While pastry shell is baking, prepare lemon custard filling: from lemon, grate 1 teaspoon zest and squeeze 2 tablespoons juice; set aside. In heavy medium saucepan over medium-low heat, heat butter, sugar and cornflour, stirring constantly, until mixture thickens and boils; boil for 1 minute longer.

5 In small bowl, with fork, beat egg yolks; stir in small amount of hot sugar mixture.

6 Slowly pour egg yolk mixture back into sugar mixture in pan, stirring rapidly with wooden spoon to prevent lumping.

7 Cook, stirring constantly, until mixture thickens and coats spoon well, about 1 minute. Remove saucepan from heat.

8 Stir lemon zest and lemon juice into custard; cool, then cover and refrigerate until very cold, about 1 hour.

9 In small bowl, whip double or whipping cream until stiff peaks form. With rubber spatula or wire whisk, fold whipped cream into chilled lemon custard.

RASPBERRIES

These small, juicy, thimble-shaped berries come in red, black, purple and yellow varieties, and are best during June to July and September to October.

- Choose plump, fresh-looking berries.

- Do not buy berries that are crushed or bruised, or that have leaked moisture through container.

- Keep refrigerated and use within 1-2 days.

- Eat raspberries plain or use in fruit salads, pies, flans, crumbles, jams, jellies and sweet sauces.

10 Evenly spoon lemon custard filling into cooled pastry shell.

Spooning lemon custard filling into pastry shell

Whipped cream is folded into egg custard to make this rich filling

11 Arrange raspberries in circular pattern round edge of tart.

12 Fill in centre with blueberries and raspberries; refrigerate for 1 hour until custard is set.

With different fruits to match the seasons, this can be a year-round treat. Use bananas and oranges in winter; pineapple and papaya in spring; apricots and cherries in summer; grapes and pears in autumn. Slice or dice fruit as necessary, to make it look as pretty as possible, and for easy serving

ROYAL RASPBERRY TART

8-10 servings
Allow 3 ½ hours preparation and cooking time

1 x 25 cm/10 inch Tart or Flan Shell (see Box, page 159)

60 g/2 oz caster sugar

20 g/ ²⁄₃ oz cornflour

1 tablespoon powdered gelatine

2 eggs plus 1 egg yolk

350 ml/12 fl oz milk

150 ml/ ¼ pint double or whipping cream

450 g/1 lb raspberries

1 Prepare and bake Tart or Flan Shell according to recipe instructions; cool on wire rack.

2 In medium saucepan, combine sugar, cornflour and gelatine. In medium bowl, with wire whisk or fork, beat eggs and egg yolk with milk until well mixed; stir into gelatine mixture. Leave to stand for 5 minutes to soften gelatine slightly.

3 Cook over low heat, stirring constantly, until mixture thickens and coats spoon well, about 20 minutes. Remove saucepan from heat.

4 Pour custard into large bowl; cool, then cover and refrigerate until mixture mounds slightly when dropped from spoon, about 1 hour, stirring occasionally.

5 In small bowl, whip double or whipping cream until stiff peaks form. With rubber spatula or wire whisk, fold whipped cream into custard.

ALTERNATIVE RASPBERRY TOPPINGS

In the main picture below, raspberries are piled high on top of custard. For a more formal effect, raspberries can be arranged in a pattern, as here.

Windmill
Arrange raspberries in 4 triangular shapes, working from centre of filling towards outside.

In the Round
Arrange raspberries in concentric circles, working from outside edge of filling to centre.

6 Carefully remove pastry shell from tin; place on serving plate. Spoon custard into pastry shell; top with raspberries.

7 Refrigerate tart for 1 hour or until custard is completely set.

Fresh summer raspberries are piled high in centre of tart; if you like, sprinkle them with caster sugar just before serving

NUTCRACKER TART

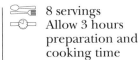

- 8 servings
- Allow 3 hours preparation and cooking time

Ginger Pastry

175 g/6 oz plain flour

2 tablespoons caster sugar

1 teaspoon ground ginger

120 g/4 oz butter

1 egg

Filling

60 g/2 oz butter

60 g/2 oz black treacle

175 g/6 oz golden syrup

60 g/2 oz caster sugar

3 eggs

120 g/4 oz shelled pecans or walnut halves

100 g/3 ½ oz shelled unsalted macadamia nuts or hazelnuts

Whipped cream and non-toxic flowers (pages 118-119) to decorate

1 Prepare ginger pastry dough: in medium bowl, with fork, stir flour, sugar and ginger. With pastry blender or with fingertips, cut or rub butter into flour mixture until mixture resembles coarse crumbs. Add egg; mix lightly with fork until dough just holds together.

Rich-tasting macadamia nuts look good arranged with pecans because of their perfect round shape, but for a less expensive alternative you could equally well use a combination of hazelnuts and walnuts

2 With hand, pat dough on to bottom and up side of 25 cm/10 inch loose-bottomed tart or flan tin. Set aside.

3 Preheat oven to 180°C/350°F/gas 4.

4 Prepare filling: in medium saucepan over low heat, melt butter; remove from heat.

5 Into melted butter, with wire whisk, beat treacle, syrup, sugar and eggs just until blended.

6 Arrange pecans or walnuts and macadamia nuts or hazelnuts on bottom of pastry shell in concentric circles.

7 Slowly pour treacle mixture over nuts in pastry shell, taking care not to disturb pattern.

8 Bake tart for 35 minutes or until knife inserted in filling 2.5 cm/1 inch from edge comes out clean. Cool tart in tin on wire rack.

9 To serve, remove side of tin; decorate centre of tart with whipped cream and flower.

FRENCH APPLE PUFFS

8 servings

Allow 1 ½ hours preparation and cooking time

---

450 g/1 lb frozen puff pastry

---

4 medium-sized dessert apples

---

3 digestive biscuits, finely crushed

---

45 g/1 ½ oz butter, melted

About 3 tablespoons orange marmalade

Icing sugar for sprinkling

Whipped cream for serving (optional)

1 Thaw puff pastry according to packet instructions.

2 Preheat oven to 220°C/425°F/gas 7. On floured surface, with floured rolling pin, roll half of the pastry out to 36 cm/14 ½ inch square.

3 Using 17.5 cm/7 inch round plate as a guide, cut out 4 rounds from pastry square.

4 Cut 2 apples in half lengthways; remove cores and peel. Cut apple halves lengthways into paper-thin slices.

5 Place pastry rounds on large baking sheet. Top each pastry round with 1 tablespoon biscuit crumbs, then with one-quarter of the apple slices.

Finely crushed digestive biscuits add crunch to apple filling, and help prevent apple juices seeping into pastry and making it soggy

6 Brush apple slices with some melted butter.

7 Bake apple puffs for 15 minutes or until pastry is lightly browned and crisp and apple slices are tender. With fish slice, transfer apple puffs to wire racks.

8 In small saucepan over low heat, heat orange marmalade until melted. Brush over apple slices while they are still hot.

9 Repeat with remaining ingredients to make 4 more apple puffs.

Icing sugar melts and caramelizes on hot marmalade glaze

TO SERVE
Sift icing sugar over apple slices. Serve puffs warm, with whipped cream.

PEACH GALETTE

 8 servings
Allow 3 hours preparation and cooking time

Pastry

| 175 g/6 oz plain flour |
| 30 g/1 oz caster sugar |
| 120 g/4 oz butter |
| 1 egg |

Filling

| 2 x 825 g/1 lb 13 oz cans peach halves |
| 1 teaspoon lemon juice |
| 1/4 teaspoon ground ginger |
| 3 heaped tablespoons peach or apricot jam |

Pastry 'scallops' follow shape of peaches

1 Prepare pastry dough: in medium bowl, with fork, stir flour and sugar. With pastry blender or with fingertips, cut or rub butter into flour mixture until mixture resembles coarse crumbs. Add egg; mix lightly with fork until dough just holds together. (Or, in food processor with knife blade attached, blend flour, sugar and butter, cut into 8 pieces, for about 10 seconds. Add egg through feed tube; blend for 15 seconds longer or until dough holds together.) Shape dough into ball. Wrap and refrigerate for 1 hour.

2 Meanwhile, prepare filling: drain peaches; set aside 8 peach halves. Slice remaining peaches.

3 Put sliced peaches in saucepan; add lemon juice, ground ginger and 1 tablespoon jam. Bring to the boil, then cook over medium heat for 5-10 minutes or until mixture is reduced to 300 ml/ 1/2 pint, mashing frequently with potato masher. Leave to cool.

4 Preheat oven to 180°C/350°F/gas 4. On lightly floured surface, with floured rolling pin, roll pastry dough out to 35 cm/14 inch round; transfer to large baking sheet.

5 With fingertips, roll edge towards centre until round measures 25 cm/10 inches and edge is 2 cm/3/4 inch high; push edge in towards centre to make 7 large, evenly spaced scallops.

6 Bake for 25 minutes or until pastry is golden. Cool on baking sheet on wire rack.

7 Melt remaining peach or apricot jam in small saucepan over medium heat, then press through sieve into small jug. Spoon cooled peach mixture over pastry.

8 Cut reserved peach halves into slices, taking care to maintain peach shape. Slip flat side of broad-bladed knife under each peach half and arrange on filling.

9 Fan peach slices slightly; brush with peach or apricot jam glaze. Transfer galette to serving plate.

Pushing pastry edge in to make 'scallop' shapes

UPSIDE-DOWN APPLE TART

 8-10 servings

Allow 1 ½ hours preparation and cooking time

300 g/10 oz frozen puff pastry

10 large Golden Delicious apples

200 g/7 oz caster sugar

120 g/4 oz butter

¼ teaspoon almond essence

Chilled pouring cream for serving (optional)

1 Thaw puff pastry according to packet instructions.

2 Meanwhile, peel and core apples (Golden Delicious apples with very green skin retain their shape best; do not use other apples). Cut each apple in half lengthways.

3 In 25 cm/ 10 inch heavy frying pan with metal handle (or with handle covered with heavy-duty foil) over medium heat, heat sugar, butter and almond essence until butter melts, stirring occasionally (do not use margarine because it will separate from sugar during cooking). Sugar will not be completely dissolved. Remove pan from heat.

4 Arrange apple halves on their sides round side and in centre of pan, fitting apples very tightly together.

5 Return frying pan to medium heat and bring to the boil; boil for 20-40 minutes, depending on juiciness of apples, until butter and sugar mixture becomes caramel-coloured. Remove from heat.

6 Preheat oven to 230°C/450°F/gas 8.

7 On lightly floured surface, with floured rolling pin, roll pastry out to 30 cm/12 inch round.

8 Carefully place pastry round over apple halves in frying pan.

9 With prongs of fork, press pastry to edge of frying pan.

10 Cut slits in pastry. Bake in the oven for 20-25 minutes until pastry is golden. Remove pan from oven; allow to cool on wire rack for 10 minutes.

11 Place dessert platter upside-down over frying pan; holding them firmly together, carefully invert tart on to dessert platter (do this over sink since tart may be extremely juicy).

> **TO SERVE**
> Serve Upside-Down Apple Tart warm or cold, with chilled cream if you like.

When tart is turned out upside-down for serving, apples are caramelized yet still retain their shape

MINCEMEAT AND PEAR FLAN

- 8-10 servings
- Allow 2 hours preparation and cooking time

Pastry

175 g/6 oz plain flour
30 g/1 oz caster sugar
120 g/4 oz butter
1 egg

Streusel Topping

30 g/1 oz plain flour
20 g/²/₃ oz light soft brown sugar
30 g/1 oz butter

Filling

450 g/1 lb mincemeat
1 x 400 g/14 oz can pear halves

Sweet and buttery streusel topping adds crunch and texture to soft mincemeat and pears

1 Prepare pastry dough: in medium bowl, with fork, stir flour and sugar. With pastry blender or with fingertips, cut or rub butter into flour mixture until mixture resembles coarse crumbs. Add egg; mix lightly with fork until dough just holds together. (Or, in food processor with knife blade attached, blend flour, sugar and butter, cut into 8 pieces, until mixture resembles coarse crumbs, about 10 seconds. Add egg through feed tube; blend for 15 seconds longer or until dough holds together and leaves side of bowl.) With hands, shape dough into ball. Wrap and refrigerate for 1 hour.

2 Prepare streusel topping: in small bowl, combine flour and brown sugar. With pastry blender or with fingertips, cut or rub butter into flour mixture until mixture resembles coarse crumbs. Refrigerate.

3 Preheat oven to 180°C/350°F/gas 4.

4 On lightly floured surface, with floured rolling pin, roll pastry dough out to round 2.5 cm/1 inch larger all round than 23 cm/9 inch loose-bottomed tart or flan tin.

5 Ease dough into tin to line evenly; trim edge. With fork, prick pastry shell liberally to prevent puffing and shrinkage during baking.

6 Line pastry shell with foil and spread evenly with dried or baking beans; bake for 10 minutes.

7 Remove foil and beans; prick dough again. Bake for a further 10 minutes. Remove pastry shell from oven; turn oven up to 220°C/425°F/gas 7.

8 Spoon mincemeat into pastry shell and spread evenly.

9 Drain pears; pat dry with kitchen paper. Cut each pear half lengthways into 5 mm/¹/₄ inch thick slices, taking care to keep slices from each half together. Arrange pears on mincemeat, fanning slices slightly.

10 With spoon, evenly sprinkle streusel topping over sliced pears in pastry shell.

11 Bake flan for 15-20 minutes until filling is heated through and pastry and topping are lightly browned. Cool flan slightly in tin on wire rack.

12 Remove side of tin. Serve flan warm or cool completely to serve cold later.

Fanning pear halves in circle on top of mincemeat filling

FRUIT TARTLETS

Petite and prettily shaped, tartlets filled with a variety of colourful fruits and topped with a sparkling glaze make an irresistible display on the table. Here are a few ideas for presentation, to inspire you to create your own filling and topping combinations. Use tartlet tins of as many different shapes as you can, and choose small whole fruits that lend themselves to the shape of the shells, or cut up larger fruits to fit. Make the pastry shells from the recipe for Tartlet Shells (see Box, page 159), leave them to cool, then fill them with Lemon Custard Filling (page 162) or sweetened whipped cream. Once fruits have been arranged on top, brush them with a little melted jelly – use redcurrant jelly for dark fruits, or sieved apricot jam for light-coloured fruits. The thin glaze will provide an instant gloss and keep fruit looking its best for a few hours if necessary.

Raspberry and blackberry

Blueberry

Strawberry

Orange and grapefruit

Red and green seedless grapes

FRUIT TOPPINGS

Choose fruits that suit the size and shape of the tartlet shell. Dainty small whole fruits such as berries and grapes can be used singly, or heaped or clustered on filling. Dice larger fruits, or cut them into slices for dramatic effect.

Grapes can be left whole or sliced, according to their size

Star fruit slices have a beautiful shape

Passion fruit pulp can be sprinkled over other fruits as a decoration

PEAR CRUMBLE TART

 8-10 servings
Allow 3 hours preparation and cooking time

Filling

30 g/1 oz caster sugar
1 teaspoon ground cinnamon
300 ml/ ½ pint double or whipping cream
2 egg yolks
2 x 400 g/14 oz cans pear halves

Crumble Crust

215 g/7 ½ oz plain flour
¼ teaspoon salt (optional)
45 g/1 ½ oz caster sugar
90 g/3 oz butter

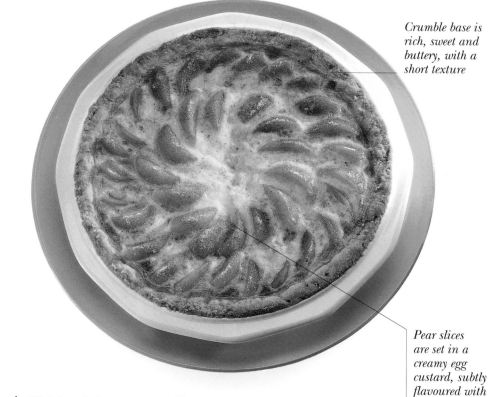

Crumble base is rich, sweet and buttery, with a short texture

Pear slices are set in a creamy egg custard, subtly flavoured with cinnamon

1 Prepare filling: in small bowl, with fork, mix sugar and cinnamon; set aside.

2 In another small bowl, with wire whisk or fork, beat double or whipping cream with egg yolks until blended; cover and refrigerate.

3 Preheat oven to 200°C/400°F/gas 6. Prepare crumble crust: in medium bowl, with fork, stir flour, salt, if using, and sugar. With pastry blender or with fingertips, cut or rub butter into flour mixture until mixture resembles coarse crumbs. (Mixture will be dry and crumbly.)

4 With hand, firmly press crumble mixture on to bottom and up side of shallow 25 cm/10 inch pie dish.

5 Drain pears; pat dry with kitchen paper. Slice pears, then arrange in pie dish, fanning slices slightly.

6 Over pear slices in bottom of crumble crust, with spoon, evenly sprinkle sugar and cinnamon mixture.

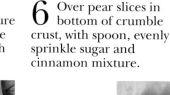

7 Bake tart for about 5 minutes or until sugar and cinnamon mixture is melted.

8 With pie dish still on oven rack, carefully pour cream mixture over pears.

9 Bake tart for 20-30 minutes until top is browned and knife inserted in centre of filling comes out clean.

10 Cool tart in dish on wire rack. Serve warm, or cover and refrigerate to serve cold later.

APRICOT LINZER TORTE

  8 servings
Allow 3 hours
preparation and
cooking time

Filling

| 350 g/12 oz dried apricot halves |
| 250 ml/8 fl oz orange juice |
| 100 g/3 ½ oz caster sugar |

Almond Pastry

| 120 g/4 oz blanched almonds, ground |
| 265 g/9 ½ oz plain flour |
| 200 g/7 oz caster sugar |
| 175 g/6 oz butter, softened |
| 30 g/1 oz cocoa powder |
| 1 teaspoon ground cinnamon |
| 1 teaspoon grated lemon zest |
| 1 egg |
| Icing sugar for sprinkling |

1 Prepare filling: in large saucepan bring apricots, orange juice, sugar and *250 ml/8 fl oz water* to the boil. Cook, uncovered, over medium heat for 30 minutes or until apricots are very tender and liquid is absorbed, stirring frequently.

2 Press apricot mixture through food mill or coarse sieve into bowl; cover and refrigerate.

3 Generously grease 28 cm/11 inch loose-bottomed tart or flan tin.

4 Prepare almond pastry dough: in large bowl, with electric mixer, beat almonds, flour, caster sugar, butter, cocoa, cinnamon, lemon zest and egg until well mixed, occasionally scraping bowl.

5 Divide dough in half; press half of the dough on to bottom and up side of tin. Spoon apricot mixture into pastry shell.

6 Preheat oven to 200°C/400°F/gas 6. On lightly floured surface, with floured rolling pin, roll out remaining dough into 25 cm/10 inch round. With knife, cut dough round into 1 cm/½ inch wide strips.

7 Carefully place half of the dough strips, about 1 cm/½ inch apart, over apricot filling.

8 Place remaining strips diagonally across first row of strips about 1 cm/½ inch apart.

9 Press down with finger on either side of each crossing to create rippled lattice effect.

10 Press ends of strips to inside edge of pastry shell.

11 Bake torte in the oven for 10 minutes. Turn oven down to 180°C/350°F/gas 4; bake for 20 minutes longer. Cool torte in tin on wire rack.

12 To serve, remove side of tin; place torte on serving platter. Sift icing sugar over lattice, covering top strips only.

If you use a small sieve and are very careful when sifting icing sugar over lattice, sugar will settle on top row of lattice strips only, and look most effective

FRESH CHERRY FLAN

8 servings
Allow 2 hours preparation and cooking time

1 x 25 cm/10 inch Tart or Flan Shell (see Box, page 159)

450 g/1 lb cherries

3 eggs

300 ml/ ½ pint double or whipping cream

60 g/2 oz caster sugar

2 tablespoons almond liqueur or 1 teaspoon almond essence

For the best creamy texture, egg custard should be firm and set at edge when removed from oven, but still slightly soft in centre; it will set throughout if left to stand for 10-15 minutes

1 Prepare and bake Tart or Flan Shell according to recipe instructions; cool. Turn oven down to 180°C/350°F/gas 4.

2 Meanwhile, with cherry stoner, remove stones from cherries.

3 In large bowl, with electric mixer, beat eggs with double or whipping cream, sugar and almond liqueur or almond essence until blended.

CUSTARDS AND CUSTARD TARTS

Because custards are so delicate in texture, and can easily be overcooked, they should be removed from the oven when they are set at the sides – and still slightly soft in the centre.

Testing Custards
When custard looks firm and set, double-check by inserting knife 2.5 cm/1 inch from edge – custard is ready if knife comes out clean. Custard will continue cooking after it has been removed from the oven, so that after 10-15 minutes it will be set throughout.

4 Place cherries in pastry shell, arranging them in concentric circles.

5 Set tin on oven rack and slowly pour egg mixture over cherries, taking care not to dislodge pattern.

6 Bake flan in the oven for 30 minutes or until knife inserted in filling 2.5 cm/ 1 inch from edge comes out clean.

7 Cool flan slightly in tin on wire rack.

8 Remove side of tin. Serve flan warm, or cover and leave to cool to serve cold later.

Sweet juicy cherries are stoned and set in an almond-flavoured creamy egg custard

CLAFOUTIS FLAN

- 8-10 servings
- Allow 4 hours preparation and cooking time

Pastry

215 g/7 ½ oz plain flour

¾ teaspoon salt (optional)

1 teaspoon caster sugar

120 g/4 oz butter, softened

1 egg

Filling

6 eggs

200 g/7 oz caster sugar

450 ml/¾ pint milk

150 ml/¼ pint soured cream

1 teaspoon vanilla essence

175 g/6 oz blueberries or stoned cherries

1 Prepare pastry dough: in medium bowl, with fork, stir flour, salt, if using, and sugar. With pastry blender or with fingertips, cut or rub butter into flour mixture until mixture resembles coarse crumbs. In cup, with fork, beat egg; add to flour mixture and mix lightly with fork until dough just holds together, adding a little water if necessary. With hands, shape dough into ball. Wrap and refrigerate for 1 hour.

Here, fresh blueberries are used for this French 'clafoutis', but you can use stoned cherries if they are more easy to obtain

2 On lightly floured surface, with floured rolling pin, roll out dough into round 2.5 cm/1 inch larger all round than 30 cm/12 inch flan dish. Ease dough into dish to line evenly; trim edge. With fork, prick pastry shell in many places to prevent puffing during baking. To prevent pastry from shrinking during baking, place shell in freezer for 15 minutes.

3 Preheat oven to 220°C/425°F/gas 7. Line pastry shell with foil and evenly spread dried or baking beans over bottom.

4 Bake pastry shell for 20 minutes. Remove beans and foil and again prick pastry shell. Bake for a further 3-4 minutes until pastry is lightly browned and no longer soft and raw (if pastry puffs up, gently press it to dish with spoon).

5 Prepare filling: in large bowl, with electric mixer, beat eggs and caster sugar until very thick and lemon-coloured, about 3 minutes. Gradually add milk, soured cream and vanilla essence; beat until well blended.

6 Place blueberries or cherries in warm pastry shell. Slowly pour over egg mixture.

Pouring egg mixture over blueberries

7 Bake in the oven for 30-35 minutes until filling is set and pastry is golden brown; cover with foil after 20 minutes to prevent overbrowning.

8 Cool flan in dish on wire rack.

Flan is served topped with extra blueberries and sifted with icing sugar

ORANGE AND ALMOND FLAN

 10 servings
Allow 2 ¹/₄ hours preparation and cooking time

Ginger Pastry

150 g/5 oz plain flour

¹/₄ teaspoon salt

¹/₄ teaspoon ground ginger

1 tablespoon caster sugar

60 g/2 oz butter

Filling

2 eggs

225 g/8 oz almond paste

125 ml/4 fl oz double or whipping cream

2 medium-sized oranges

2 tablespoons golden syrup

60 g/2 oz caster sugar

1 First prepare pastry dough: in medium bowl, with fork, stir flour, salt, ginger and sugar. With pastry blender or with fingertips, cut or rub butter into flour mixture until it resembles coarse crumbs.

2 Sprinkle 2-3 table-spoons cold water, a tablespoon at a time, into mixture, mixing lightly with fork after each addition until dough is just moist enough to hold together. Shape dough into ball. Wrap and chill in refrigerator for 1 hour.

3 Preheat oven to 190°C/375°F/gas 5. On lightly floured surface, with floured rolling pin, roll out dough into round about 2.5 cm/1 inch larger all round than 24 cm/ 9 ¹/₂ inch loose-bottomed tart or flan tin. Ease dough into tin; trim edge.

4 Prepare filling: in large bowl, with electric mixer, beat eggs, almond paste and double or whipping cream until mixture is smooth, occa-sionally scraping bowl with rubber spatula.

5 Pour almond mixture into pastry shell. Bake for 35 minutes or until filling and pastry are golden brown. Cool flan in tin on wire rack.

6 While flan is cooling, prepare candied orange zest: with vegetable peeler, thinly pare zest from oranges in long strips. Cut orange zest into matchstick-thin strips.

7 With knife, cut white pith from oranges; cut along both sides of each dividing membrane and lift out segments from centre. Place orange segments on kitchen paper to absorb excess juice.

8 In medium saucepan over medium heat, bring orange zest, golden syrup, sugar and 5 table-spoons water to the boil, stirring frequently. Reduce heat to medium-low; cook for 15 minutes or until zest is tender.

9 With fork, remove orange zest and place in single layer on wire rack to drain.

10 Brush flan with sugar syrup remaining in saucepan.

11 Carefully remove side of tin; slide flan on to serving plate.

> **TO SERVE**
> Arrange candied orange zest round edge of flan; arrange orange segments in centre.

Matchstick-thin strips of candied orange zest are arranged round circle of orange segments to make the pretty topping for this superb-tasting flan

ITALIAN WALNUT TART

 8 servings
Allow 3 hours
preparation and
cooking time

Sweet Cornmeal Pastry

215 g/7 ¹/₂ oz plain flour
40 g/1 ¹/₃ oz cornmeal
60 g/2 oz caster sugar
175 g/6 oz butter
1 egg
1 tablespoon milk

Filling

150 g/5 oz caster sugar
250 ml/8 fl oz double cream
90 g/3 oz liquid honey
450 g/1 lb walnut pieces, coarsely chopped

Sweet cornmeal pastry gives this lattice-topped tart a golden colour and accentuates the nutty flavour of the filling

1 Prepare sweet cornmeal pastry dough: in large bowl, with fork, stir flour, cornmeal and sugar. With pastry blender or with fingertips, cut or rub butter into flour and cornmeal mixture until mixture resembles coarse crumbs.

2 Add egg to flour and cornmeal mixture; mix lightly with fork until dough just holds together.

3 With your hands, press two-thirds of dough on to bottom and 3 cm/1 ¹/₄ inches up side of 25 cm/10 inch springform cake tin.

4 Place pastry shell and remaining pastry dough in refrigerator to chill while preparing filling.

5 Prepare filling: in large frying pan over medium heat, heat sugar, without stirring, just until it begins to melt. Cook, stirring constantly, for 6-8 minutes until golden brown. Remove pan from heat; slowly and carefully stir in double cream (mixture will spatter). Return pan to medium heat; cook for 5 minutes or until mixture is smooth, stirring frequently.

Stirring walnuts into filling

6 Remove frying pan from heat; stir in honey until well blended. Stir in chopped walnuts until evenly mixed.

7 Leave walnut filling in frying pan to cool slightly.

8 Preheat oven to 180°C/350°F/gas 4. Evenly spread walnut filling in pastry shell. On lightly floured surface, with floured rolling pin, roll out remaining dough into 25 x 12.5 cm/ 10 x 5 inch rectangle; cut lengthways into ten 1 cm/¹/₂ inch wide strips.

9 Twist strips; arrange in lattice design on top of filling.

10 Brush strips lightly with milk. Bake tart for 45 minutes or until golden brown. Cool tart in tin on wire rack.

11 To serve, carefully remove side from springform tin. Serve warm, or leave to cool, cover and refrigerate to serve cold later.

DELUXE APPLE FLAN

This beautiful apple flan is a classic piece of French pâtisserie, yet it is easy to make at home. Take care to cut the apple slices really thinly, and take time to arrange them in overlapping circles; your efforts will be rewarded.

 8-10 servings

 Allow 4 hours preparation and cooking time

Pastry

150 g/5 oz plain flour

75 g/2 ½ oz butter, softened

30 g/1 oz caster sugar

⅛ teaspoon salt (optional)

Filling

6 large dessert apples

120 g/4 oz apricot jam

1 teaspoon lemon juice

1 Prepare pastry dough: in medium bowl, combine flour, butter, sugar, salt, if using, and *2 tablespoons cold water*. With fingertips, mix together just until blended, adding more water, 1 teaspoon at a time, if needed.

2 Press dough on to bottom and up side of 23 cm/9 inch loose-bottomed tart or flan tin; refrigerate.

3 Prepare filling: peel and core 3 apples; cut into chunks. In saucepan, cook apple chunks with half of the apricot jam and *4 tablespoons water* until apples are tender.

4 In food processor or blender, blend apple mixture until smooth. Pour apple purée into medium non-stick saucepan; cook, uncovered, until very thick, stirring frequently to prevent purée catching on bottom of pan.

5 Peel remaining 3 apples. Cut each apple into quarters lengthways; remove cores.

Removing cores from apples

FILLING AND GLAZING FLAN

Spreading apple purée in pastry shell: spoon apple purée into pastry shell, then spread evenly with back of spoon.

Arranging apples in centre of flan: place apple slices, closely overlapping, in small circle in centre of apple purée filling.

Arranging remaining apple slices: place remaining apple slices, closely overlapping, in large circle round first small circle, to cover apple purée completely and fill pastry shell.

Glazing apples: with pastry brush, gently spread hot apricot glaze over apple slices until evenly coated.

6 Cut each quarter lengthways into 3 mm/⅛ inch thick slices.

7 In large bowl, gently toss apple slices with lemon juice.

8 Preheat oven to 200°C/400°F/gas 6.

9 Fill pastry shell with apple purée and cover with apple slices (see Box, page 178).

10 Bake flan in the oven for 45 minutes or until apple slices are tender and browned. Transfer tin to wire rack.

11 In small saucepan, melt remaining apricot jam; with spoon, press through sieve if liked.

12 Brush jam glaze evenly over apple slices (see Box, page 178). Cool flan in tin on wire rack.

13 To serve, carefully remove side of tin.

VIENNESE CARAMEL NUT TART

 8 servings
Allow 3 hours preparation and cooking time

Filling

225 g/8 oz shelled pecans or walnut halves

135 g/4 ½ oz caster sugar

300 ml/ ½ pint double or whipping cream

15 g/ ½ oz butter

Pastry

300 g/10 oz plain flour

30 g/1 oz caster sugar

½ teaspoon salt (optional)

175 g/6 oz butter

Chocolate Coating

175 g/6 oz plain chocolate, broken into pieces

60 g/2 oz butter

Tart is turned upside-down after baking; pastry on top is then glazed and piped

1 Prepare filling: reserve 10 pecan or walnut halves for decoration; finely chop remaining nuts. Set aside.

2 In medium saucepan over high heat, bring sugar and *4 tablespoons water* to the boil, stirring frequently until sugar completely dissolves. Reduce heat to medium; cook sugar syrup for 10 minutes, without stirring, until syrup turns medium amber in colour. Remove saucepan from heat; slowly and carefully pour in double or whipping cream (mixture will spatter). Return saucepan to heat; cook until caramel dissolves, stirring occasionally. Increase heat to high; cook, stirring frequently, until mixture boils and thickens slightly.

3 Remove saucepan from heat; stir in chopped nuts and butter. Set aside to cool.

4 Prepare pastry dough: in medium bowl, with fork, stir flour, sugar and salt, if using. With pastry blender or with fingertips, cut or rub butter into flour mixture until mixture resembles coarse crumbs. Sprinkle *4-6 tablespoons cold water*, a tablespoon at a time, into mixture, mixing lightly with fork after each addition until dough holds together. With hands, shape dough into ball.

5 Preheat oven to 200°C/400°F/gas 6. On lightly floured surface, with floured rolling pin, roll out two-thirds of pastry dough into round about 5 cm/2 inches larger all round than 20 cm/8 inch loose-bottomed tart or flan tin. Ease dough into tin to line evenly (you will have a 2.5 cm/1 inch overhang).

6 Spoon nut mixture into pastry shell. Roll out remaining dough into 19 cm/7 ½ inch round; place on top of nut filling. Fold overhang over round; press gently to seal.

7 Bake tart in the oven for 40 minutes or until lightly browned. Cool tart in tin on wire rack.

8 When tart is cool, prepare chocolate coating: in bowl over saucepan of gently simmering water, heat pieces of chocolate and butter, stirring frequently, until melted and smooth. Remove bowl from pan; cool chocolate mixture slightly.

9 Carefully turn tart out upside-down on to cake plate; remove tin. Spoon 4 tablespoons chocolate mixture into piping bag fitted with small writing tube; spread remaining chocolate mixture over top and sides of tart. Arrange reserved pecan or walnut halves on top. Drizzle chocolate mixture in piping bag over top of tart to make pretty design. Leave for 15 minutes until chocolate sets before serving.

LEMON CUSTARD TART

 8 servings

Make day before and keep in refrigerator

Pastry

90 g/3 oz butter, softened

45 g/1 ¹/₂ oz caster sugar

¹/₂ teaspoon grated lemon zest

1 egg yolk

120 g/4 oz plain flour

Filling

4 eggs

4 egg yolks

175 ml/6 fl oz lemon juice

190 g/6 ¹/₂ oz caster sugar

60 g/2 oz butter

2 tablespoons apricot jam

Lemon slices to decorate

1 Prepare pastry dough: in medium bowl, with electric mixer, beat butter, sugar and lemon zest until well blended; beat in egg yolk. Stir in flour until just blended. Shape pastry dough into ball; wrap and refrigerate for 1 hour.

2 Preheat oven to 220°C/425°F/gas 7. On lightly floured surface, with floured rolling pin, roll out dough into round 2.5 cm/1 inch larger all round than 23 cm/9 inch loose-bottomed tart or flan tin. Ease dough into tin to line evenly; trim edge even with rim. With fork, prick pastry shell in many places to prevent puffing and shrinkage during baking. Line pastry shell with foil and spread evenly with dried or baking beans.

3 Bake pastry shell for 10 minutes; remove beans and foil and again prick shell. Bake for a further 5 minutes or until pastry is golden (if pastry puffs up, gently press it to tin with spoon). Cool pastry shell in tin on wire rack.

4 Prepare filling: in non-stick saucepan, with wire whisk or fork, beat eggs and egg yolks until blended; stir in lemon juice and 150 g/5 oz sugar. Cook over medium-low heat, stirring constantly, until mixture thickens and coats a spoon well, about 15 minutes (do not boil or mixture will curdle). Stir in butter until melted.

5 Into baked pastry shell, pour lemon custard filling.

6 Refrigerate tart overnight so that filling is well chilled and firm.

Here lemon slices are 'vandyked' with canelle knife to make cartwheel shapes – see page 62 for instructions

7 About 1-2 hours before serving, preheat grill to high. Cover edge of pastry shell with foil to prevent overbrowning. Evenly sprinkle remaining caster sugar over chilled lemon custard filling.

8 Place tart under grill for 6-8 minutes until sugar melts and begins to brown, making a shiny crust. (Take care not to let filling scorch.) Cool, then refrigerate.

9 Carefully remove side of tin; slide tart on to cake plate. Melt apricot jam, then work through sieve. Brush top of tart with jam glaze and decorate with lemon slices.

GRAPE AND KIWI FRUIT FLAN

8 servings

Allow 3 1/2 hours preparation and cooking time

1 x 25 cm/10 inch Tart or Flan Shell (see Box, page 159)

60 g/2 oz caster sugar

25 g/ 3/4 oz plain flour

1 tablespoon powdered gelatine

2 eggs plus 1 egg yolk

450 ml/ 3/4 pint milk

2 tablespoons almond liqueur or 1/2 teaspoon almond essence

About 225 g/8 oz seedless green or red grapes

3 medium-sized kiwi fruit

150 ml/1/4 pint double or whipping cream

2 tablespoons redcurrant jelly

1 Prepare and bake Tart or Flan Shell according to recipe instructions; cool on wire rack.

2 While pastry shell is baking, prepare filling: in heavy medium saucepan, combine sugar, flour and gelatine. In small bowl, with wire whisk or fork, beat eggs and egg yolk with milk until well mixed; stir into gelatine mixture. Leave to stand for 5 minutes to soften gelatine slightly.

3 Cook over low heat, stirring constantly, until mixture thickens and coats a spoon well, about 15 minutes (do not boil or mixture will curdle).

The contrasting shades of two green fruits look stunning in Grape and Kiwi Fruit Flan

4 Remove saucepan from heat; stir in almond liqueur or almond essence. Cool, then cover and refrigerate until mixture mounds slightly when dropped from a spoon, about 1 hour, stirring occasionally.

5 Meanwhile, cut each grape in half lengthways. Peel and thinly slice kiwi fruit. Set grapes and kiwi fruit aside.

6 In small bowl, whip double or whipping cream until stiff peaks form. With rubber spatula or wire whisk, fold whipped cream into almond custard.

Melted redcurrant jelly gives these artfully arranged fruits a glossy finish

7 Carefully remove side of flan tin; slide pastry shell on to serving plate. Evenly spoon custard into cooled pastry shell. Arrange grapes, cut side down, and kiwi fruit slices on custard to make attractive design.

8 In small saucepan over medium heat, melt redcurrant jelly, stirring occasionally. With pastry brush, carefully brush fruit with melted jelly. Refrigerate flan until filling is completely set, about 1 hour.

PASTRIES

All pastries are made with some kind of dough; and the different doughs, coupled with the wide variety of fillings that can be used, add up to an almost limitless choice of eye-catching, taste-tempting desserts. Melt-in-the-mouth shortcrust can be used for fruit-filled rolls and dumplings.

Flaky puff pastry makes handsome pies, tarts and turnovers. Light and airy shells made from choux pastry take to luscious fillings from whipped cream to ice cream; and delicious desserts made with paper-thin phyllo range from classic Strudel to the incomparable Baklava.

PEARS EN CROÛTE À LA CRÈME

 Makes 6
Allow 1 ½ hours preparation and cooking time

Filling

15 g/ ½ oz caster sugar	
¼ teaspoon ground cinnamon	
3 medium-sized William's pears	
6 whole cloves	

Pastry

215 g/7 ½ oz plain flour	
120 g/4 oz butter, softened	
1 x 85 g/3 oz package full-fat soft cheese, softened	
1 egg white	

Custard

1 egg yolk	
450 ml/ ¾ pint single or half cream	
4 teaspoons cornflour	
45 g/1 ½ oz caster sugar	
¼ teaspoon almond essence	

1 Prepare filling: in cup, with fork, stir sugar with cinnamon; set aside. Peel pears. Cut each pear in half lengthways; remove cores.

2 Prepare pastry dough: in medium bowl, combine flour, butter and soft cheese; with fingertips, mix together just until blended.

3 On lightly floured surface, with floured rolling pin, roll out half of the dough 3 mm/⅛ inch thick. Using 18 cm/7 inch round plate as a guide, cut 3 rounds from dough; reserve trimmings.

4 Sprinkle rounds of dough with half of the sugar and cinnamon mixture; place a pear half, cut side up, on each round. Carefully fold round of dough over each pear half. Pinch dough edges to seal.

5 Place wrapped pears, seam side down, on ungreased large baking sheet. Repeat with remaining pears and dough to make 6 altogether.

Pastry made with soft cheese is rich and melt-in-the mouth, an ideal casing for a sweet William's pear

6 Preheat oven to 190°C/375°F/gas 5. Reroll dough trimmings; cut to make leaves. Brush dough with egg white; decorate with dough leaves and brush them with egg white.

7 Bake pears for 35 minutes or until pastry is golden. Transfer to wire rack; cool slightly.

8 Meanwhile, make custard: in medium saucepan, combine egg yolk, single or half cream, cornflour and sugar.

9 Cook over medium-low heat, stirring constantly, until mixture thickens and coats a spoon well, about 15 minutes. Remove saucepan from heat; stir in almond essence. Cool custard slightly.

> **TO SERVE**
> On to each of 6 dessert plates, spoon some custard. Place pear in centre of custard; insert whole clove in tip of each to resemble stalk. Or refrigerate pears and custard separately to serve chilled later.

PEAR JALOUSIE

 8 servings
Allow 1 ½ hours
preparation and
cooking time

Pastry

2 x 225 g/8 oz packets
  frozen puff pastry

1 egg

Caster sugar for sprinkling

Filling

6 medium-sized pears

45 g/1 ½ oz currants

100 g/3 ½ oz caster sugar

To Serve

Spiced Cream (see Box,
  below)

Thinly sliced pears and
currants peep through
slats in pastry jalousie
(jalousie means 'Venetian
blind' in French)

Jalousie is best served sliced on
individual plates, as it is
difficult to find a serving
plate that is the right shape
and size for the whole dessert

1 Thaw puff pastry
according to packet
instructions.

2 Meanwhile, prepare
pear filling: core and
thinly slice pears (do not
peel them). In large
bowl, toss pear slices with
currants and caster sugar.

3 Preheat oven to
220°C/425°F/gas 7.
On lightly floured surface,
with floured rolling pin,
roll 1 packet of pastry out
into 33 x 25 cm/
13 x 10 inch rectangle;
place on ungreased large
baking sheet.

SPICED CREAM

In large saucepan over
high heat, bring 350 ml/
12 fl oz double cream,
2 tablespoons caster sugar
and 1 teaspoon ground
cinnamon to the boil,
stirring occasionally.
Boil until cream is
reduced to about
300 ml/½ pint. Strain
cream into serving
bowl. Leave cream to
cool slightly to serve
warm, or refrigerate
to serve cold later.

4 On lightly floured
surface, with floured
rolling pin, roll out
remaining packet of
pastry into 35 x 28 cm/
14 x 11 inch rectangle;
sprinkle lightly with flour.
Fold pastry in half
lengthways.

5 Cut pastry crossways
through folded edge
to within 2.5 cm/1 inch
of unfolded edge at 1 cm/
½ inch intervals.

6 In cup, with fork, beat
egg and 1 teaspoon
water. Spoon pear filling
on to pastry rectangle on
baking sheet to about
2.5 cm/1 inch from edges.
Brush edges of pastry with
some egg mixture.

7 Place folded piece
of pastry over filling
with fold at centre; unfold
pastry. Press edges of
pastry together to seal.

8 Brush pastry all over
with remaining egg
mixture; sprinkle lightly
with caster sugar. Bake in
the oven for 30 minutes or
until pastry is golden and
puffed.

9 While jalousie is
baking, prepare
Spiced Cream.

10 Cut jalousie into
slices; serve warm,
or cool on wire rack to
serve cold later. Serve
Spiced Cream separately.

CONTINENTAL FRUIT SLICE

- 8 servings
- Allow 4 hours preparation and cooking time

Filling

225 g/8 oz dried figs, coarsely chopped

150 g/5 oz stoned dates, coarsely chopped

120 g/4 oz dried apricots, coarsely chopped

30 g/1 oz sultanas

2 tablespoons lemon juice

1 teaspoon ground cinnamon

100 g/3 ¹/₂ oz caster sugar

120 g/4 oz walnut pieces, chopped

Pastry

300 g/10 oz plain flour

1 teaspoon salt (optional)

30 g/1 oz caster sugar

175 g/6 oz butter

1 egg

1 tablespoon milk

1 Make filling: in large saucepan over high heat, bring figs, dates, apricots, sultanas, lemon juice, cinnamon, sugar and *600 ml/1 pint water* to the boil. Reduce heat to low; simmer, uncovered, stirring occasionally, for 30 minutes or until mixture is thick. Remove saucepan from heat; stir in chopped walnuts. Leave to cool for at least 1 hour.

2 Meanwhile, prepare pastry dough: in medium bowl, with fork, stir flour, salt, if using, and sugar. With pastry blender or with fingertips, cut or rub butter into flour mixture until mixture resembles coarse crumbs. Sprinkle *5-6 tablespoons cold water*, a tablespoon at a time, into flour mixture, mixing lightly with fork after each addition until dough just holds together. With hands, shape dough into ball. Wrap and refrigerate until dried fruit filling is cool.

3 Preheat oven to 220°C/425°F/gas 7. Reserve a little dough for making leaves and berries. On lightly floured surface, with floured rolling pin, roll out remaining dough into 40 x 30 cm/ 16 x 12 inch rectangle.

4 Transfer dough rectangle to ungreased large baking sheet. Spoon dried fruit filling lengthways in 10 cm/4 inch wide strip over centre of rectangle to about 6 cm/ 2 ¹/₂ inches from each end. Fold one long side of dough rectangle over filling, then roll over to enclose filling, seam side down. Fold dough under on each end of roll.

5 In cup, with fork, beat egg and milk. Brush roll with some egg mixture. With tip of knife, cut few shallow lines in top of roll. On floured surface, with floured rolling pin, roll out reserved dough. With knife, cut out small leaves and roll small pieces of dough into berries. Arrange leaves and berries on top of roll; brush with some egg mixture.

6 Bake roll for 25-30 minutes until pastry is golden. With fish slices, transfer pastry roll to wire rack to cool completely. Serve at room temperature.

Sweet and juicy filling of dried fruits and nuts is revealed when generous slices are cut for serving

APPLE TURNOVERS

 Makes 8

Allow 5 hours preparation and cooking time

Flaky Pastry

300 g/10 oz plain flour
1 teaspoon salt (optional)
225 g/8 oz butter
1 egg

Filling

2 large cooking apples
100 g/3 ¹/₂ oz caster sugar
1 tablespoon cornflour
1 teaspoon lemon juice
¹/₄ teaspoon ground cinnamon

Topping

Glacé Icing (see Box, below)

Triangles of flaky pastry encase apples flavoured with cinnamon and lemon; glacé icing is drizzled over before serving

1 Prepare pastry dough: in medium bowl, with fork, stir flour and salt. With pastry blender or with fingertips, cut or rub half of the butter into flour mixture until mixture resembles coarse crumbs. Sprinkle *125 ml/4 fl oz cold water,* a tablespoon at a time, into mixture, mixing lightly with fork after each addition until dough just holds together. With hands, shape dough into ball.

2 On lightly floured surface, with floured rolling pin, roll out pastry dough into 45 x 20 cm/ 18 x 8 inch rectangle. Cut 60 g/2 oz butter into thin slices.

3 Starting at one of the 20 cm/8 inch sides, place butter slices over two-thirds of rectangle to within about 1 cm/¹/₂ inch of edge of dough.

4 Fold unbuttered third of dough over middle third.

5 Fold opposite end of dough over to make 20 x 15 cm/8 x 6 inch rectangle.

6 Roll out dough again into 45 x 20 cm/ 18 x 8 inch rectangle. Slice remaining butter; place slices on dough and fold as before. Wrap dough and refrigerate for 15 minutes.

7 Roll out folded dough into 45 x 20 cm/ 18 x 8 inch rectangle. Fold rectangle lengthways and then crossways; wrap and refrigerate for 1 hour.

8 Meanwhile, prepare filling: peel, core and slice apples. In small saucepan over low heat, cook apples with sugar, cornflour, lemon juice and cinnamon, stirring frequently, until apples are tender. Set aside until filling is cool.

9 Preheat oven to 230°C/450°F/gas 8. Cut dough in half cross-ways. On lightly floured surface, with floured rolling pin, roll out half into 30 cm/12 inch square (keep remaining dough refrigerated); cut into four 15 cm/6 inch squares. In cup, with fork, beat egg and *1 tablespoon water;* brush some egg mixture over dough squares.

10 Spoon one-eighth of apple mixture in centre of each square; fold diagonally in half and press edges to seal. Place on ungreased baking sheet; refrigerate. Repeat with remaining dough and apple mixture.

11 Brush turnovers with egg mixture. Bake for 20 minutes or until pastry is golden. Cool on wire rack.

12 Prepare Glacé Icing; with spoon, drizzle over turnovers; leave to set before serving.

GLACÉ ICING

In small bowl, mix together *60 g/2 oz icing sugar, sifted,* and *about 1 tablespoon water.*

RASPBERRY CREAM SLICES

Makes 6
Allow 2 hours preparation and cooking time

1 x 225 g/8 oz packet frozen puff pastry

325 g/11 oz caster sugar

150 ml/¼ pint single cream

300 ml/½ pint double or whipping cream

300 g/10 oz raspberries

1 Thaw pastry according to packet instructions.

2 Preheat oven to 220°C/425°F/gas 7. On lightly floured surface, with floured rolling pin, roll out pastry to 24 x 20 cm/9½ x 8 inch rectangle. With sharp knife, cut thin strip of pastry, about 5 mm/¼ inch wide, from each side of pastry (freshly cut edges give maximum puffing). Cut pastry into 6 rectangles in all.

3 Place pastry rectangles on ungreased large baking sheet. Bake for 15 minutes or until pastry is puffed and golden. Cool on wire rack.

4 About 30 minutes before serving, prepare caramel sauce: in large saucepan over medium heat, bring 300 g/10 oz sugar and 5 tablespoons water to the boil, stirring frequently. Cook, without stirring, until mixture becomes caramel-coloured. Remove saucepan from heat; gradually stir in single cream (sugar mixture will harden). Cook over medium heat, stirring constantly, until caramel sauce is smooth; keep sauce warm.

5 In small bowl, with mixer on medium speed, whip double or whipping cream with remaining caster sugar until soft peaks form.

6 With serrated knife and using a sawing action, carefully split each puff pastry rectangle in half horizontally.

Splitting puff pastry rectangles in half

7 Spoon whipped cream on to bottom half of each puff pastry rectangle, spreading it out evenly.

8 With fingers, carefully place raspberries on top of whipped cream, spacing them evenly.

9 Gently replace pastry tops over whipped cream and raspberries.

> ### TO SERVE
> Pour warm caramel sauce on to 6 dessert plates. Arrange pastries on plates; decorate with remaining raspberries.

FRESH FRUIT PUFF PASTRY TARTS

The melt-in-the-mouth layers of puff pastry in these glorious French tarts are filled with cream and juicy, colourful fruits. Here there's a mixture of fresh and *canned fruits – fresh strawberries, apples, grapes and kiwi fruit with canned mandarin oranges and peaches, but you can ring the changes according to the season.*

 Makes 16

Pastry can be made up to 1 week ahead; allow about 3 hours to make tarts

Rough Puff Pastry

550 g/1 lb 3 oz plain flour
1 teaspoon salt (optional)
450 g/1 lb cold butter
1 egg, beaten

Filling

300 ml/ 1/2 pint double or whipping cream
30 g/1 oz caster sugar
1/4 teaspoon almond essence
Fresh or canned fruits
Mint leaves to decorate

MAKING PASTRY TARTS

1 Fold 1 square of dough in half diagonally to form triangle.

2 Starting at folded side, cut 1 cm/¹/₂ inch border strip on both sides of triangle, leaving 1 cm/ ¹/₂ inch uncut dough at triangle point so strips remain attached.

3 Unfold triangle. Lift up both loose border strips and slip one under the other, gently pulling to matching corners on base. Attach points of dough with drop of water.

1 First make pastry dough: in medium bowl, with fork, stir flour and salt, if using. With pastry blender or with fingertips, cut or rub 120 g/4 oz butter into flour until mixture resembles coarse crumbs. Add *250 ml/8 fl oz cold water*, a few tablespoons at a time, mixing lightly with fork after each addition until soft dough is formed (add more water if needed, a tablespoon at a time).

2 With hands, shape dough into ball. Wrap and refrigerate for 30 minutes.

3 Meanwhile, between 2 sheets of grease-proof paper, roll remaining butter into 15 cm/ 6 inch square; wrap and refrigerate.

4 On lightly floured surface, with floured rolling pin, roll out dough into 30 cm/12 inch square.

5 Place square of butter diagonally in centre of dough; fold corners of dough over butter so that they meet edges in centre, overlapping slightly.

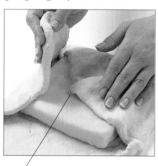

Square of butter is placed diagonally in centre of dough, then corners of dough are folded over butter to meet in the centre

6 Press dough with rolling pin to seal seams.

7 Roll into 45 x 30 cm/ 18 x 12 inch rectangle. Fold one-third over centre, then fold opposite third over first to form 30 x 15 cm/ 12 x 6 inch rectangle of three layers.

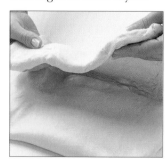

8 Press rectangle of dough with rolling pin to seal seam. Give dough quarter turn. Roll out dough into 37.5 x 20 cm/ 15 x 8 inch rectangle; fold into thirds to form 20 x 12.5 cm/8 x 5 inch rectangle. Wrap and refrigerate, at least 1 hour.

9 Repeat, rolling out dough into 37.5 x 20 cm/15 x 8 inch rectangle and folding into thirds, twice. Wrap and refrigerate for 2 hours.

10 Repeat rolling, folding and refrige-rating twice more, or 6 times in all. After sixth time, wrap well and refrigerate for at least 4 hours (or up to 1 week) before using.

11 Cut dough cross-ways in half. On floured surface, with floured rolling pin, roll out half of the dough into rectangle of 51 x 26 cm/ 20 ¹/₂ x 10 ¹/₂ inches, gently lifting dough occasionally.

12 With sharp knife or pastry wheel, trim edges to make 50 x 25 cm/20 x 10 inch rectangle.

13 Cut rectangle into eight 12.5 cm/ 5 inch squares; place on large baking sheet. Refrigerate for 30 minutes.

14 Repeat with remaining dough. (Or wrap and freeze remaining dough for up to 6 months; thaw dough in refrigerator overnight before using.)

15 Make pastry tarts (see Box, page 188). Refrigerate for 30 minutes.

16 Preheat oven to 200°C/400°F/gas 6. Bake tarts for 20 minutes. Turn oven down to 190°C/375°F/gas 5; brush top of borders with beaten egg. Bake for 20 minutes longer or until centres of tarts are lightly browned. Cool tarts on wire rack.

17 In small bowl, whip double or whipping cream with sugar and almond essence until soft peaks form. Fill tarts with whipped cream; top with fruit and decorate with mint leaves.

Sliced fresh strawberries, canned mandarin orange segments and fresh mint leaves make a colourful combination

Apple, kiwi, peach slices and grapes fit neatly into puff pastry tarts

BAKLAVA

Makes 24

Allow 3 ½ hours preparation and cooking time

| 450 g/1 lb walnut pieces, finely chopped |
| 100 g/3 ½ oz caster sugar |
| 1 teaspoon ground cinnamon |
| 450 g/1 lb fresh or frozen (thawed) phyllo pastry |
| 225 g/8 oz butter, melted |
| 350 g/12 oz liquid honey |

In Baklava, layer upon layer of phyllo pastry and chopped walnuts are made sweet and sticky with melted butter and honey

1 In large bowl, with fork, mix finely chopped walnuts, sugar and cinnamon; set aside.

2 Cut sheets of phyllo into 33 x 23 cm/ 13 x 9 inch rectangles. In greased 33 x 23 cm/ 13 x 9 inch baking dish, place 1 phyllo sheet; brush with some melted butter. Repeat with more phyllo and butter until there are 6 rectangular sheets of phyllo in dish.

3 Over phyllo pastry in baking dish, sprinkle one-quarter of chopped walnut mixture.

4 Repeat steps 2 and 3 to make 3 more layers (4 layers in total). Place remaining phyllo on top of last amount of walnuts; brush with butter.

5 Preheat oven to 150°C/300°F/gas 2. With sharp knife, cut just halfway through layers in triangle pattern to make 24 servings (cut lengthways into 3 strips; cut each strip crossways into 4 rectangles; then cut each rectangle diagonally into 2 triangles).

6 Bake for 1 hour and 25 minutes or until top is golden brown.

7 In small saucepan over medium-low heat, heat honey until hot but not boiling. Evenly spoon hot honey over hot Baklava.

ALTERNATIVE SHAPES

For a change from triangles, you can cut Baklava into diamond shapes, which are more traditional.

Diamond Baklava
In step 5, with sharp knife, cut just halfway through layers in diamond pattern (cut lengthways into 4 strips, then cut diagonally across strips in parallel lines); finish cutting through layers in step 9.

8 Cool Baklava in dish on wire rack for at least 1 hour; cover with foil and leave at room temperature until serving.

9 To serve, with sharp knife, finish cutting through layers to make 24 Baklava triangles.

Spooning honey over Baklava

APPLE STRUDEL

🍴 10 servings
⏰ Allow 2 hours preparation and cooking time

3 large cooking apples

100 g/3 ¹/₂ oz caster sugar

75 g/2 ¹/₂ oz seedless raisins

60 g/2 oz walnut pieces, chopped

¹/₂ teaspoon ground cinnamon

¹/₄ teaspoon grated nutmeg

About 75 g/2 ¹/₂ oz white breadcrumbs

225 g/8 oz fresh or frozen (thawed) phyllo pastry

120 g/4 oz butter, melted

Icing sugar for sprinkling

Icing sugar is sifted over top of strudel to help hide cracks in phyllo pastry

1 Grease large baking sheet. Peel, core and thinly slice apples. In bowl, toss apples with caster sugar, raisins, walnuts, cinnamon, nutmeg and 25 g/³/₄ oz breadcrumbs.

2 Cut two 60 cm/24 inch lengths of greaseproof paper. Place 2 long sides together, overlapping them by about 5 cm/2 inches; join with adhesive tape.

3 On sheet of grease-proof paper, arrange 1 sheet of phyllo. (It should be a 43 x 30 cm/ 17 x 10 inch rectangle; if necessary, trim or overlap small pieces of phyllo to make it this size.) Brush with some melted butter.

4 Sprinkle phyllo with scant tablespoon breadcrumbs. Continue layering phyllo, brushing each sheet with melted butter and sprinkling every other sheet with crumbs.

5 Preheat oven to 190°C/375°F/gas 5. Spoon apple mixture along 1 long side of phyllo rectangle to within 1 cm/ ¹/₂ inch of edges to cover about half of rectangle.

Spooning apple mixture on to phyllo

6 From apple mixture side, roll phyllo, Swiss roll fashion, using grease-proof to help lift roll.

7 Place roll on baking sheet, seam side down. Brush with remaining melted butter. Bake for 40 minutes or until golden. Cool on baking sheet for 30 minutes.

SWAN CHOUX PUFFS

🥄 Makes 8
⏱ Allow 3 hours
    preparation and
    cooking time

*Choux Pastry Dough (see
    Box, below right)*

*300 ml/ ½ pint double
    cream*

*150 ml/ ¼ pint canned
    Devon custard*

*Pretty as a picture, Swan
Choux Puffs are filled with
the most luscious cream
and custard mixture*

1 Preheat oven to
190°C/375°F/gas 5.
Prepare Choux Pastry
Dough. Spoon some
dough into piping bag
fitted with large writing
tube (tip about 1 cm/
½ inch in diameter). On
to greased large baking
sheet, pipe eight 7.5 cm/
3 inch long 'question
marks' for swans' necks,
making small dollop at
beginning of each for
head.

*Piping 'question
mark' shapes for
swans' necks*

2 Drop remaining
dough by large
spoonfuls, pushing off with
rubber spatula, into
8 large mounds on baking
sheet, about 7.5 cm/
3 inches apart.

3 With moistened
finger, gently smooth
dough to round slightly.

4 Bake swans' necks
and choux puffs in
the oven for 20 minutes
or until necks are golden.
Transfer necks to wire
rack to cool.

5 Continue baking
choux puffs for
45-50 minutes until
golden; transfer to racks
and leave to cool.

6 When choux puffs are
cool, prepare filling:
in small bowl, whip double
cream until stiff peaks
form. With rubber spatula
or wire whisk, gently fold
into custard.

7 Cut off top third
from each choux puff;
set aside.

CHOUX PASTRY DOUGH

In medium saucepan
over medium heat, heat
120 g/4 oz butter and
250 ml/8 fl oz water until
butter melts and
mixture boils. Remove
saucepan from heat.
Add *150 g/5 oz plain
flour* all at once; with
wooden spoon, vigor-
ously stir until mixture
leaves side of pan and
forms a ball. Add *4 eggs*,
1 egg at a time, beating
well with wooden spoon
after each addition until
choux pastry dough is
smooth and satiny.

8 Spoon some filling
into each of the
choux puff bottoms
(swans' bodies). Cut each
reserved top piece in half;
set into filling for wings.
Place swans' necks into
filling. Refrigerate if not
serving immediately.

PARIS-BREST

 10 servings
Allow 3 hours preparation and cooking time

Choux Pastry Dough (see Box, page 192)

450 ml/ ³/4 pint double cream

2 tablespoons brandy

Chocolate Glaze (see Box, above right)

1 Preheat oven to 200°C/400°F/gas 6. Grease and flour large baking sheet.

2 Prepare Choux Pastry Dough according to recipe instructions. Using 17.5 cm/7 inch plate as guide, trace circle in flour on baking sheet. Drop dough by heaping tablespoons, pushing off with rubber spatula, into 10 mounds, inside circle, to form ring.

3 Bake ring for 40 minutes or until golden. Turn oven off; leave ring in oven for 15 minutes. Cool ring on wire rack.

4 With long serrated knife, slice ring horizontally in half.

CHOCOLATE GLAZE
In heavy non-stick saucepan, gently heat *90 g/ 3 oz plain chocolate, broken into pieces, 15 g/ ¹/2 oz butter, 1 ¹/2 teaspoons golden syrup* and *1 ¹/2 teaspoons milk,* stirring often, until melted and smooth.

5 In small bowl, whip double cream until stiff peaks form; fold in brandy. Spoon on to bottom of pastry ring.

6 Replace top of pastry ring.

7 Prepare Chocolate Glaze; with spoon, carefully drizzle glaze over top of choux pastry ring to give it a smooth, glossy coating.

8 Refrigerate Paris-Brest if not serving immediately.

Paris-Brest, a ring of choux pastry filled with brandy-flavoured whipped cream and coated with a rich chocolate glaze, was created by a Parisian baker in 1891. The wheel-shaped cake was designed in honour of the annual bike race between the cities of Paris and Brest.

APPLE DUMPLINGS WITH CHEDDAR PASTRY

Makes 6

Allow 2 hours preparation and cooking time

Pastry

365 g/12 ½ oz plain flour
1 teaspoon salt (optional)
175 g/6 oz butter
120 g/4 oz mature Cheddar cheese, grated
1 egg
6 whole cloves

Filling

75 g/2 ½ oz light soft brown sugar
30 g/1 oz seedless raisins
30 g/1 oz walnut pieces
60 g/2 oz butter, softened
1 teaspoon ground cinnamon
6 small Golden Delicious apples

Sauce

300 ml/ ½ pint apple juice
125 ml/4 fl oz maple syrup

1 Prepare pastry dough: in large bowl, with fork, stir flour and salt, if using. With pastry blender or with fingertips, cut or rub butter into flour mixture until mixture resembles coarse crumbs; stir in cheese. Sprinkle *8-9 tablespoons cold water*, a tablespoon at a time, into mixture, mixing lightly with fork after each addition until dough just holds together. With hands, shape dough into ball.

2 In small bowl, with fork, mix brown sugar, raisins, walnuts, butter and cinnamon.

TO SERVE
Serve apple dumplings hot on individual plates, with hot sauce spooned round.

---

3 Peel apples; remove cores but do not cut all the way through apples.

4 Preheat oven to 200°C/400°F/gas 6. Reserve 45 g/1 ½ oz pastry dough. On well-floured surface, with floured rolling pin, roll out remaining dough into 52.5 x 35 cm/21 x 14 inch rectangle. Cut dough into six 17.5 cm/7 inch squares.

5 In cup, with fork, beat egg and *1 teaspoon water*. Centre an apple on square of dough.

6 Spoon one-sixth of sugar mixture into cavity in apple. Brush edges of dough square with some egg mixture.

7 Bring points of dough square up over apple, pinching edges together to seal well.

8 Repeat with remaining dough squares, apples and sugar mixture. With fish slice, place dumplings in greased 33 x 23 cm/13 x 9 inch baking dish.

9 On floured surface, with floured rolling pin, roll out reserved dough 5 mm/¼ inch thick. Cut 12 leaves from dough; score with tip of knife to make 'veins'. Brush dumplings with some egg mixture; press 2 leaves on top of each dumpling and brush them with egg mixture. Press cloves, rounded side down, into dumplings to look like stalks. Bake dumplings for 35 minutes.

10 In bowl, with spoon, stir apple juice and maple syrup; pour mixture over dumplings. Bake dumplings for 15 minutes longer (cover with foil after 5 minutes if dumplings are browning too much), basting occasionally with sauce in baking dish, until pastry is golden brown and apples are tender when pierced with skewer.

PROFITEROLES GLACÉES

 Makes 18

Can be made up to 1 month ahead and kept in freezer

Sauce

225 g/8 oz frozen raspberries

60 g/2 oz caster sugar

1 scoop vanilla ice cream

Choux Pastry

60 g/2 oz butter

75 g/2 ¹/₂ oz plain flour

2 eggs

Filling and Topping

60 g/2 oz plain chocolate, broken into pieces

2 tablespoons milk

15 g/ ¹/₂ oz butter

600 ml/1 pint vanilla ice cream

30 g/1 oz shelled pistachio nuts, chopped

1 Sprinkle raspberries with sugar; set aside to thaw. Preheat oven to 200°C/400°F/gas 6. Grease and flour large baking sheet.

2 Prepare choux pastry dough: in medium saucepan over medium heat, heat butter and 125 ml/4 fl oz water until butter melts and mixture boils. Remove from heat. Add flour all at once; with wooden spoon, vigorously stir until mixture leaves side of pan and forms a ball. Add eggs, 1 at a time, beating well after each addition until dough is smooth and satiny.

TO SERVE
Spoon raspberry sauce on to 6 dessert plates; arrange 3 profiteroles on each plate.

3 Drop 18 teaspoonfuls of dough on baking sheet, 5 cm/2 inches apart.

4 Bake for 30 minutes or until golden. Turn oven off; leave puffs in oven for 10 minutes. Cool on wire rack.

5 While puffs are cooling, make sauce: over large bowl, with back of spoon, press and scrape thawed raspberries with their juice firmly against medium-mesh sieve to purée; discard pips left in sieve. Add ice cream to raspberry purée; stir to mix. Cover sauce and refrigerate.

ALTERNATIVE SERVING IDEA

As an alternative to raspberry sauce, you can serve Profiteroles Glacées with other fruit sauces such as strawberry, apricot or mango. This peach sauce goes especially well, both in colour and flavour.

Peach Sauce
In blender at low speed, blend *450 g/1 lb ripe peaches, peeled and stoned, ¹/₄ teaspoon almond essence* and *¹/₈ teaspoon grated nutmeg* until all ingredients are smooth.

6 When puffs are cool, make topping: in non-stick saucepan over low heat, heat pieces of chocolate, milk and butter, stirring frequently, until melted and smooth.

7 Cut each puff in half horizontally; fill bottom halves with ice cream; replace tops. Drizzle profiteroles with chocolate mixture and sprinkle with nuts. Freeze.

Profiteroles nestled together on a pool of raspberry sauce are drizzled with chocolate sauce and sprinkled with nuts

HOT FRUIT PUDDINGS

Here you'll find homely and satisfying puddings: sweet fruit blanketed with a crunchy topping in a crumble, or covered with a tender scone crust in a cobbler, or layered with buttered breadcrumbs, sugar and spices in a 'brown Betty'. Reheating at the same temperature at which they were baked will give puddings made ahead, or leftovers, a freshly baked goodness.

BANANA BROWN BETTY

4 servings
Allow 40 minutes preparation and cooking time

2 large oranges

6 medium-sized bananas

45 g/1 1/2 oz caster sugar

90 g/3 oz butter

25 g/ 3/4 oz fresh breadcrumbs

20 g/ 2/3 oz rolled oats

45 g/1 1/2 oz soft brown sugar

1/2 teaspoon ground cinnamon

Whipped cream (optional)

1 From oranges, grate 1 teaspoon zest and squeeze 175 ml/6 fl oz juice. Cut bananas into chunks.

2 In large frying pan over medium-high heat, cook caster sugar, 3 tablespoons orange juice and 30 g/1 oz butter, stirring frequently, until light caramel colour, about 3-4 minutes. To orange juice mixture, add banana chunks; toss until banana is evenly coated.

3 Remove frying pan from heat; set aside. Preheat oven to 200°C/400°F/gas 6.

4 Divide half of the caramelized banana mixture equally among four 250 ml/8 fl oz ramekins or baking dishes.

5 Sprinkle each with 1 tablespoon breadcrumbs. Top with remaining banana mixture. Spoon 2 tablespoons orange juice over banana mixture in each ramekin.

Chunks of juicy, caramelized bananas peep through crunchy topping

6 Into remaining breadcrumbs, with fingertips, mix oats, brown sugar, cinnamon, orange zest and remaining butter until mixture resembles coarse crumbs; sprinkle over bananas.

7 Place ramekins in baking tray for easier handling. Bake for 15 minutes or until topping is crisp and golden. Serve warm, with whipped cream if you like.

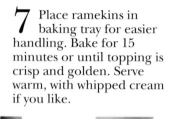

Spooning cinnamon-flavoured oat and breadcrumb topping over bananas

APPLE COBBLER

RHUBARB CRUMBLE

🍴 6 servings

⏰ Allow 50 minutes preparation and cooking time

700 g/1 ¹/₂ lb rhubarb

1 teaspoon lemon juice

100 g/3 ¹/₂ oz caster sugar

Custard or pouring cream for serving

Crumble Topping

185 g/6 ¹/₂ oz plain flour

45 g/1 ¹/₂ oz caster sugar

120 g/4 oz butter

1 Wash rhubarb; trim and discard leaves and discoloured ends. Cut rhubarb into 2.5 cm/1 inch pieces. In saucepan over medium heat, bring rhubarb, lemon juice, sugar and *4 tablespoons water* to the boil. Reduce heat to low; cover and simmer for about 10 minutes or until rhubarb is tender.

2 Preheat oven to 220°C/425°F/gas 7. While rhubarb is cooking, make crumble mixture: in medium bowl, with fork, stir flour and sugar. With pastry blender or with fingertips, cut or rub butter into flour mixture until mixture resembles coarse crumbs.

3 Pour rhubarb mixture into 20 cm/8 inch square baking dish. Sprinkle crumble mixture over rhubarb.

4 Bake for 25 minutes or until crumble topping is golden.

> *TO SERVE*
> *Serve Rhubarb Crumble hot with custard or pouring cream.*

🍴 6 servings

⏰ Allow 1 hour preparation and cooking time

225 g/8 oz light soft brown sugar

45 g/1 ¹/₂ oz plain flour

30 g/1 oz butter

1 teaspoon lemon juice

¹/₄ teaspoon ground cinnamon

Pinch of grated nutmeg

5 large cooking apples

Pouring cream or vanilla ice cream (optional)

Dough

150 g/5 oz plain flour

2 teaspoons baking powder

45 g/1 ¹/₂ oz butter

175 ml/6 fl oz milk

1 In small saucepan, mix brown sugar and flour; stir in *250 ml/8 fl oz water*. Bring to the boil over medium heat, stirring constantly; cook until thick.

2 Remove pan from heat. Stir butter, lemon juice, cinnamon and nutmeg into sauce.

3 Peel, core and thinly slice apples. Arrange in 30 x 20 cm/12 x 8 inch baking dish; pour sauce mixture over apples.

4 Preheat oven to 190°C/375°F/gas 5. Make dough: in medium bowl, combine flour and baking powder. With pastry blender or with fingertips, cut or rub butter into flour mixture until size of peas. Add milk; stir until moistened but still lumpy.

5 Evenly drop large spoonfuls of cobbler dough on top of apples, not covering completely. Bake for 40 minutes or until topping is golden.

> *TO SERVE*
> *Serve Apple Cobbler warm, with cream or ice cream, if you like.*

INDIVIDUAL PEACH COBBLERS

 Makes 4

Allow 1 hour preparation and cooking time

4 large peaches

25 g/ ³/₄ oz plain flour

60 g/2 oz caster sugar

Scone Dough

120 g/4 oz plain flour

1 teaspoon baking powder

2 teaspoons caster sugar

45 g/1 ¹/₂ oz butter

5-6 tablespoons whipping cream plus extra for glazing

1 Peel peaches (see Box, page 53); slice thinly. In large bowl, toss peaches, flour and sugar. Spoon into four 250 ml/ 8 fl oz ramekins. Set aside.

2 Prepare scone dough: in large bowl, with fork, mix flour, baking powder and sugar. With pastry blender or with fingertips, cut or rub in butter until mixture resembles coarse crumbs. Stir in 5-6 tablespoons whipping cream; quickly mix just until a stiff dough is formed that leaves side of bowl.

3 Preheat oven to 200°C/400°F/gas 6. Turn dough on to lightly floured surface. With floured rolling pin, roll out dough to about 2 cm/ ³/₈ inch thickness.

4 Using floured pastry cutter with diameter about 5 mm/¹/₄ inch smaller than diameter of top of ramekin, cut out 4 rounds.

Cutting out rounds of scone dough for cobbler topping

5 Place dough rounds over peaches; brush dough rounds lightly with whipping cream.

6 If you like, press trimmings together; roll and cut into desired shapes to decorate top of cobblers.

7 Place cobblers in baking tray for easier handling. Bake for 15-20 minutes until peach mixture begins to bubble and scone topping is golden.

Tiny aspic cutters are used to cut dough trimmings into pretty shapes to top cobbler dough

BISCUITS AND COOKIES

199-216

BISCUITS AND COOKIES

Biscuits and cookies – perfect for after school, as a snack, with dessert, for anytime! Around the holidays, festive Gingerbread Christmas Biscuits and Sweet and Spicy Peppernuts are crowd-pleasers for children and adults alike. Elegant Chocolate and Nut Shortbread and Almond Butter Shortbread are ideal to accompany afternoon tea or after-dinner coffee, and delicate Brandy Snaps and dainty Waffle Hearts taste as good as they look – why not make a second batch to wrap as take-home gifts for guests? For all-round favourites, nothing can beat Apricot Croissants and Nutty Oat Crunchies – home-baked goodness your family and friends will love.

CONTENTS

BISCUITS AND COOKIES

In this biscuit collection, you'll find dainty, elegant morsels for the tea table, sturdy favourites for the school lunchbox, and jolly sugary snowmen to delight the children at Christmas. There are different shapes, sizes and decorations to catch the eye and match any occasion. Every palate is sure to be pleased with the choice of buttery, nutty, chocolatey or sugar-and-spicy flavours and the variety of textures, from tender and chewy to crisp and crunchy.

BRANDY SNAPS

  Makes about 36
Allow 2 hours preparation and cooking time

120 g/4 oz butter

3 tablespoons golden syrup

75 g/2 ½ oz plain flour

100 g/3 ½ oz caster sugar

1 teaspoon ground ginger

2 tablespoons brandy

Lacy-textured Brandy Snaps are good served with after-dinner coffee and liqueurs

1 Preheat oven to 180°C/350°F/gas 4. Line large baking sheet with non-stick baking parchment. In small saucepan over medium heat, heat butter and golden syrup, stirring occasionally, until butter melts. Remove saucepan from heat; with spoon, stir in flour, sugar, ginger and brandy until smooth. Return saucepan to very low heat to keep mixture warm.

2 Drop 1 teaspoon mixture on to baking sheet; spread in circular motion to make 10 cm/4 inch round (mixture spreads during baking to fill in any thin areas). Repeat to make 3 more rounds, about 5 cm/2 inches apart.

3 Bake biscuits for about 5 minutes or until golden brown. Remove baking sheet from oven; allow biscuits to cool briefly, only until edges set. With fish slice, flip biscuits over quickly so lacy texture will be on outside after rolling.

4 Working as quickly as possible, roll each biscuit into cylinder around handle of wooden spoon (1 cm/½ inch in diameter). If biscuits become too hard to roll, return to oven briefly to soften. As each biscuit is shaped, remove from spoon handle; cool on wire racks.

5 Repeat until all mixture is used.

TWO-TONE HEARTS

Makes 30

Allow 4 hours preparation and cooking time

60 g/2 oz plain chocolate, broken into pieces

325 g/11 oz plain flour

175 g/6 oz butter, softened

1 tablespoon milk

1 ½ teaspoons baking powder

1 egg

150 g/5 oz caster sugar plus extra for sprinkling

1 Place pieces of chocolate in bowl over pan of gently simmering water and heat, stirring frequently, until melted and smooth. Remove bowl from pan.

2 In large bowl, combine flour, butter, milk, baking powder, egg and 150 g/5 oz sugar. With electric mixer, beat ingredients until well blended, occasionally scraping bowl with rubber spatula. With hands, shape half of the dough into ball; wrap and refrigerate for 2 hours or until dough is firm enough to handle. (Or place dough in freezer for 40 minutes.)

Eye-catching Two-Tone Hearts are rich and buttery, the perfect present for your sweetheart on Valentine's Day

3 With electric mixer, beat melted chocolate into dough remaining in bowl until blended. With hands, shape chocolate dough into ball; wrap and refrigerate for 2 hours.

4 Grease and flour 2 large baking sheets. On lightly floured surface, with floured rolling pin, roll out half of the plain dough 3 mm/⅛ inch thick; keep remaining dough refrigerated. With floured 8 cm/3 ¼ inch heart-shaped cutter, cut dough into hearts. Place hearts, about 5 mm/¼ inch apart, on 1 baking sheet. Repeat with remaining plain dough and trimmings. Repeat with chocolate dough, placing hearts on second baking sheet. Refrigerate until hearts are firm, about 20 minutes.

5 Preheat oven to 180°C/350°F/gas 4. With 2.5 cm/1 inch heart-shaped pastry cutter, cut small heart in centre of each plain and chocolate heart biscuit; set small hearts aside. With 5 cm/2 inch heart-shaped pastry cutter, cut another heart in centre of each biscuit. Remove medium-sized heart from each plain biscuit and replace it with one from chocolate biscuit. Fit 2.5 cm/1 inch plain hearts into centres of medium-sized chocolate hearts; repeat with 2.5 cm/1 inch chocolate hearts and medium-sized plain hearts.

6 Sprinkle biscuits lightly with sugar. Bake biscuits for 10 minutes or until golden. With fish slice, transfer biscuits to wire racks to cool. Store in airtight container.

CHRISTMAS SUGAR COOKIES

Makes about 48
Can be made several days before and kept in airtight container

525 g/1 lb 2 ½ oz plain flour
225 g/8 oz butter, softened
150 g/5 oz caster sugar
125 ml/4 fl oz golden syrup
1 tablespoon lemon juice
2 eggs
Ornamental Icing (see Box, right)

1 In large bowl, combine flour, butter, sugar, golden syrup, lemon juice and eggs. With electric mixer, beat ingredients until well blended, occasionally scraping bowl with rubber spatula. Wrap dough; refrigerate for 2 hours or until dough is firm enough to handle. (Or place dough in freezer for 40 minutes.)

2 Preheat oven to 180°C/350°F/gas 4. On well floured surface, with floured rolling pin, roll out one-quarter of dough 3 mm/⅛ inch thick, keeping remaining dough refrigerated. With floured pastry cutters, cut dough into different shapes (or use 7.5 cm/3 inch round cutter). With fish slice, place cookies, about 1 cm/½ inch apart, on ungreased baking sheet.

3 Bake cookies for 5-7 minutes until golden. With fish slice, transfer cookies to wire racks to cool. Repeat with remaining dough and trimmings.

ORNAMENTAL ICING

In large bowl, with electric mixer, beat 450 g/1 lb icing sugar, sifted, 5 tablespoons warm water and 3 tablespoons albumen powder. Beat until mixture is so stiff that when knife is drawn through mixture it will leave a clean path.

Divide icing among small bowls; tint each bowl of icing with *food colouring* as liked. Keep all bowls covered with damp tea towels or cling film, to prevent icing drying out during standing.

4 Prepare Ornamental Icing.

5 Place cookies on baking sheets lined with non-stick baking parchment. With small palette knife or small and medium artist's paint brushes and piping bags fitted with writing tubes, decorate cookies with Ornamental Icing as desired. (If icing is too stiff for brushing on cookies, dilute it with a little water.) Set cookies aside to allow icing to dry completely, about 2 hours. Store cookies in airtight container.

Jingle Bells
With skewer, make small hole in dough at top of each bell before baking. After cookies have cooled, coat with yellow icing; leave to dry. With piping bag and small writing tube, pipe decorative designs in different colours on top of yellow; leave to dry. Thread string or ribbon through holes.

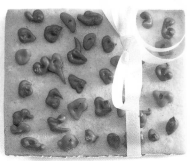

Holly Wreaths
Coat each wreath shape with green icing; leave to dry. With piping bag and small writing tube, pipe white icing in zig-zag design over green. Pipe red dots in between white icing to resemble holly berries.

Christmas Presents
With piping bag and small writing tube, pipe decorative designs in different coloured icings on plain rectangular-shaped cookies. If you like, tie presents with ribbon.

Jolly Snowmen
Coat each cookie with white icing; leave to dry. With piping bag and small writing tube and different coloured icings, pipe hats, faces, scarves, buttons and other trimmings on snowmen.

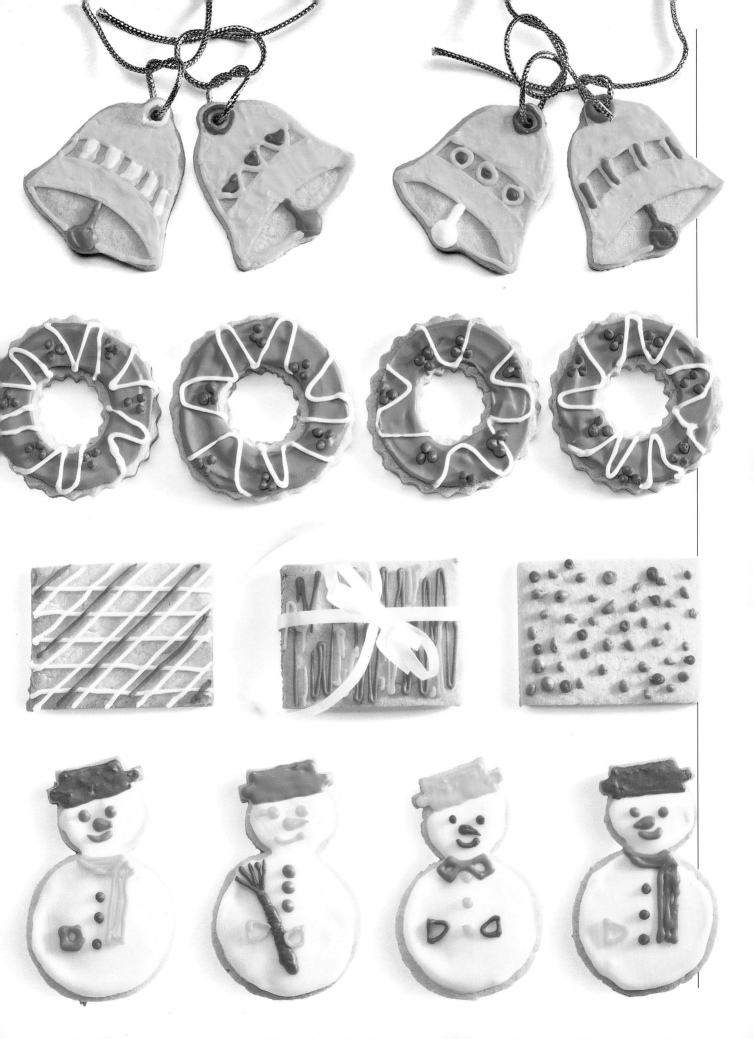

CHOCOLATE AMARETTI

Makes about 30
Allow 1 ½ hours preparation and cooking time

140 g/4 ½ oz blanched whole almonds

100 g/3 ½ oz caster sugar

2 egg whites

⅛ teaspoon cream of tartar

½ teaspoon vanilla essence

½ teaspoon almond essence

15 g/ ½ oz cocoa powder

30 g/1 oz icing sugar plus extra for sifting

1 In large frying pan over medium heat, cook almonds until lightly browned, shaking pan frequently. Remove from heat; cool almonds.

2 In food processor, blend almonds with half of the caster sugar, pulsing on and off, until almonds are finely ground.

3 Preheat oven to 170°C/325°F/gas 3. Line large baking sheet with non-stick baking parchment or foil.

4 In small bowl, with electric mixer on full speed, beat egg whites with cream of tartar until soft peaks form; gradually sprinkle in remaining caster sugar, beating until sugar completely dissolves and whites stand in stiff, glossy peaks. Beat in both vanilla and almond essences. With rubber spatula or wire whisk, gently fold in ground almond mixture, cocoa powder and 30 g/1 oz sifted icing sugar.

5 Spoon almond mixture into piping bag fitted with medium writing tube (tip about 1 cm/ ½ inch in diameter). On to baking sheet, pipe mixture in 4 cm/1 ½ inch mounds, about 2.5 cm/ 1 inch apart.

6 Bake for 15 minutes or until amaretti are crisp. Cool for 10 minutes on baking sheet on wire rack; with fish slice, transfer amaretti to wire rack to cool completely. Sift icing sugar over amaretti until coated. Store in airtight container.

CAPPUCCINO SQUARES

Makes 24
Allow 2 hours preparation and cooking time

225 g/8 oz butter

225 g/8 oz plain chocolate, broken into pieces

700 g/1 ½ lb caster sugar

6 eggs

225 g/8 oz walnut pieces

250 g/9 oz plain flour

30 g/1 oz instant coffee powder

½ teaspoon ground cinnamon

Icing sugar to decorate

1 Preheat oven to 180°C/350°F/gas 4. Grease and flour 33 x 23 cm/13 x 9 inch baking tin.

2 In heavy non-stick saucepan over low heat, heat butter and chocolate, stirring often, until melted and smooth; remove saucepan from heat. With wire whisk or spoon, beat in caster sugar and eggs until well blended. Stir in walnuts, flour, coffee powder and cinnamon.

3 Evenly spread mixture in baking tin. Bake for 45-50 minutes until skewer inserted in centre comes out clean. Cool completely in tin on wire rack.

4 When cold, cut crossways into 6 strips, then cut each strip into 4 pieces. With fish slice, remove squares from tin; carefully sift icing sugar over half of each square. Store in single layer in airtight container.

APRICOT CROISSANTS

Makes 36

Allow 2 ½ hours preparation and cooking time

300 g/10 oz plain flour

275 g/9 oz butter

175 ml/6 fl oz soured cream

120 g/4 oz apricot jam

60 g/2 oz plain chocolate chips or polka dots

30 g/1 oz flaked almonds

30 g/1 oz caster sugar

1 Into large bowl, sift flour. With pastry blender or with fingertips, cut or rub 225 g/8 oz butter into flour until mixture resembles fine breadcrumbs. Add soured cream and mix lightly with fork until dough just holds together. Divide dough into 3 pieces. Wrap and refrigerate for 1 hour or until firm enough to handle.

2 On lightly floured surface, with floured rolling pin, roll out 1 piece of dough into 27.5 cm/11 inch round, keeping remaining pieces of dough refrigerated.

3 Spread dough round with one-third of apricot jam; sprinkle with one-third of chocolate chips. Cut dough round into 12 equal wedges; starting at curved edge, roll up each wedge croissant fashion. Place croissants, point side up, about 4 cm/1 ½ inches apart, on large ungreased baking sheet. Repeat with remaining dough, jam and chocolate chips.

4 Preheat oven to 190°C/375°F/gas 5. In small saucepan over low heat, melt remaining butter; remove saucepan from heat. In small bowl, mix almonds and sugar.

5 Brush croissants with melted butter, then sprinkle with almond mixture. Bake croissants for 25 minutes or until golden brown. With fish slice, immediately transfer croissants to wire racks to cool.

These miniature 'croissants' are perfectly divine – melt-in-the-mouth buttery pastry around a gooey chocolate and apricot filling; they are best served warm

CHOCOLATE AND NUT SHORTBREAD

Makes about 18

Allow 2 hours preparation and cooking time

180 g/6 ¼ oz plain flour

90 g/3 oz icing sugar, sifted

30 g/1 oz cornflour

45 g/1 ½ oz shelled pecans or walnut pieces, finely chopped

175 g/6 oz butter

175 g/6 oz plain chocolate, broken into pieces

1 Preheat oven to 170°C/325°F/gas 3. In large bowl, with fork, stir flour, icing sugar, cornflour and chopped nuts. With knife, cut butter into small pieces; add to flour mixture. With hand, rub in ingredients until well blended, then knead together.

2 Pat dough evenly into 28 x 18 cm/11 x 7 inch Swiss roll tin. Bake shortbread for 35-40 minutes or until golden. With sharp knife, immediately cut shortbread lengthways into 3 strips, then cut each strip crossways into 12 pieces. Cool shortbread in dish on wire rack. When cold, with fish slice, remove shortbread from baking dish.

3 Place pieces of chocolate in bowl over pan of gently simmering water and heat, stirring often, until melted and smooth; remove bowl from pan. Dip 1 corner of each piece of shortbread diagonally into chocolate until half is coated with chocolate. Place shortbread on baking sheet lined with greaseproof paper or foil. Refrigerate until chocolate is set, about 15 minutes.

FUNNEL CAKES

Makes 7

Allow 30 minutes preparation and cooking time

Oil for deep frying

165 g/5 ¹/₂ oz plain flour

175 ml/6 fl oz milk

1 teaspoon baking powder

1 teaspoon almond essence

1 egg

Icing sugar for sifting

1 In deep-fat fryer or deep frying pan over medium heat, heat oil to 170°C/325°F on a deep-frying thermometer.

2 Meanwhile, in bowl, with wire whisk or fork, mix flour, milk, baking powder, almond essence and egg until well blended.

Funnel Cakes are a speciality from Pennsylvania Dutch country in the USA

3 Holding funnel with 1 cm/¹/₂ inch narrow spout, close spout with finger; pour about 4 tablespoons batter into funnel. Over hot oil, remove finger to let batter run out in a stream, to make a spiral about 15 cm/ 6 inches in diameter.

4 Fry for 3-5 minutes until golden brown, turning once with tongs. Drain well on kitchen paper; keep warm. Repeat with remaining batter, stirring well each time before pouring.

5 Sift icing sugar lightly over Funnel Cakes. Serve warm.

Crisp and dainty, these deep-fried bow ties are sprinkled with icing sugar for extra sweetness

FRIED BOW TIES

Makes about 40

Allow 4 hours preparation and cooking time

2 size-6 eggs

2 tablespoons caster sugar

2 tablespoons milk

185 g/6 ¹/₂ oz plain flour

Oil for deep frying

Icing sugar for sifting (optional)

1 In medium bowl, combine eggs, caster sugar, milk and 135 g/ 4 ¹/₂ oz flour. With wooden spoon, stir until ingredients are well blended; stir in enough of remaining flour until mixture holds together. With hands, shape dough into ball; wrap dough and refrigerate for 2 hours or until easy to handle. (Or place dough in freezer for 40 minutes.)

2 On floured surface, with floured rolling pin, roll out half of the dough until paper thin, keeping remaining dough refrigerated. Cut dough into 10 x 4 cm/ 4 x 1¹/₂ inch rectangles. Twist each strip to form bow tie shape, pinching centre firmly to flatten and seal. Repeat with remaining dough.

3 In deep-fat fryer or deep frying pan over medium heat, heat oil to 180°C/350°F on a deep-frying thermometer.

4 Gently place several bow ties in hot oil; fry for about 1¹/₂ minutes or until golden. Drain bow ties on kitchen paper; cool. Fry remaining bow ties in batches; drain and cool. Store in airtight container.

5 If you like, sift icing sugar over bow ties just before serving.

CRISPY SNOWFLAKES

Makes 32

Allow 4 hours preparation and cooking time

3 eggs

400 g/14 oz plain flour

50 g/1 ²/₃ oz caster sugar

4 tablespoons milk

Oil for deep frying

Icing sugar for sifting (optional)

1 In medium bowl, combine eggs, flour, caster sugar and milk. With wooden spoon, stir ingredients until well blended and mixture holds together. With hands, shape dough into ball; wrap and refrigerate for 2 hours or until dough is easy to handle. (Or place dough in freezer for 40 minutes.)

2 Divide dough into 32 pieces. On lightly floured surface, with floured rolling pin, roll out 16 dough pieces into 13.5 cm/5 ¹/₂ inch rounds; cover and refrigerate remaining dough pieces. Allow dough rounds to stand, uncovered, until tops are fairly dry.

3 Fold each dough round in half, folding dry top side together; fold again into quarters, then into eighths. With sharp knife, scissors or petit four cutter, cut designs along edges of dough. Unfold snowflakes and set aside at room temperature. Meanwhile, repeat with remaining dough.

4 In deep-fat fryer or deep frying pan over medium heat, heat oil to 180°C/350°F on deep-frying thermometer.

5 Gently place 2 or 3 snowflakes in hot oil; fry for about 1 ¹/₂ minutes or until golden. Drain snowflakes on kitchen paper; cool. Fry remaining snowflakes in batches; drain and cool. Store in airtight container.

6 If you like, sift icing sugar over snowflakes just before serving.

Snowflake shapes are made by folding dough and cutting out design exactly as you would when making paper snowflakes. One helpful tip: it is essential to let the dough get really dry before folding and cutting or you will not get good shapes

WAFFLE HEARTS

Makes about 48 heart- or wedge-shaped waffles

Allow 2 hours preparation and cooking time

250 g/8 ¹/₂ oz plain flour
150 g/5 oz caster sugar
120 g/4 oz butter, melted
2 teaspoons baking powder
3 eggs

WAFFLE IRON
Waffle irons are available in electric and non-electric models in various shapes and sizes. Be sure to follow manufacturer's instructions for exact amount of batter to use, and cooking times.

1 Preheat 17.5 cm/ 7 inch waffle iron according to manufacturer's instructions (see Box, above right).

2 In large bowl, mix all ingredients. With electric mixer, beat ingredients until blended, occasionally scraping bowl with rubber spatula.

3 Pour about 2 tablespoons batter at a time on to waffle iron. Cover; cook according to manufacturer's instructions (do not lift cover during cooking).

4 When done, lift cover and loosen waffle with fork; transfer to wire rack to cool.

5 When waffles are cold, break each into 4 pieces to serve. (The 17.5 cm/7 inch iron makes round waffles, each with 4 heart- or wedge-shaped sections.)

These waffles are made in a heart-shaped waffle iron; if you do not have a waffle iron, use a frying pan, and turn the waffles halfway through cooking

NUTTY OAT CRUNCHIES

Makes about 30

Allow 2 hours preparation and cooking time

175 g/6 oz butter, softened
165 g/5 ¹/₂ oz light soft brown sugar
1 tablespoon grated lemon zest
1 teaspoon baking powder
1 egg
260 g/9 oz quick-cooking porridge oats
45 g/1 ¹/₂ oz ground almonds
2 egg yolks, lightly beaten, or a little milk

1 In bowl, combine first 5 ingredients. With electric mixer, beat ingredients for 10 minutes or until light and fluffy, occasionally scraping bowl with rubber spatula. Add oats and almonds; with hand, knead until well blended and mixture holds together.

2 Preheat oven to 180°C/350°F/gas 4. Grease well 2 large baking sheets. Between 2 sheets of non-stick baking parchment, roll out half of the dough until 5 mm/¹/₄ inch thick. With 6 cm/2 ¹/₂ inch round cutter, cut dough into as many rounds as possible; place rounds, 2.5 cm/1 inch apart, on baking sheets. Brush tops with egg yolk or milk.

3 Bake for 12 minutes or until golden. Quickly, with fish slice, transfer oat crunchies to wire racks to cool. Repeat with remaining dough and trimmings. Store in airtight container.

ALMOND BUTTER SHORTBREAD

🍴 Makes 30

⏱ Allow 1 ½ hours preparation and cooking time

300 g/10 oz plain flour

300 g/10 oz butter, softened

150 g/5 oz cornflour

150 g/5 oz caster sugar

½ teaspoon almond essence

60 g/2 oz flaked almonds

Icing sugar or caster sugar

1 Preheat oven to 170°C/325°F/gas 3. In food processor, combine flour, butter, cornflour, sugar and almond essence until mixture is well blended and will hold together.

2 Form dough roughly into a ball. Place in ungreased 33 x 23 cm/ 13 x 9 inch Swiss roll tin. With fingers, pat and press dough into tin (if dough is sticky, cover with cling film and press through it). Prick dough all over with fork; sprinkle with almonds and sifted icing sugar or caster sugar.

3 Bake shortbread for 40-45 minutes or until very pale golden. Leave in tin until lukewarm, then cut into 30 pieces. Leave in tin until almost cold, then lift out and place on wire rack; leave to cool completely. Store in airtight container.

Shortbread must be made with butter to taste really good; it keeps extremely well, so it is worth baking a big batch

Toasted sesame seeds give these crunchy cookies a distinctive 'oriental' flavour

TOASTED SESAME COOKIES

🍴 Makes about 36 small cookies

⏱ Allow 2 hours preparation and cooking time

130 g/4 ¼ oz sesame seeds

300 g/10 oz plain flour

150 g/5 oz caster sugar

120 g/4 oz butter, softened

1 teaspoon baking powder

½ teaspoon vanilla essence

1 egg

1 In large frying pan over medium heat, cook sesame seeds until golden, shaking pan and stirring often. Remove pan from heat; set aside.

2 In large bowl, combine flour, sugar, butter, baking powder, vanilla essence, egg and *2 tablespoons water.* With electric mixer, beat ingredients until well blended, occasionally scraping bowl with rubber spatula. With wooden spoon, stir in half of the toasted sesame seeds.

3 Preheat oven to 180°C/350°F/gas 4. Shape 2 teaspoons dough at a time into 5 cm/2 inch long oval; roll ovals in remaining sesame seeds. Place ovals, about 2.5 cm/ 1 inch apart, on ungreased baking sheets.

4 Bake cookies for 20 minutes or until lightly browned. With fish slice, transfer cookies to wire rack to cool. Store in airtight container.

SWEET AND SPICY PEPPERNUTS

These Canadian biscuits are richly flavoured with maple syrup; serve them with morning coffee

Makes about
8 large cupfuls

Allow 2 ½ hours
preparation and
cooking time

250 g/8 ½ oz plain flour

200 g/7 oz light soft brown
sugar

60 g/2 oz butter, softened

¼ teaspoon bicarbonate of
soda

¼ teaspoon ground
cinnamon

¼ teaspoon ground cloves

¼ teaspoon ground ginger

Good pinch of white pepper

1 egg, beaten

1 Preheat oven to
190°C/375°F/gas 5.
In large bowl, combine all
ingredients. With electric
mixer, beat ingredients
until well blended, occa-
sionally scraping bowl with
rubber spatula. (Mixture
may be crumbly; if neces-
sary, add a little more egg
and, with hand, knead
lightly until mixture holds
together.) Shape dough
into ball.

2 For each peppernut,
pinch off walnut-sized
pieces of dough; with
hands, shape into ball.
Place dough balls, about
1 cm/½ inch apart, on
baking sheets lined with
non-stick baking parch-
ment.

3 Bake peppernuts for
about 7 minutes or
until lightly browned.
Leave to cool on baking
sheets. Store in airtight
container.

*These German
sweetmeats are perfect as
petits fours with after-
dinner coffee and
liqueurs*

MAPLE LEAVES

Makes about 24

Allow 3 ½ hours
preparation and
cooking time

300 g/10 oz plain flour

120 g/4 oz butter, softened

75 g/2 ½ oz light soft
brown sugar

4 tablespoons maple syrup

1 teaspoon cream of tartar

½ teaspoon bicarbonate of
soda

1 egg

1 In large bowl, mix
all ingredients.
With electric mixer, beat
ingredients until blended,
occasionally scraping bowl
with rubber spatula.

2 With hands, shape
dough into ball; wrap
and refrigerate for 1 hour
or until dough is easy to
handle. (Or place dough
in freezer for 30 minutes.)

3 Preheat oven to
180°C/350°F/gas 4.
Grease large baking sheet.
On lightly floured surface,
with floured rolling pin,
roll out half of the dough
3 mm/⅛ inch thick; keep
remaining dough in
refrigerator. With floured
8 cm/3½ inch leaf-shaped
pastry cutter, cut dough
into leaves; score leaf
'veins' in dough with tip of
knife. Place leaf shapes,
2.5 cm/1 inch apart, on
baking sheet.

4 Bake leaf shapes for
10 minutes or until
golden. With fish slice,
transfer to wire racks; cool.
Repeat with remaining
dough and trimmings.
Store in airtight container.

POPPYSEED CATHERINE WHEELS

Makes about 30
Allow about 4 hours preparation and cooking time

50 g/1 ²/₃ oz caster sugar

90 g/3 oz butter, softened

135 g/4 ¹/₂ oz plain flour

¹/₂ beaten egg

¹/₄ teaspoon vanilla essence

30 g/1 oz walnut pieces

40 g/1 ¹/₄ oz poppy seeds

45 g/1 ¹/₂ oz honey

¹/₂ teaspoon grated orange zest

Pinch of ground cinnamon

1 In large bowl, with electric mixer, beat sugar and 60 g/2 oz butter for 10 minutes or until light and fluffy, scraping bowl often with rubber spatula. Add flour, egg and vanilla essence; beat just until blended, occasionally scraping bowl. With hands, shape dough into ball; wrap and refrigerate for 1 hour or until dough is firm enough to handle. (Or place dough in freezer for 30 minutes.)

2 Meanwhile, in food processor, finely grind walnuts. In small bowl, stir walnuts, poppy seeds, honey, orange zest, cinnamon and remaining butter until mixed; set aside.

3 On sheet of non-stick baking parchment, with floured rolling pin, roll out dough into a 25 x 20 cm/10 x 8 inch rectangle; spread rectangle with poppy seed mixture. Starting at a 20 cm/8 inch side, roll dough Swiss roll fashion. Wrap roll and refrigerate for 1 hour or until dough is firm enough to slice. (Or place roll in freezer for 30 minutes.)

4 Preheat oven to 190°C/375°F/gas 5. With sharp knife, slice roll crossways into slices about 5 mm/¹/₄ inch thick. Place slices, about 1 cm/¹/₂ inch apart, on ungreased baking sheets.

5 Bake for 10-12 minutes until lightly browned. With fish slice, transfer to wire racks to cool. Store in airtight container.

Poppy seeds spiral their way through these crisp, nutty cookies

WINDMILLS

Makes about 36
Allow 3 ¹/₂ hours preparation and cooking time

300 g/10 oz plain flour

225 g/8 oz light soft brown sugar

120 g/4 oz butter, softened

¹/₂ teaspoon bicarbonate of soda

1 egg

45 g/1 ¹/₂ oz walnut pieces, chopped

1 In large bowl, mix all ingredients except nuts. With electric mixer, beat ingredients until well blended, occasionally scraping bowl with rubber spatula.

2 With hands, shape dough into ball; wrap and refrigerate for 1 hour or until dough is easy to handle. (Or place dough in freezer for 30 minutes.)

3 Preheat oven to 180°C/350°F/gas 4. Grease large baking sheet. On lightly floured surface, with floured rolling pin, roll out one-third of dough 3 mm/¹/₈ inch thick; keep remaining dough in refrigerator. With floured 8 cm/3 ¹/₂ inch round pastry cutter, cut dough into rounds. Place rounds, 2.5 cm/1 inch apart, on baking sheet. With knife, cut 4 lines from edge of each round almost to centre, forming quarters; fold left corner of each quarter to centre; press to form windmill. Sprinkle with nuts.

4 Bake windmills for 10-12 minutes until golden. Transfer windmills to wire racks to cool. Repeat with remaining dough and nuts. Store in airtight container.

GINGERBREAD CHRISTMAS BISCUITS

 Makes about 24

Can be made up to 1 week before and kept in airtight container

75 ml/2 ¹/₂ fl oz black treacle

60 g/2 oz dark soft brown sugar

60 g/2 oz butter, softened

³/₄ teaspoon bicarbonate of soda

¹/₄ teaspoon ground allspice

¹/₄ teaspoon ground cinnamon

¹/₄ teaspoon ground cloves

¹/₄ teaspoon ground ginger

1 egg

About 325 g/11 oz plain flour

Ornamental Icing (see Box, above right)

ORNAMENTAL ICING

In large bowl, with electric mixer, beat *450 g/1 lb icing sugar, sifted, 5 tablespoons warm water* and *3 tablespoons albumen powder*. Beat until mixture is so stiff that when knife is drawn through mixture it will leave a clean path.

If not using icing immediately, keep bowl covered with damp tea towel or cling film.

Christmas Tree

Twinkling Star

1 In large bowl, combine black treacle, brown sugar, butter, bicarbonate of soda, allspice, cinnamon, cloves, ginger, egg and 100 g/ 3 ¹/₂ oz flour. With electric mixer, beat ingredients for 2 minutes, frequently scraping bowl with rubber spatula. With wooden spoon, stir in enough of remaining flour to make stiff dough. Shape dough into ball; wrap. Use dough immediately or refrigerate to use within 2 days.

2 Preheat oven to 180°C/350°F/gas 4. On lightly floured surface, with floured rolling pin, roll out half of the dough 3 mm/¹/₈ inch thick.

3 With desired shape pastry cutter (about 8.5 cm/3¹/₂ inches), cut out as many biscuits as possible. With fish slice, place biscuits, about 1 cm/¹/₂ inch apart, on ungreased large baking sheet.

4 Bake biscuits for 12 minutes or until edges are firm. With fish slice, immediately loosen biscuits from baking sheet and transfer to wire racks to cool. Repeat with remaining dough and trimmings.

5 If not decorating biscuits immediately, wrap in freezer paper or foil, seal, label and freeze. Before decorating, unwrap frozen biscuits and thaw for 1 hour.

6 Prepare Ornamental Icing. Spoon icing into piping bag with small writing tube, or use paper piping bag with tip cut to make 3 mm/¹/₈ inch hole; pipe decorative outlines and designs on each biscuit. Set biscuits aside to allow icing to dry completely, about 1 hour.

Rocking Horse

Father Christmas

Reindeer

PINOLIS

Makes 16
Allow 2 ½ hours preparation and cooking time

120 g/4 oz plain flour

75 g/2 ½ oz butter, softened

50 g/1 ⅔ oz caster sugar

4 tablespoons golden syrup

1 egg

90 g/3 oz pine kernels

1 Preheat oven to 180°C/350°F/gas 4. In medium bowl, combine flour, 60 g/2 oz butter and 40 g/1 ⅓ oz sugar. With hand, knead ingredients until well blended and mixture holds together.

2 Divide dough into 16 pieces. Press dough pieces on to bottom and up sides of each of sixteen 4.5 cm/1 ¾ inch holes in deep bun tin.

3 In small saucepan over low heat, heat remaining butter until just melted. Remove saucepan from heat; into melted butter, stir golden syrup, egg and remaining caster sugar.

4 Into dough cups in deep bun tin, sprinkle pine kernels.

5 Spoon syrup mixture over pine kernels. Bake pinolis for about 25 minutes or until edges are browned and skewer inserted in centre of filling comes out clean.

6 Cool pinolis in tin on wire rack for about 5 minutes or until firm. With tip of knife or small palette knife, loosen pinolis from bun tin holes; place on wire racks to cool completely.

HAZELNUT CRESCENTS

Makes about 18
Allow about 2 hours preparation and cooking time

15 g/ ½ oz shelled hazelnuts

90 g/3 oz plain flour

60 g/2 oz butter, softened

30 g/1 oz icing sugar, sifted

1 Preheat oven to 200°C/400°F/gas 6. Place hazelnuts in small baking tray. Bake for 8-10 minutes until lightly toasted. Remove nuts from oven; turn oven down to 180°C/350°F/gas 4. Cool nuts; chop finely.

2 In large bowl, combine flour, butter and icing sugar; add hazelnuts. With hand, knead ingredients until well blended and mixture holds together. (Mixture may be crumbly; if necessary, add *1 tablespoon water* while kneading ingredients together.)

3 Shape dough into 4.5 x 1 cm/1 ¾ x ½ inch crescents (about 2 level teaspoons each). Place crescents, about 2.5 cm/1 inch apart, on ungreased baking sheets.

4 Bake crescents for 10 minutes or until lightly browned. With fish slice, transfer crescents to wire racks to cool. Store in airtight container.

FROZEN
DESSERTS
217-240

FROZEN DESSERTS

Summertime or winter, cool and creamy frozen desserts will delight everyone. Many of the fabulous frozen cakes and bombes are made with bought ice cream, making them much easier than they look, while pretty decorations, such as mint leaves, fruit slices, and chocolate 'coffee beans' give even the simplest of iced drinks a sophisticated look. Florida Fruit Cups and Lemon Ice in Lemon Cups are ideal for casual entertaining and everyday eating. On the lighter side, Raspberry Sorbet and Two-Tone Granitas – elegant layers of icy coffee and citrus sorbet – are so refreshing in hot weather or to balance out a lavishly rich meal. When you're feeling especially creative, try Hazelnut Icebox Cake, smooth, frozen coffee and chocolate custards with a hazelnut crunch topping. Or, for a special treat, Fudge Sundae Pie, a deluxe concoction of vanilla and chocolate ice creams with a rich and chewy fudge centre, all in a walnut crust. Scrumptious!

CONTENTS

FROZEN DESSERTS

Nothing beats ice cream, frozen yogurt or sorbet for an 'instant' dessert: just dish it up, serve and enjoy. You'll find all your favourite flavours in this chapter, plus recipes to turn them (or their bought counterparts) into chilly treats that money can't buy, such as dacquoises, frozen tortes and more. For freezer storage, wrap them well to prevent freezer burn, and keep them on hand to serve with easy elegance at very short notice, or to end a feast superbly.

CHESTNUT GLACÉ

Makes 6

Allow 15 minutes preparation, plus freezing time

300 ml/ 1/2 pint double or whipping cream

1 x 439 g/15 1/2 oz can unsweetened chestnut purée

120 g/4 oz caster sugar

2 tablespoons brandy

Dark Chocolate Curls (page 142) and lemon leaves (optional) to decorate

1 In small bowl, whip double or whipping cream until stiff peaks form. In large bowl, with fork, mash chestnut purée; stir in sugar and brandy until smooth.

Gold foil tartlet tins give these quick-and-easy frozen desserts a ritzy look

2 With rubber spatula or wire whisk, fold whipped cream into chestnut mixture.

3 Spoon chestnut and cream mixture into foil tartlet tins or small freezerproof ramekins. Cover; freeze until firm, at least 3 hours.

4 Leave to stand at room temperature for about 10 minutes to soften slightly for easier eating.

> **TO SERVE**
> *Decorate with chocolate curls and lemon leaves, if you like.*

RAINBOW ICE CREAM TORTE

 16 servings

Allow about 2 hours preparation, plus final freezing time

600 ml/1 pint chocolate ice cream

600 ml/1 pint mint chocolate chip ice cream

600 ml/1 pint strawberry ice cream

600 ml/1 pint vanilla ice cream

15 gingernut biscuits

60 g/2 oz butter, softened

1 x 425 g/15 oz can stoned black cherries, drained

60 g/2 oz walnut pieces, chopped

This party cake is a bit of a cheat in that it is made from bought ice cream, but it looks so spectacular that your guests are bound to be impressed!

1 Place ice creams in refrigerator to soften slightly.

2 Meanwhile, place biscuits in polythene bag; with rolling pin, roll biscuits into fine crumbs.

3 Or in food processor or blender, blend gingernut biscuits until fine crumbs form.

4 In 23 cm/9 inch springform cake tin, with hand, mix biscuit crumbs with butter; press mixture firmly on to bottom of tin. Freeze until firm, about 10 minutes.

5 Evenly spread chocolate ice cream on top of crumb mixture. Place tin in freezer to harden ice cream slightly, about 15 minutes.

6 Spread mint chocolate chip ice cream on chocolate ice cream layer; top with cherries.

7 Return springform tin to freezer to harden ice creams and cherries slightly.

8 With palette knife, evenly spread strawberry ice cream over layer of cherries.

Spreading strawberry ice cream over cherries

9 Place tin in freezer to harden ice cream slightly, about 15 minutes. Evenly spread vanilla ice cream on strawberry ice cream layer. Sprinkle top with walnuts. Cover and freeze until firm.

10 To serve, run knife or palette knife, dipped in hot water, round edge of tin to loosen ice cream cake; remove side of tin. Leave cake to stand at room temperature for about 10 minutes for easier slicing.

VANILLA ICE CREAM

 8-10 servings
Allow 30 minutes preparation, plus freezing time

4 eggs, separated

120 g/4 oz vanilla sugar, or caster sugar and 1 teaspoon vanilla essence

300 ml/ ¹/₂ pint double cream

1 In small bowl, with wire whisk, beat egg yolks until well blended.

2 In large bowl, with electric mixer on full speed, beat egg whites until soft peaks form.

3 Into beaten egg whites, gradually sprinkle vanilla sugar, 1 tablespoon at a time, beating well after each addition. (This will take about 10 minutes.)

4 In another large bowl, whip cream until soft peaks form. (If using vanilla essence, add to cream before whipping.)

5 With rubber spatula or wire whisk, fold beaten egg whites and egg yolks into whipped cream.

6 If you are making one of the variations (see right and Box, right), add the extra ingredients.

7 Turn mixture into 1.5 litre/2 ¹/₂ pint plastic container; cover and freeze overnight.

8 To serve, scoop ice cream into individual dessert bowls or dishes; serve immediately.

SIMPLE VARIATIONS

If you are making one of the following variations on basic vanilla ice cream, use caster sugar instead of vanilla sugar (or omit vanilla essence). Add extra ingredients after folding beaten egg whites and egg yolks into whipped cream.

Ginger Ice Cream
Add *1 teaspoon ground ginger* and *120 g/4 oz stem ginger in syrup, drained and chopped,* to basic ice cream.

Mocha Ice Cream
Add *2 tablespoons coffee essence* and *2 tablespoons coffee liqueur* to basic ice cream.

Fresh Lemon Ice Cream
Add *grated zest* and *juice of 2 lemons* to basic ice cream.

Mango Ice Cream
Peel and stone *1 ripe mango*; lightly mash flesh and add to basic ice cream.

Passion Fruit Ice Cream
Halve *3 passion fruit*; with small spoon, scoop out flesh and add to basic ice cream.

Tutti Frutti Ice Cream
Chop *120 g/4 oz mixed glacé pineapple, raisins, dried apricots, glacé cherries* and *angelica*; in small bowl, soak overnight in *4 tablespoons brandy* to plump them. Add to basic ice cream.

Blackcurrant Ice Cream
Add *3 tablespoons blackcurrant cordial* and *3 tablespoons crème de cassis* to basic ice cream.

SPECIAL VARIATIONS

Once you've mastered the art of ice cream making, you can ring the changes by adding different fresh fruits, chocolate, nuts or fudge to vanilla ice cream. Here are 3 special varieties for you to try.

Chocolate Ice Cream
Make basic vanilla ice cream using caster sugar instead of vanilla sugar (or omit vanilla essence). In small bowl, with spoon, stir *15 g/ ¹/₂ oz cocoa powder, 30 g/1 oz caster sugar* and about *3 tablespoons boiling water* to a smooth paste; cool. Stir sweetened cocoa paste mixture into ice cream until evenly blended.
Makes 8-10 servings

Fudge-Swirl Ice Cream
Make basic vanilla ice cream using caster sugar instead of vanilla sugar (or omit vanilla essence); freeze until softly set.
  Meanwhile, prepare fudge sauce: in heavy saucepan over medium-high heat, bring *200 g/7 oz caster sugar, 300 ml/ ¹/₂ pint double or whipping cream, 30 g/1 oz butter, 1 tablespoon golden syrup* and *120 g/4 oz plain chocolate, chopped*, to the boil, stirring constantly. Reduce heat to medium; cook for 5 minutes, stirring occasionally. Remove saucepan from heat; stir in *1 teaspoon vanilla essence*.
  Leave sauce to cool, stirring occasionally, then with spoon or knife, quickly swirl fudge sauce into ice cream to create marbled design. Cover container of ice cream again, return to freezer and freeze overnight.
Makes 8-10 servings

Strawberry Ice Cream
Make basic vanilla ice cream using caster sugar instead of vanilla sugar (or omit vanilla essence). Add *150 ml/ ¹/₄ pint strawberry purée*, beating well to mix.
  For Raspberry Ice Cream, substitute *raspberry purée* for strawberry. For Gooseberry, Plum or Rhubarb Ice Cream, add *150 ml/ ¹/₄ pint sweetened cooked gooseberry, plum or rhubarb purée*.
Makes 8-10 servings

Chocolate Ice Cream
A piped chocolate design only hints at the rich taste of Chocolate Ice Cream. Make the designs as shown, using directions for Chocolate Squiggles (page 101); chill and place on servings at the last minute.

Vanilla Ice Cream
Home-made Vanilla Ice Cream is everybody's favourite, so delicious that it can be served absolutely plain. Yet it's equally good topped with sweet sauces, fruit, nuts, honey, liqueur or even crumbled biscuits.

Strawberry Ice Cream
For incomparable flavour, use the reddest, ripest (but not over-ripe), juiciest berries you can find for Strawberry Ice Cream. Here, scoops of varied sizes make a pretty plateful.

Fudge-Swirl Ice Cream
The decoration is built right into Fudge-Swirl Ice Cream, with thick, fudgy sauce rippled through the frozen mixture. Elegant rolled biscuits make a perfect partner.

HAZELNUT ICEBOX CAKE

 10 servings

Allow about 2 ½ hours preparation, plus final freezing time

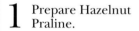

Hazelnut Praline (see Box, below right)

12 egg yolks

175 ml/6 fl oz golden syrup

2 tablespoons coffee liqueur

2 teaspoons instant coffee powder

175 g/6 oz plain chocolate, broken into pieces

750 ml/1 ¼ pints double or whipping cream

Toasted hazelnuts for decoration

1 Prepare Hazelnut Praline.

2 In large bowl, with electric mixer, beat egg yolks and golden syrup until slightly thickened and light-coloured, about 4 minutes.

3 Pour egg yolk mixture into large non-stick saucepan. Cook over low heat, stirring constantly, until mixture thickens and coats a spoon well, about 30 minutes. Remove saucepan from heat.

4 Pour two-thirds of egg yolk mixture into large bowl.

5 In cup, stir coffee liqueur and coffee powder; stir into egg yolk mixture in large bowl.

6 In bowl over pan of gently simmering water, heat half of the chocolate, stirring frequently, until melted and smooth.

7 Stir melted chocolate into remaining egg yolk mixture in saucepan until blended.

8 In another large bowl, whip 600 ml/1 pint double or whipping cream until stiff peaks form.

9 With rubber spatula or wire whisk, fold two-thirds of whipped cream into coffee mixture until blended. Fold remaining whipped cream into chocolate mixture.

10 Spoon half of the coffee mixture into 23 cm/9 inch springform cake tin, spreading evenly; freeze until set, about 15 minutes.

11 Evenly spread chocolate mixture over coffee layer in springform tin; freeze until set, about 15 minutes.

12 Sprinkle chocolate layer with hazelnut praline; evenly spread with remaining coffee mixture. Cover and freeze until firm, at least 4 hours.

13 In bowl over pan of gently simmering water, heat remaining chocolate, stirring often, until melted and smooth; remove saucepan from heat. Cut non-stick baking parchment into two 10 cm/4 inch squares. Moisten large baking sheet with water; place parchment squares on baking sheet (water will prevent paper from slipping). Use melted chocolate and parchment squares to make Chocolate Triangles (see Box, page 225); refrigerate.

14 In small bowl, whip remaining double or whipping cream until stiff peaks form. Spoon whipped cream into piping bag fitted with star tube.

HAZELNUT PRALINE

Coarsely chop 135 g/ 4 ½ oz shelled hazelnuts.

In large frying pan over medium heat, heat 60 g/2 oz caster sugar until sugar melts and turns golden brown. Stir in chopped hazelnuts; toss to coat well.

Pour into baking tin; leave to cool. Break into small pieces.

15 Run knife or palette knife, dipped in hot water, round edge of springform tin to loosen cake; remove side of tin.

16 Pipe whipped cream into 8 'flowers' round edge on top of cake; place chocolate triangles between whipped cream flowers. Decorate with toasted hazelnuts.

17 Leave cake to stand at room temperature for about 10 minutes for easier slicing.

CHOCOLATE TRIANGLES

Removing baking parchment: *carefully peel parchment from chocolate squares.*

Spreading melted chocolate: *with small palette knife, evenly spread chocolate to cover baking parchment squares. Refrigerate until chocolate is firm but not brittle, about 10 minutes. Remove chocolate from refrigerator; leave to stand for about 5 minutes to soften slightly.*

Cutting triangles: *with sharp knife, quickly but gently cut each chocolate square into 8 triangles.*

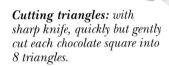

Cutting chocolate into triangle shapes

Top of cake is beautifully decorated with whipped cream 'flowers', toasted hazelnuts and chocolate triangles

DACQUOISE GLACÉE

 10 servings
Allow about 4 hours preparation, plus freezing time

5 egg whites

300 g/10 oz caster sugar

25 g/¾ oz cocoa powder, sifted

60 g/2 oz flaked almonds

1 litre/2 pints coffee ice cream

450 ml/¾ pint double or whipping cream

30 g/1 oz icing sugar, sifted

2 tablespoons coffee liqueur

1 Line 1 large and 1 small baking sheet with non-stick baking parchment or foil.

2 Using 20 cm/8 inch round plate as guide, outline 2 circles on parchment or foil on large baking sheet and 1 circle on small baking sheet.

3 In large bowl, with electric mixer on full speed, beat egg whites until soft peaks form.

4 Into beaten egg whites, gradually sprinkle caster sugar, 1 tablespoon at a time, beating well after each addition until sugar completely dissolves and whites stand in stiff, glossy peaks.

5 With rubber spatula or wire whisk, gently fold sifted cocoa into meringue until blended.

6 Preheat oven to 140°C/275°F/gas 1. Spoon one-third of meringue inside each circle on baking sheets; spread to fill circle.

7 Bake layers for 1¼ hours or until meringue is crisp.

8 Cool meringue layers on baking sheets on wire racks for 10 minutes; carefully loosen and lift meringue layers from parchment or foil.

9 Place meringue layers on wire racks; leave to cool completely.

ASSEMBLING DACQUOISE GLACÉE

Spreading meringue with ice cream: *with palette knife, quickly and evenly spread first meringue layer with softened ice cream.*

Topping with second meringue layer: *carefully lift chilled meringue round and place it over ice cream layer.*

Icing frozen dessert: *evenly swirl whipped cream all over side and top of frozen dessert.*

10 While meringue is cooling, turn oven up to 180°C/350°F/gas 4. Spread almonds in baking tray. Bake almonds for 10-15 minutes until browned, stirring occasionally. Cool; set aside.

11 Chill meringue layers in freezer for about 30 minutes for easier handling. Place half of the coffee ice cream in refrigerator to soften slightly, about 30 minutes.

12 On freezerproof cake plate, place 1 meringue layer; spread with softened ice cream (see Box, page 226).

13 Place meringue with ice cream in freezer until firm, about 30 minutes. Meanwhile, place remaining coffee ice cream in refrigerator to soften.

14 Remove meringue with ice cream from freezer. Top with second meringue layer (see Box, page 226).

15 Quickly and evenly spread with remaining ice cream; place remaining meringue layer on top. Return to freezer until completely frozen, at least 4 hours.

16 In bowl, whip double or whipping cream with icing sugar and coffee liqueur until stiff peaks form.

17 Ice frozen dessert with whipped cream (see Box, page 226). Evenly sprinkle toasted almonds on top of whipped cream.

Sprinkling toasted almonds on top of frozen dessert

18 Return dessert to freezer; when whipped cream has hardened, cover. Keep in freezer until ready to serve.

Ridged effect on whipped cream is made by drawing a serrated icing spreader round side of cake

TO SERVE
Leave cake to stand at room temperature for about 10 minutes for easier slicing.

AMERICAN ICED DRINKS

VELVET HAMMER

 4 servings

 Make just before serving

600 ml/1 pint vanilla ice cream, slightly softened

2 tablespoons orange liqueur

2 tablespoons brandy

Orange wedges and curls (see Citrus Curls, page 62) to decorate

1 In food processor or blender on medium speed, blend all ingredients just until smooth. Do not overblend; mixture should be thick.

2 Pour immediately into chilled wine glasses for sipping; decorate each serving with orange wedge and curls.

STRAWBERRY SODA

 6-8 servings

Make just before serving

300 ml/ ½ pint milk

300 g/10 oz frozen sliced strawberries, partially thawed

600 ml/1 pint strawberry ice cream

450 ml/ ³/4 pint soda water or fizzy strawberry drink, chilled

1 In food processor or blender on high speed, blend milk and strawberries for 15 seconds until smooth. Pour into 5 tall glasses.

2 Add scoop of straw-berry ice cream to each; slowly add soda or fizzy drink to fill almost to top. Serve immediately.

Strawberry Soda is topped with scoop of strawberry ice cream

Milk and strawberries are blended to a very smooth consistency

Velvet Hammer looks coolly elegant with orange wedge and curl on rim of glass

DECORATIONS FOR ICED DRINKS

A pretty decoration on top of an iced drink, or arranged on the rim of the glass, adds greatly to its appeal. Sprigs of fresh herbs and fruit slices go well with fruity drinks, while chocolate 'coffee beans' taste good with chocolate- and coffee-flavoured drinks.

Mint sprig

Star fruit slice

Chocolate 'coffee beans'

BLACK COW

🍴 1 serving
⏱ Make just before serving

150 ml/ ¹/₄ pint root beer or cola, chilled

Scoop of vanilla ice cream

Black Cow, a very popular soft drink in America, is a dark soda, root beer or chocolate drink with white ice cream floating on top

1 Into chilled tall glass, pour chilled root beer or cola.

2 Top with generous scoop of slightly softened vanilla ice cream. Serve immediately with straw and long-handled spoon.

Scoop of slightly softened ice cream makes a delicious froth on the top of root beer or cola

MOCHA FLOAT

🍴 1 serving
⏱ Make just before serving

1 teaspoon drinking chocolate powder

³/₄ teaspoon instant coffee powder

¹/₂ teaspoon caster sugar

Soda water, chilled

2 small scoops of chocolate ice cream

Chocolate ice cream tops this coffee- and chocolate-flavoured drink

1 In 300 ml/ ¹/₂ pint glass, combine first 3 ingredients. Gradually add enough soda to fill glass three-quarters full; stir vigorously until sugar is dissolved.

2 Add chocolate ice cream; stir. Serve with spoon and straw.

FLORIDA FRUIT CUPS

12 servings
Allow 20 minutes preparation, plus freezing time

600 ml/1 pint plain yogurt

3 tablespoons liquid honey

Grated zest of 1 small lemon

300 g/10 oz assorted fresh fruit (halved strawberries, chopped peaches, chopped nectarines, blueberries or raspberries)

Decoration: lemon leaves, halved strawberries, blueberries, raspberries and nectarine wedges

1 Place fluted paper cake cases in each of 12 holes in deep bun tin.

2 Into large bowl, pour yogurt; add honey and grated lemon zest (honey prevents yogurt from crystallizing in freezer). With wire whisk, mix until blended. Gently stir in 175 g/6 oz fruit.

3 Spoon fruit and yogurt mixture into paper cake cases; top with remaining fruit (some fruit will stay above mixture for pretty colour).

4 Cover bun tin; freeze until firm, about 3 hours.

5 With your fingers, carefully peel off paper cake cases from dessert.

Ridges from paper cases look attractive

6 Leave fruit cups to stand at room temperature for 10-15 minutes to soften slightly for easier eating.

> *TO SERVE*
> *Decorate each serving with lemon leaves, strawberry halves, blueberries, raspberries and nectarine wedges.*

RASPBERRY ARCTIC ROLL

🍴 8 servings

⏱ Allow 2 ½ hours preparation, plus freezing time

100 g/3 ½ oz self-raising flour

120 g/4 oz caster sugar

15 g/ ½ oz cocoa powder plus extra for sprinkling

4 eggs

300 ml/ ½ pint Cornish dairy ice cream

300 ml/ ½ pint raspberry or strawberry ice cream

1 Preheat oven to 220°C/425°F/gas 7. Line 33 x 23 cm/ 13 x 9 inch Swiss roll tin with non-stick baking parchment.

2 In small bowl, stir flour, 60 g/2 oz sugar and 15 g/ ½ oz cocoa powder until evenly blended; set aside.

3 In large bowl, with electric mixer, beat eggs with remaining sugar until thick and lemon-coloured, occasionally scraping bowl with rubber spatula.

4 With wire whisk or rubber spatula, gently fold flour mixture into egg mixture.

5 Spoon mixture into tin, spreading evenly. Bake for about 12 minutes until top of cake springs back when lightly touched with finger.

6 Sprinkle clean tea towel with cocoa. When cake is done, immediately turn out on to towel. Carefully peel baking parchment from cake. If you like, cut off crisp edges. Starting at 1 narrow end, roll cake with towel, Swiss roll fashion. Place cake roll, seam side down, on wire rack; cool completely.

7 Place ice creams in refrigerator to soften slightly, about 30 minutes. Carefully unroll cooled cake; with palette knife, spread half of the cake crossways with one flavour ice cream; evenly spread other half of the cake with remaining flavour ice cream.

8 Starting at same narrow end, roll cake without towel.

9 Place rolled cake, seam side down, on long freezerproof platter. Cover and freeze cake until firm, at least 4 hours.

FLAVOURING ICE CREAM

Cornish dairy ice cream is rich and very creamy. If you want to keep this flavour throughout the filling for Raspberry Arctic Roll, use it for the raspberry or strawberry layer and make your own flavouring: after softening the ice cream in step 7, beat in *150 ml/ ¼ pint puréed strawberries or raspberries, sweetened with icing sugar to taste.*

TO SERVE
Leave arctic roll to stand at room temperature for 15 minutes for easier slicing.

LEMON ICE IN LEMON CUPS

🍴 6 servings

⏱ Allow 45 minutes preparation, plus freezing time

6 large lemons

1 tablespoon powdered gelatine

200 g/7 oz caster sugar

Lemons are cut lengthways to make deep cup shapes

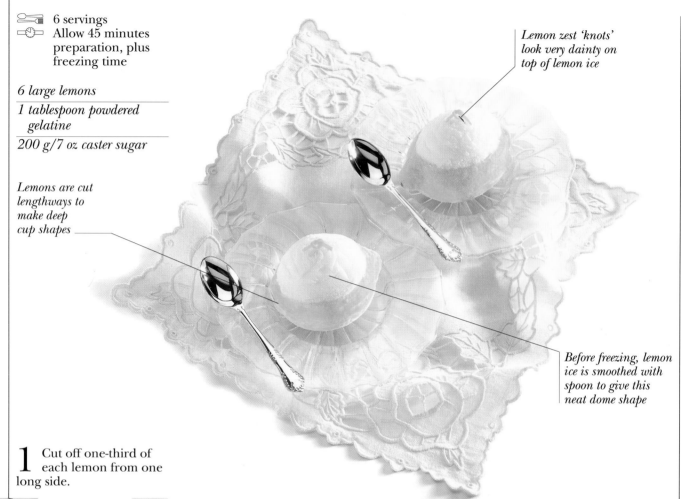

Lemon zest 'knots' look very dainty on top of lemon ice

Before freezing, lemon ice is smoothed with spoon to give this neat dome shape

1 Cut off one-third of each lemon from one long side.

2 With canelle knife, remove 6 strips of zest from cut off pieces of lemons. Wrap; refrigerate for decoration. Grate remaining zest from cut off pieces of lemons; set aside.

3 Squeeze 175 ml/ 6 fl oz juice from bottom pieces of lemons. Remove all crushed pulp and membrane.

4 Cut thin slice off base of each lemon cup so it can stand level. Place lemon cups in polythene bag; refrigerate until ready to fill.

5 In medium saucepan, with wire whisk, mix gelatine and sugar; stir in *550 ml/18 fl oz water*. Leave to stand for 1 minute to soften gelatine slightly. Cook over medium heat, stirring constantly, until gelatine completely dissolves. Remove saucepan from heat; stir in grated lemon zest and juice.

6 Pour lemon mixture into 23 cm/9 inch baking tin; cover with foil or cling film. Freeze until partially frozen, about 2 hours, stirring occasionally.

7 Spoon lemon mixture into chilled large bowl; with electric mixer, beat mixture until smooth but still frozen.

8 Return mixture to baking tin; cover and freeze until partially frozen, about 2 hours. Spoon mixture into chilled large bowl; beat again as before. Cover and freeze until firm.

9 With spoon, fill lemon cups with lemon ice.

10 Tie each strip of reserved lemon zest into loose knot; use to decorate top of each lemon ice. Serve immediately or freeze to serve later. If not serving on same day, when filled cups have hardened, wrap and return to freezer.

ITALIAN TARTUFO

6 servings

Allow 2 ³/₄ hours
preparation, plus
final freezing time

---

*900 ml/1 ¹/₂ pints vanilla
ice cream*

---

6 amaretti biscuits

---

*2 tablespoons almond
liqueur or orange juice*

---

*175 g/6 oz plain chocolate,
broken into pieces*

---

45 g/1 ¹/₂ oz butter

---

1 tablespoon golden syrup

---

*90 g/3 oz walnut pieces,
toasted*

---

1 Place ice cream in
refrigerator to soften
slightly. Chill small baking
sheet in freezer.

2 Meanwhile, place
amaretti biscuits on
plate; pour over almond
liqueur or orange juice.
Leave to stand until
liqueur is absorbed,
turning biscuits
occasionally.

3 Line chilled baking
sheet with non-stick
baking parchment. Work-
ing quickly, with large ice
cream scoop, scoop a ball
of ice cream. Gently press
an amaretti into centre.

4 Reshape ice cream
into ball around
amaretti; place on lined
baking sheet. Repeat with
remaining ice cream and
amaretti to make 6 ice
cream balls. Freeze until
firm, about 1 ¹/₂ hours.

5 In bowl over pan
of gently simmering
water, heat chocolate
pieces, butter and golden
syrup, stirring frequently,
until melted and smooth.
Remove bowl from pan.

6 Remove baking sheet
with ice cream balls
from freezer.

7 Place 1 ice cream ball
on metal spatula over
bowl of melted chocolate.
With large metal spoon,
quickly scoop up melted
chocolate and pour over
ice cream ball to coat
completely.

8 Place chocolate-
coated ice cream ball
on same baking sheet.
Firmly pat some walnuts
on to chocolate coating.

9 Repeat with remain-
ing ice cream balls,
chocolate mixture and
nuts. Freeze until ice
cream balls are firm, about
1 hour.

10 If not serving on
same day, wrap ice
cream balls with foil;
return to freezer to use
within 1 week.

---

*TO SERVE
Leave ice cream balls to
stand at room tempera-
ture for about 10 minutes
to soften slightly for
easier eating.*

---

*Toasted walnuts are pressed
on to chocolate coating before
ice cream ball is frozen, so they
will be secure for serving*

ICE CREAM BOMBE

 8-10 servings

Allow 3 hours preparation, plus final freezing time

3 eggs

90 g/3 oz caster sugar, warmed

75 g/2 ¹/₂ oz self-raising flour

15 g/ ¹/₂ oz cocoa powder

300 ml/ ¹/₂ pint strawberry ice cream

600 ml/1 pint vanilla ice cream

3 tablespoons coffee liqueur (optional)

1 x 425 g/15 oz can stoned black cherries, drained

300 ml/ ¹/₂ pint chocolate ice cream

Chocolate Bow and Ribbon Streamers (see Box, right)

60 g/2 oz desiccated coconut

120 g/4 oz icing sugar, sifted

120 g/4 oz butter, softened

¹/₄ teaspoon vanilla essence

1 Preheat oven to 220°C/425°F/gas 7. Lightly grease 33 x 23 cm/ 13 x 9 inch Swiss roll tin and line with non-stick baking parchment.

2 In large bowl, with electric mixer, beat eggs and caster sugar until very thick and lemon-coloured. Sift over flour and cocoa powder; with large metal spoon, fold into egg mixture. Spoon mixture into tin, spreading evenly. Bake for 10 minutes or until top of cake springs back when lightly touched with finger. Immediately turn cake out on to wire rack; peel off baking parchment and leave cake to cool.

3 Place both strawberry and vanilla ice creams in refrigerator to soften slightly.

4 Line medium bowl with cling film. Cut chocolate cake into pieces to line bowl, keeping large piece aside for top; trim pieces of cake to fit, if necessary and press trimmings into gaps. Brush cake with coffee liqueur.

5 Spoon half of the strawberry ice cream into cake-lined bowl. Spoon one-quarter of vanilla ice cream in dollops on to strawberry ice cream. Scatter one-quarter of cherries between vanilla ice cream dollops.

6 Repeat with remaining strawberry ice cream, one-quarter of vanilla ice cream and one-quarter of cherries; press down mixture to eliminate air pockets. Place bowl in freezer to harden ice cream slightly, about 20 minutes.

DECORATION FOR ICE CREAM BOMBE

The bow and ribbon streamers on the Ice Cream Bombe (page 235) add a professional touch to the finished dessert, yet they are simple to make. If you use white marzipan or almond paste rather than yellow, you will get a better 'chocolate' colour.

Chocolate Bow and Ribbon Streamers
Knead 2 teaspoons sifted cocoa powder into 120 g/ 4 oz marzipan or almond paste until evenly blended. If mixture seems very dry, lightly dampen hands, but do not use too much water or paste will be too sticky to roll.

Sift a very little extra cocoa powder on to work surface; with rolling pin, roll out paste to 20 x 11 cm/ 8 x 4 ¹/₂ inch rectangle.

Trim edges; cut paste into 8 long strips of equal width. Use 5 strips for ribbon streamers; cut ends on the diagonal. Arrange on bombe, some full length and some shorter. Make loops with remaining strips; place on top of bombe to resemble bow.

7 Meanwhile, place chocolate ice cream in refrigerator to soften slightly, and return remaining vanilla ice cream to freezer.

8 Remove bowl from freezer. Repeat layering as for strawberry ice cream, but use chocolate ice cream with remaining vanilla ice cream and cherries.

9 Place reserved chocolate cake on top of chocolate ice cream, pressing cake down firmly against ice cream. Cover bowl with freezer film; place bowl in freezer until ice cream is firm, at least 4 hours.

10 Prepare Chocolate Bow and Ribbon Streamers.

Spooning vanilla ice cream over chocolate ice cream in bowl

11 Heat grill. Evenly sprinkle coconut in baking tray; grill for 3 minutes or until lightly toasted, stirring frequently. Set aside.

12 Prepare butter cream: in medium bowl, with electric mixer, beat icing sugar, butter and *2 teaspoons hot water* until light and fluffy, scraping bowl often with rubber spatula. Beat in vanilla essence until smooth.

13 Remove ice cream cake from freezer. Turn cake out on to chilled freezerproof cake stand or platter; remove cling film. With palette knife, thinly spread butter cream over cake, covering a small area at a time and immediately pressing toasted coconut on to butter cream.

14 Continue until cake is completely covered with butter cream and toasted coconut. Decorate cake with chocolate bow and ribbon streamers. Keep cake in freezer until ready to serve.

> *TO SERVE*
> *Leave cake to stand at room temperature for 20 minutes for easier slicing.*

When Ice Cream Bombe is cut, it reveals its pretty coloured layers of cake, ice cream and cherries

MELON SORBET

6-8 servings

Allow 15 minutes preparation, plus freezing time

1 ripe gallia, charentais or cantaloupe melon (800 g/1 ³/₄ lb)

Juice of ¹/₂ lemon

4 egg whites

100 g/3 ¹/₂ oz caster sugar

1 Remove and discard rind and seeds from melon; cut melon into chunks. In food processor, blend melon chunks and lemon juice until smooth.

2 Turn blended melon and lemon mixture into 1.7 litre/3 pint rigid freezer container and level surface; place in freezer until mixture is just beginning to set round edges.

3 In large bowl, with electric mixer on full speed, beat egg whites until soft peaks form.

4 Into beaten egg whites, gradually sprinkle caster sugar, 1 tablespoon at a time, beating well after each addition until sugar completely dissolves and whites stand in stiff, glossy peaks.

5 Return partially frozen melon mixture to food processor; blend until mixture is broken down. Fold in beaten egg whites until evenly blended. Return melon mixture to rigid container; cover and freeze until firm, about 3 hours.

6 Leave sorbet to stand at room temperature for 10 minutes for easier scooping.

Colourful wedges of melon are arranged like spokes of a wheel round edge of serving bowl

For this attractive presentation, different-sized scoops of sorbet were placed on chilled baking sheet lined with non-stick baking parchment and put in freezer to harden; they were then lifted off and piled on top of each other

TWO MELON GRANITA

🍴 8 servings
🕐 Allow 30 minutes preparation, plus freezing time

200 g/7 oz caster sugar

4 tablespoons lemon juice

1 ripe charentais or gallia melon (about 900 g/2 lb)

1 ripe honeydew melon (about 900 g/2 lb)

1 In small saucepan over high heat, bring sugar and *500 ml/16 fl oz water* to the boil. Reduce heat to medium; cook for 5 minutes. Remove saucepan from heat; stir in lemon juice.

2 Remove and discard rind and seeds from charentais or gallia melon; cut flesh into chunks. In food processor or blender, blend melon flesh until smooth; pour into rigid freezer container.

3 Repeat with honeydew melon; pour into another rigid freezer container.

4 Pour half of the sugar mixture into each rigid container; stir until well mixed. Cover with lids; freeze melon mixtures until firm, about 5 hours, stirring occasionally so mixtures freeze evenly.

5 Leave granitas to stand at room temperature for about 10 minutes to soften slightly.

6 With spoon, scrape across surface of granitas to create pebbly texture.

7 Spoon some charentais granita and some honeydew granita into each of 8 chilled dessert bowls.

WATERMELON ICE

🍴 8 servings
🕐 Allow 20 minutes preparation, plus final freezing time

1 x 900 g/2 lb piece watermelon

15 g/ ¹/₂ oz icing sugar, sifted

1 ¹/₂ teaspoons lemon juice

1 Remove and discard rind and seeds from watermelon; cut watermelon flesh into bite-sized chunks. In food processor, blend half of the watermelon chunks with icing sugar and lemon juice until smooth.

2 Pour watermelon mixture into rigid freezer container. Blend remaining watermelon chunks until smooth. Stir into mixture in container. Cover with lid; freeze until partially frozen, about 2 hours, stirring occasionally.

3 Return partially frozen watermelon mixture to food processor; blend until mixture is broken down. Return mixture to rigid container; cover and freeze until firm, about 3 hours.

4 Leave ice to stand at room temperature for about 10 minutes to soften slightly. Then, with spoon, scrape across surface of ice to create fine 'snow-like' texture; spoon into dessert dishes.

'Snow-like' texture is made by scraping spoon across surface of water ice when removing it from container for serving

RASPBERRY SORBET

🍴 8 servings

⏱ Allow 20 minutes preparation, plus freezing time

2 x 250 g/8.8 oz packets frozen raspberries

120 g/4 oz caster sugar

1 tablespoon powdered gelatine

4 tablespoons golden syrup, dissolved in 4 tablespoons hot water

5 tablespoons raspberry liqueur

3 tablespoons lemon juice

Kiwi fruit, papaya and fresh raspberries

1 Sprinkle raspberries with sugar; set aside to thaw.

2 In small saucepan, evenly sprinkle gelatine over 250 ml/ 8 fl oz water; allow to stand for 1 minute to soften. Cook over medium heat until gelatine completely dissolves, stirring often. Remove saucepan from heat.

3 Over large bowl, with back of spoon, press and scrape rasp-berries with their syrup firmly against medium-mesh sieve to purée; discard pips left in sieve.

4 Stir golden syrup, liqueur and lemon juice into raspberry purée, then stir in dissolved gelatine, a little at a time, until well mixed.

5 Pour raspberry mixture into rigid freezer container. Freeze until partially frozen, about 2 hours, stirring occasionally.

6 Transfer partially frozen raspberry mixture to food processor; blend until mixture is broken down. Return mixture to rigid container; cover and freeze until firm, about 3 hours.

7 Arrange some kiwi fruit, papaya and fresh raspberries on individual plates. Place small scoops of sorbet next to fruit.

Adding dissolved gelatine to raspberry mixture

Slices of peeled papaya and kiwi fruit add extra colour to individual servings of sorbet

SERVING SORBET AND ICE CREAM

For an attractive presen-tation, sorbet and ice cream look best served in scoops. For easy serving, with ice cream scoop, take balls of sorbet or ice cream from container and place on chilled baking sheet lined with non-stick baking parchment.

Immediately place baking sheet in freezer; leave until sorbet or ice cream hardens. To serve, lift scoops off parchment and place on dessert plates or in dishes at last minute.

FUDGE SUNDAE PIE

🥄 8-10 servings

🕐 Allow about 3 hours preparation, plus freezing time

120 g/4 oz digestive biscuits, finely crushed

60 g/2 oz walnut pieces, finely chopped

60 g/ 2 oz soft brown sugar

90 g/3 oz butter, softened

600 ml/1 pint vanilla ice cream

175 g/6 oz caster sugar

45 g/1 ¹/₂ oz cocoa powder

450 ml/ ³/₄ pint double or whipping cream

600 ml/1 pint chocolate or coffee ice cream

Chocolate Curls (page 104) to decorate

1 Preheat oven to 200°C/400°F/gas 6. In shallow 23 cm/9 inch pie dish, with hand, mix biscuits, walnuts, brown sugar and 75 g/2 ¹/₂ oz butter. Press mixture on to bottom and up side of pie dish. Bake for 8 minutes. Cool crust on wire rack.

2 Meanwhile, place vanilla ice cream in refrigerator to soften slightly.

3 With rubber spatula or palette knife, evenly spread softened vanilla ice cream in crust; freeze until firm, about 1 ¹/₂ hours.

4 In non-stick saucepan over medium heat, place 150 g/5 oz caster sugar, cocoa powder, 125 ml/4 fl oz double or whipping cream and remaining butter. Bring to the boil, stirring constantly until smooth. Remove saucepan from heat. Cool fudge sauce to room temperature.

5 Over vanilla ice cream layer in biscuit crust, pour fudge sauce.

6 Return pie to freezer; freeze until fudge sauce hardens, about 30 minutes.

7 Remove chocolate or coffee ice cream from container to medium bowl; leave to stand at room temperature, stirring occasionally, until a smooth spreading consistency (but not melted). Spread chocolate or coffee ice cream over fudge layer; return pie to freezer.

8 In small bowl, whip remaining double or whipping cream with remaining caster sugar until stiff peaks form.

9 With palette knife, spread whipped cream smoothly and evenly over pie.

TO SERVE
Let pie stand at room temperature 15 minutes for easier slicing.

10 Decorate pie with chocolate curls.

11 Return pie to freezer, uncovered; freeze until firm, about 3 hours. If not serving pie same day, wrap frozen pie with foil and freeze until ready to serve.

Spreading whipped cream over pie

TWO-TONE GRANITAS

COFFEE

🥄 6 servings
⏱ Allow 10 minutes preparation, plus freezing time

60 g/2 oz caster sugar

4 tablespoons instant coffee powder

1 In medium saucepan over high heat, bring sugar, coffee powder and *750 ml/1 ¼ pints water* to the boil, stirring occasionally. Reduce heat to medium; cook for 5 minutes.

2 Pour mixture into rigid freezer container.

3 Cool mixture. Cover with container lid; freeze until firm, about 5 hours, stirring occasionally.

TO SERVE
Leave granitas to stand at room temperature for 10 minutes to soften slightly. Then, with spoon, scrape across surface of granitas to create pebbly texture; spoon into tall glasses, alternating layers.

LEMON

🥄 6 servings
⏱ Allow 15 minutes preparation, plus freezing time

200 g/7 oz caster sugar

4 large lemons

1 In medium saucepan over high heat, bring sugar and *500 ml/16 fl oz water* to the boil, stirring occasionally. Reduce heat to medium; cook for 5 minutes. Cool.

2 From lemons, grate 2 teaspoons zest and squeeze 175 ml/6 fl oz juice. Stir lemon zest and juice into cooled sugar syrup.

3 Pour mixture into freezer container.

4 Cover and freeze until firm, about 5 hours, stirring occasionally.

USEFUL INFORMATION AND BASIC RECIPES

241-259

DESSERTS

The recipes in this book fall into the following categories: mousses and soufflés, custards and creams, meringues, pancakes and crêpes, fruit desserts, puddings, cakes and gâteaux, cheesecakes, fruit cakes, sweet pies, tarts and flans, pastries, hot fruit puddings, biscuits and cookies, and frozen desserts. Within each category the recipes range from simple everyday desserts to classic dishes, and popular recipes calling for slightly more advanced techniques. On these two pages, you will find useful information on general dessert-making techniques.

USING GELATINE

Many desserts, such as mousses and cold soufflés, depend on gelatine to make them set. Gelatine is available as powder or leaf, and the two can be used interchangeably. To substitute leaf gelatine for powder, use 2 leaves for each 7 g/ ¹/₄ oz powdered gelatine (1 tablespoon).

DISSOLVING GELATINE

For properly set, jellied mixtures, gelatine must be dissolved completely in hot liquid such as water, milk or fruit juice in a bowl or saucepan; no visible bits of gelatine should remain in the mixture or they will spoil its clarity and/or smoothness.

Constant stirring is essential to make sure gelatine is completely dissolved.

Gelatine granules that splash up the side of bowl or saucepan are difficult to dissolve, so always stir mixture steadily but not too vigorously.

For best results, powdered gelatine should not be added directly to hot liquid. The granules could lump together and not dissolve completely, and could then spoil the dessert.

Leaf gelatine should always be soaked in water to soften it, then squeezed out before being added to hot liquid.

To check powdered gelatine has dissolved completely: *run rubber spatula through mixture, next to side of pan or bowl, to see if granules are all dissolved*

TURNING OUT GELATINE DESSERTS

Individual desserts set with gelatine can be turned out right on to dessert plates for serving. Turn out large desserts on to serving platter (moisten platter first so that if dessert comes out off-centre on platter, it can be moved easily to centre).

• Fill sink or large basin with warm, not hot, water.

• Carefully loosen edges of dessert from mould with palette knife.

• Dip mould into warm water just to rim for about 10 seconds. Be careful not to melt dessert.

• Lift mould out of water and shake it gently to loosen dessert.

• Invert serving platter on top of mould.

• Quickly invert mould and platter together; gently lift off mould.

ADDING INGREDIENTS TO GELATINE

In most recipes, a gelatine mixture should be partially set before other ingredients are added, or solid ingredients such as sliced fruit might sink to the bottom, and whipped cream could lose its volume by the time it is thoroughly blended in. When solids are to be added, gelatine mixture should have thickened to consistency of unbeaten egg white. This partially thickened stage allows for even distribution of solids. When adding whipped cream, chill mixture slightly longer, until it mounds when dropped from spoon.

If gelatine mixture thickens too much before other ingredients are folded in or it is turned into a mould, place bowl of mixture in hot water and stir occasionally for 1 minute or less to melt gelatine. Then chill mixture again, stirring occasionally.

CHILLING GELATINE DESSERTS

In order to set, a gelatine mixture must be chilled. Stir mixture occasionally while it chills, so that it cools and thickens evenly. For faster thickening, place saucepan or bowl containing mixture in larger bowl of iced water. Stir mixture often until it reaches desired consistency. Or place saucepan or bowl in freezer and stir often until mixture is of desired consistency. Do not leave mixture in freezer until it sets; ice crystals will form and make mixture watery, spoiling the dessert.

To test consistency of gelatine mixture: *take up spoonful of mixture and drop it on top. It should 'mound', not disappear*

EGGS: HANDLE WITH CARE

Raw or undercooked eggs may pose a risk of salmonellosis, food poisoning caused by salmonella bacteria found in some eggs. While this risk is extremely small, it does exist, so it is a good idea to follow some simple rules. When making a custard, be sure that the eggs are cooked and the custard thickened properly, but do not allow the custard to boil or it will curdle. Proper storage and cooking of eggs and handling of egg-rich foods is necessary to prevent growth of potentially harmful bacteria. For safety first, take these precautions.

• Buy only clean, uncracked eggs from a reputable source.

• Don't buy too many eggs at a time; buy only as many as you need.

• When you bring eggs home, put them a cool place or in the refrigerator as soon as possible.

• Keep eggs in their box, pointed ends downwards.

• Use eggs within 1 week of purchase.

• To test an egg for freshness: place in a bowl of cold water; if it begins to float, it is not fresh.

• If an egg is fresh, its white will not be runny.

• If a speck of yolk gets into egg whites while separating eggs, use a spoon, not the egg shell, to remove it. The egg shell might not be clean.

• Serve eggs and egg-rich foods as soon as they are cooked; or, if you've made them ahead, refrigerate them at once and use within 3 days.

• The following, in particular, are advised not to eat raw or undercooked eggs:
  a) elderly whose immune systems are weakened with age
  b) infants whose immune systems are not yet fully developed
  c) pregnant women
  d) anyone with an immune system weakened by disease or anticancer treatments.

THICKENING WITH EGGS

Many different desserts use eggs as a thickening agent in the form of a custard. The key to successful custards is careful control of heat; too high a heat causes eggs to curdle, resulting in a lumpy, thin mixture. However, it is also important that the heat is high enough (see Eggs: Handle with Care, left).

For successful custards, always use a heavy, non-stick saucepan, or double boiler, and stir mixture constantly with a whisk until it thickens and coats a metal spoon well. Take care not to let mixture boil or it will curdle. Check thickness by lifting spoon from custard and holding it up for 15-20 seconds; if back of spoon does not show through it, custard has thickened to right consistency.

To test consistency of custard: *lift spoon from pan and hold it up for 15-20 seconds; back of spoon should not show through mixture*

HOT SOUFFLÉS

Raised high with beaten egg whites, light, fluffy, hot dessert soufflés need to be carefully timed since they should be served as soon as they are taken from the oven: they tend to collapse if left to stand for more than a few minutes. Both the basic sauce and the soufflé dish itself can be prepared well in advance. Don't open oven door before end of specified baking time; a rush of cold air into the oven could cause soufflé to collapse.

With wire whisk, gradually folding soufflé mixture into egg whites

With back of spoon, making 2.5 cm/1 inch indentation round top of soufflé for 'top hat' effect

MOUSSES

The light, creamy texture of a mousse comes from eggs, custard or whipped cream, or a combination of these, blended into melted chocolate, fruit purée or nuts.

To achieve a smooth, creamy texture, it is essential to fold and blend ingredients in as evenly as possible; for best results, use a wire whisk or rubber spatula when folding in or blending, and a 'figure of eight' action.

SAUCES

A repertoire of sweet sauces enables the cook to put a special finishing touch to a wide variety of desserts. On these pages you will find sauces to enhance the flavour and appeal of fresh, canned and frozen fruits; home-made or bought pastries, flans and cakes; frozen desserts; and bread and rice puddings.

Today's sauces aren't just poured over foods. They can be puddled on the plate or spooned round food to frame it like in a picture. More, sauces themselves can be decorated, with designs piped or stirred in; see Decorating with Sauces (pages 24-25) for ideas to copy or to spark your own imagination.

CHOCOLATE SAUCES

CHOCOLATE CREAM SAUCE

175 g/6 oz plain chocolate, broken into pieces

125 ml/4 fl oz golden syrup

4 tablespoons single cream

15 g/ 1/2 oz butter

1 In bowl over saucepan of gently simmering water, melt pieces of chocolate with golden syrup, stirring. Remove bowl from pan; stir in remaining ingredients.

2 Serve warm over profiteroles or ice cream.

CHOCOLATE RUM SAUCE

120 g/4 oz plain chocolate, broken into pieces

3 tablespoons caster sugar

30 g/1 oz butter

1 tablespoon rum

1 In non-stick saucepan over medium heat, bring *5 tablespoons water* to the boil with all the other ingredients, stirring. Reduce heat to medium-low; simmer, stirring, until mixture thickens and is smooth, about 3 minutes. Remove from heat; stir in rum.

2 Serve warm over bananas, ice cream or poached pears.

CHOCOLATE MARSHMALLOW SAUCE

60 g/2 oz plain chocolate, broken into pieces

100 g/3 1/2 oz marshmallows, cut into small pieces

5 tablespoons double or whipping cream

5 tablespoons honey

1 In non-stick saucepan over low heat, cook chocolate, marshmallows, cream and honey, stirring, until both chocolate and marshmallows have melted.

2 Serve hot over bananas or ice cream.

CREAM AND CUSTARD SAUCES

CHANTILLY CREAM

300 ml/ 1/2 pint double or whipping cream

1-2 tablespoons caster sugar

1/2 teaspoon vanilla essence

1 In bowl, with whisk, rotary beater or electric mixer, whip cream with sugar and vanilla essence until soft peaks form. (Over-whipping causes cream to curdle and turn to butter.)

2 On hot days, chill bowl and beaters. Serve cream on fruit or nut pies or ice cream sundaes.

Brandy Chantilly Cream
Whip cream with sugar as above until soft peaks form; fold in *2 tablespoons brandy*.

Chocolate Chantilly Cream
Place *2 tablespoons drinking chocolate powder* (or 2 table-spoons caster sugar and 2 tablespoons cocoa powder) in bowl; add 300 ml/ 1/2 pint double or whipping cream. Whip as above.

Coffee Chantilly Cream
Place *2 teaspoons instant coffee powder* and 2 tablespoons caster sugar in bowl; add 300 ml/ 1/2 pint double or whipping cream. Whip as above.

CUSTARD SAUCE

3 tablespoons caster sugar

450 ml/ 3/4 pint milk

1 egg yolk

1 tablespoon cornflour

1/2 teaspoon vanilla essence

1 In heavy non-stick saucepan, combine all ingredients except vanilla essence. Cook over medium heat, stirring, until mixture coats back of spoon well, about 15 minutes (do not boil or custard will curdle).

2 Remove from heat; stir in vanilla essence. Chill. Serve with fruit pies and crumbles, fruit tarts and flans and poached or stewed fruit.

EGG CUSTARD SAUCE

4 egg yolks

5 tablespoons caster sugar

450 ml/³/4 pint milk

1 teaspoon vanilla essence

1 In heavy non-stick saucepan over low heat, or in double boiler over hot, not boiling, water, with wire whisk, stir egg yolks and sugar.

2 Gradually add milk and cook, stirring, until mixture thickens and coats back of spoon well, about 25 minutes (do not boil or custard will curdle). Stir in vanilla essence. Serve warm or cold with apple or other fruit pies, or with poached or stewed fruit.

SUGAR SAUCES

BUTTERSCOTCH SAUCE

225 g/8 oz light soft brown sugar

125 ml/4 fl oz single cream

30 g/1 oz butter

2 tablespoons golden syrup

1 In non-stick saucepan over medium heat, heat brown sugar, single cream, butter and golden syrup just to boiling point, stirring occasionally.

2 Serve warm over vanilla or rum and raisin ice cream, or with baked custard.

HOT FUDGE SAUCE

300 g/10 oz caster sugar

125 ml/4 fl oz milk

5 tablespoons golden syrup

60 g/2 oz plain chocolate, broken into pieces

15 g/¹/2 oz butter

1 teaspoon vanilla essence

1 In non-stick saucepan over medium heat, bring first 4 ingredients to the boil, stirring constantly. Set sugar thermometer in place and continue boiling, stirring occasionally, until temperature reaches 109°C/228°F or until small amount of mixture dropped from tip of spoon back into mixture spins 5 mm/¹/4 inch thread.

2 Remove from heat; stir in butter and vanilla essence. Serve hot over vanilla ice cream or poached pears.

CARAMEL SAUCE

30 g/1 oz butter

2 tablespoons plain flour

450 ml/³/4 pint single cream

165 g/5 ¹/2 oz light soft brown sugar

150 g/5 oz caster sugar

1 In medium saucepan over medium heat, melt butter; stir in flour.

2 Gradually stir in cream; cook, stirring constantly, until mixture thickens.

3 Stir in brown and caster sugars. Serve warm or cover and refrigerate to serve cold; serve over baked bananas or apples, or vanilla or chocolate ice cream.

PRALINE SAUCE

225 g/8 oz light soft brown sugar

125 ml/4 fl oz golden syrup

15 g/¹/2 oz butter

60 g/2 oz shelled pecan or walnut pieces, finely chopped

1 In small saucepan over medium heat, stir all ingredients, except nuts, with 2 tablespoons water until sugar dissolves. Stir in nuts.

2 Serve hot over rice pudding, ice cream or waffles.

BRANDY BUTTER

120 g/4 oz icing sugar, sifted

90 g/3 oz butter, softened

2 tablespoons brandy

1 In medium bowl, with electric mixer, beat icing sugar with butter until creamy; beat in brandy.

2 Spoon into small bowl and refrigerate if not serving immediately. Serve with hot mince pies or Christmas pudding.

Deluxe Brandy Butter
Prepare as above; fold in 4 tablespoons double or whipping cream, whipped, after brandy.

Rum Butter
Prepare as for Brandy Butter, but using rum instead of brandy.

FRUIT SAUCES

BLACKBERRY SAUCE

600 g/1 ¼ lb fresh or frozen blackberries

120 g/4 oz caster sugar

2 tablespoons lemon juice

1 In medium saucepan over medium heat, heat berries, sugar and lemon juice, stirring occasionally, until hot and bubbly. Work through sieve. Cover; chill.

2 Serve over ice cream and other fruits.

CHERRY SAUCE

450 g/1 lb cherries, stoned

4 tablespoons caster sugar

1 In medium saucepan over medium heat, in *150 ml/¼ pint water*, bring cherries to the boil.

2 Reduce heat to low; cover pan and simmer cherries for about 5 minutes or until tender.

3 During last minute of cooking, add sugar. Serve hot, poured over pancakes; or serve cold over ice cream or creamy puddings.

PEACH SAUCE

1 x 400 g/14 oz can peaches in natural juice

¼ teaspoon almond essence

1 In food processor or blender, blend ingredients together until smooth.

2 Serve over ice cream.

RASPBERRY SAUCE

300 g/10 oz raspberries

1 tablespoon caster sugar

1 In food processor or blender, blend raspberries and sugar until smooth, adding *a little water* if needed to thin sauce.

2 Press sauce through fine sieve with wooden spoon to remove pips. Serve with peaches or strawberries, or over ice cream.

COMPOTE SAUCE

3 large nectarines

3 large plums

125 ml/4 fl oz orange juice

100 g/3 ½ oz caster sugar

2 tablespoons brandy

1 Cut fruit into wedges, discarding stones.

2 In medium saucepan over low heat, cook fruit and juice for 10 minutes or until tender, stirring occasionally. Remove from heat.

3 Add sugar and brandy; stir until sugar is dissolved. Serve over vanilla ice cream.

MAPLE AND ORANGE SAUCE

1 x 325 g/11 oz can mandarin orange segments, drained and chopped

175 ml/6 fl oz maple syrup

30 g/1 oz butter

1 In medium saucepan over low heat, heat all ingredients until hot and butter melts.

2 Serve warm over pancakes, French toast or ice cream sundaes.

MELBA SAUCE

75 g/2 ½ oz redcurrant jelly

300 g/10 oz raspberries

30 g/1 oz icing sugar, sifted

Juice of 1 lemon

1 In small saucepan over low heat, heat redcurrant jelly until melted.

2 In food processor, blend raspberries, melted redcurrant jelly, icing sugar and lemon juice until smooth. Press through sieve.

3 Serve over ice cream or poached peaches or pears.

ORANGE SAUCE

60 g/2 oz butter

175 g/6 oz icing sugar, sifted

5 tablespoons orange juice

2 tablespoons grated orange zest

1 In small saucepan over low heat, melt butter. Stir in icing sugar, orange juice and orange zest.

2 Cook over low heat, stirring frequently, until heated through. Serve over pancakes.

CAKES

The cake recipes in this book generally follow one of two basic methods. Most contain butter or soft margarine and are mixed and beaten in one bowl. Others, such as sponges, roulades and angel cakes, have beaten egg whites folded in at the end to give them a light and fluffy texture. Whichever type you bake, if you follow the directions given here you can be assured of success every time.

Before you start, read the recipe carefully and assemble all ingredients and equipment. Prepare tins, put oven racks in correct position, and preheat oven if necessary.

BEFORE YOU START

INGREDIENTS
In the recipes in this book size 3 eggs are used. Don't be tempted to substitute different ingredients for the ones given in the recipe; they will give different results.

MEASURING
Weigh and measure dry and liquid ingredients carefully. Spoon measures used in the recipes are metric spoons (1 tablespoon = 15 ml and 1 teaspoon = 5 ml). All spoon measures of dry ingredients are level.

TINS
Use shiny metal tins or tins with non-stick finish. Avoid old-fashioned tins with insulated bases. If using glass or porcelain-coated aluminium tins with a non-stick finish, reduce oven temperature by 10°C/25°F. Cake tins are available in round, square or rectangular shapes. Be sure your tins are the size and shape called for in the recipe. Measure the top inside of a tin for length, width or diameter; measure perpendicular inside for depth. Prepare tins according to recipe instructions (see How to Grease and Line Tins, page 248).

Springform tin: has side section which can be removed without disturbing contents

Angel cake or tube tin: has centre tube; may or may not have removable bottom

Swiss roll tin: shallow rectangular tin, usually 2.5 cm/1 inch deep

German Bundt or kugelhopf mould: fluted, with centre tube; for elegant cakes and desserts

STORING AND FREEZING CAKES

Storing
Sandwich cakes and ring cakes filled and/or iced with butter cream or glacé icing should be kept under an inverted bowl or tin to protect icing; store cakes filled and/or iced with butter cream in a cool place or the refrigerator, to prevent butter from becoming rancid.

Cakes covered with whipped cream or soft cheese icing, or those that have any sort of cream filling, should be kept refrigerated and are best eaten within 1-2 days.

Wrap rich fruit cakes closely and store in airtight containers in cool place; they will improve with storage. For very rich cakes, before storing, sprinkle cake with wine or brandy, or wrap in wine- or brandy-dampened cloth, then overwrap and store in airtight container for up to 2 months. Re-dampen cloth weekly with more wine or brandy, if you like. Ice or decorate cake just before serving.

Freezing
Cakes in the freezer make wonderful standby desserts. For freezer storage, all cakes must be wrapped or packaged in materials specifically designed for freezer use. Wrapping materials for foods must be moisture-proof: use heavy-duty freezer foil, freezer paper or freezer wrap. Secure packages with freezer or masking tape. Use waterproof felt-tip pens or markers for writing on labels, freezer tape or freezer paper.

Un-iced cakes should be closely wrapped in freezer paper, freezer wrap or foil, and securely sealed with tape.

Most cakes will keep in the freezer for 4-6 months, fruit cakes for up to 12 months.

Open freeze cakes iced and/or piped with butter cream or whipped cream on tray or sheet of card covered with foil until icing hardens, then place frozen cake in rigid container, seal and return to freezer. Iced cakes can be stored in the freezer for 2-3 months.

Do not freeze cakes which have either jam or fruit fillings; they can become soggy when thawed.

Never freeze uncooked cake mixture or cakes with fillings made with cornflour or flour.

Thaw un-iced cakes and fruit cakes in their freezer wrappings at room temperature. Un-iced cakes take about 1 hour to thaw, fruit cakes, 2-3 hours.

Cakes with butter cream and whipped cream icings should be carefully unpacked before they are thawed and placed on their serving plate so that their decoration will not be spoiled. Thaw in refrigerator for 3-4 hours and keep refrigerated until serving time. Be sure to cover and refrigerate leftovers.

MEASURING TINS

Be sure your tins are the kind and size specified in recipe. Measure top inside for length, width or diameter; measure perpendicular inside for depth.

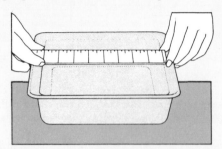

HOW TO GREASE AND LINE TINS

Make sure tins are size called for in recipe, and prepare them before you start mixing cake ingredients. Prepare tins according to instructions in individual recipes.

If tins are to be greased and floured, grease both bottom and sides with softened butter or margarine, using brush, crumpled greaseproof paper or kitchen paper. You can also grease tins with melted butter or margarine using pastry brush to grease evenly. Sprinkle tin with a little flour or, for dark-coloured cakes, with sifted cocoa powder so cake does not have white coating. Shake tin until coated, then invert it and tap to remove excess flour or cocoa. For fruit cakes, grease tins well, line with foil, then grease foil. Some recipes call for bottoms of tins to be lined with baking parchment; grease tin first, then parchment will stick to bottom.

Greasing tin: using brush, crumpled greaseproof paper or kitchen paper, spread tins evenly with melted butter or margarine

Lining tin: where specified, line bottom of greased tin with non-stick baking parchment

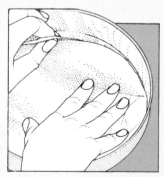

Flouring tin: in some recipes, tins are floured after greasing. Sprinkle with flour and shake and turn tin until evenly coated; knock out surplus

HOW TO BEAT MIXTURE

When preparing cake mixture, beat it with electric mixer for length of time specified in recipe. During beating, scrape bowl frequently with rubber spatula so that all cake ingredients are well mixed together. If you use a wooden spoon instead of mixer, you will need to give ingredients a very good beating until mixture is smooth and ingredients are blended thoroughly. Before adding large fruits and nuts to mixture, toss them in about 1 tablespoon of the measured flour, so that they do not sink in mixture.

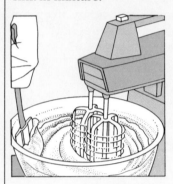

To beat mixture: beat with electric mixer for specified time, constantly scraping sides of bowl with rubber spatula to make sure ingredients are well mixed in

HOW TO FOLD IN

For cakes made with egg whites, beat egg whites into stiff peaks in bowl. In separate bowl, beat remaining ingredients according to recipe instructions. Using rubber spatula, gently fold egg whites into beaten mixture, cutting down through centre, across bottom and up side of bowl. Give bowl a quarter turn and repeat until mixture is uniformly blended, but do not overfold or egg whites will break down.

To fold mixture: use rubber spatula to fold egg whites into beaten ingredients

FILLING TINS

Pour mixture into prepared tin and tap tin sharply on work surface or cut through it several times with rubber spatula or knife to break any large air bubbles. Spread evenly with spatula.

For mixtures containing beaten egg white, push mixture into tin with rubber spatula. Smooth and level it very lightly, then cut through it with rubber spatula to break any large air bubbles.

To fill tin: with rubber spatula, push mixture into tin, then smooth and level it very lightly

BASIC SANDWICH CAKE RECIPES

The cake recipes on this page provide a good basis for making a variety of different desserts at short notice. Sandwiched together with jam, lemon curd or fresh fruit and whipped cream – nothing could be more simple. The ingredients are carefully balanced, so follow instructions exactly for successful results every time.

VICTORIA SANDWICH

Made by the all-in-one method, this cake is a great stand-by for quick-and-easy desserts and party cakes.

175 g/6 oz soft margarine	**1** Preheat oven to 180°C/350°F/gas 4.
175 g/ 6 oz caster sugar	**2** Grease bottoms of two 18 cm/7 inch straight-sided sandwich tins; line with non-stick baking parchment.
3 eggs, beaten	
175 g/ 6 oz self-raising flour	
1 rounded teaspoon baking powder	**3** In large bowl, beat margarine, sugar, eggs, flour and baking powder for about 2 minutes or until mixture is smooth and all ingredients are thoroughly blended.

4 Divide mixture evenly between prepared tins and smooth tops. Bake for 25-30 minutes or until cake is pale golden and centre springs back when lightly pressed with finger.

5 Turn cakes out on to wire rack. Carefully peel off baking parchment; leave cakes to cool.

Orange or Lemon Sandwich
To creamed mixture, add *finely grated zest of 1 orange or lemon.*

Chocolate Sandwich
In large bowl, blend *1 rounded tablespoon cocoa powder* with *2 tablespoons hot water.* Cool; add remaining cake ingredients and proceed as above.

Coffee Sandwich
Dissolve *1 heaped teaspoon instant coffee powder* in beaten eggs before adding to mixture.

WHISKED SPONGE

4 eggs	**1** Preheat oven to 190°C/375°F/gas 5. Grease bottoms of two 20 cm/8 inch straight-sided sandwich tins; line with non-stick baking parchment.
120 g/4 oz caster sugar	
120 g/4 oz self-raising flour	

2 Put eggs and sugar in large bowl; beat with electric mixer until mixture is thick, white and creamy and leaves a thick ribbon trail. Sift in flour; carefully fold in with large metal spoon.

3 Divide mixture between tins. Bake for 20 minutes or until centres spring back when lightly pressed. Turn cakes out on to wire rack. Peel off parchment; leave cakes to cool.

CHOCOLATE CAKE

2 eggs	**1** Preheat oven to 170°C/325°F/gas 3. Grease bottoms of two 20 cm/8 inch straight-sided sandwich tins; line with non-stick baking parchment.
150 ml/ 1/4 pint sunflower oil	
150 ml/ 1/4 pint milk	
2 tablespoons golden syrup	**2** Break eggs into large bowl; add all other ingredients. Beat well for about 2 minutes or until mixture is smooth and all ingredients are thoroughly blended.
150 g/5 oz caster sugar	
190 g/6 1/2 oz self-raising flour	
30 g/1 oz cocoa powder, sifted	**3** Divide mixture between tins. Bake for 30-35 minutes or until cakes shrink away slightly from sides of tins and wooden cocktail stick inserted in centres comes out clean.
1 teaspoon baking powder	
1 teaspoon bicarbonate of soda	

4 Turn cakes out on to wire rack; cool, then peel off parchment.

When using electric mixer, occasionally scrape side of bowl with rubber spatula

To test if cake is done, insert wooden cocktail stick in centre – it should come out clean

ICINGS AND FROSTINGS

Most uncooked icings such as butter cream can be made in advance and stored until needed in a tightly covered container to prevent a crust forming on top. If they are refrigerated and become too firm to spread easily, leave them to stand at room temperature, or stir well to soften to spreading consistency.

Allow your cake to cool completely before icing or filling. Trim off any crisp edges with knife or kitchen scissors and brush away all loose crumbs. Keep cake plate clean by covering edges with strips of greaseproof paper. Lay cake on paper strips, placing it in centre of plate. After icing cake, carefully slide out paper strips. Cakes iced with soft cheese, soured cream or whipped cream icings should be refrigerated until served.

Recipes on this and the following page make enough to ice a 33 x 23 cm/13 x 9 inch cake or fill and ice a 20-23 cm/8-9 inch sandwich cake.

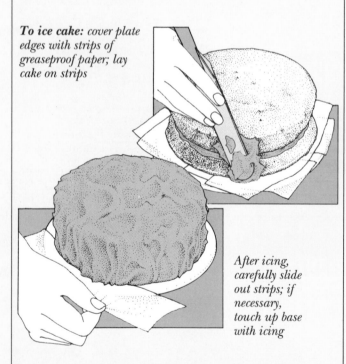

To ice cake: cover plate edges with strips of greaseproof paper; lay cake on strips

After icing, carefully slide out strips; if necessary, touch up base with icing

WHIPPED CREAM 'ICING'

450 ml/ ³/4 pint double or whipping cream	In small bowl, with whisk or electric mixer, whip double or whipping cream with sugar until stiff peaks form; fold in vanilla essence, if you like. Keep iced cake refrigerated until ready to serve.
30 g/1 oz icing sugar, sifted	
1 teaspoon vanilla essence (optional)	

TECHNIQUES

Sandwich cake
Place one layer of cake, top side down, on serving plate. Cover this layer with either filling or icing, spreading it almost to edge. If filling is soft, spread it only to within 2.5 cm/1 inch of edge. Place second cake layer, top side up, on filling, so that flat bases of two layers face each other, keeping top layer from cracking or sliding off. Ice sides of cake thinly to set any loose crumbs, then apply second, more generous layer of icing, swirling it up to make 1 cm/¹/₂ inch ridge above rim of cake. Finally, ice top of cake, swirling icing or leaving it smooth, as you like. Decorate iced cake if desired.

Oblong cake
Ice top and sides of cake as for sandwich cake, or leave cake in tin and just ice top.

Tube or ring cake
Ice sides, then top and inside centre of cake as for sandwich cake.

Cup cakes
Dip top of each cake in icing, turning it slightly to coat evenly.

Glazing
Brush crumbs from top of cake. Spoon or pour glaze on to top of cake, letting it drip down sides. Spread thicker glazes over top and sides of cake with palette knife.

Drizzling
To make decorative pattern, pour thin icing or glaze from spoon, quickly waving spoon back and forth over cake.

Chocolate Whipped Cream 'Icing'
Prepare as left; fold in *2 tablespoons drinking chocolate powder*, instead of vanilla essence.

Coffee Whipped Cream 'Icing'
Prepare as left; add *1 teaspoon instant coffee powder* with sugar and omit vanilla essence.

Orange Whipped Cream 'Icing'
Prepare as left; add *1 teaspoon grated orange zest* and *¹/₂ teaspoon orange flower water* instead of vanilla essence.

Peppermint Whipped Cream 'Icing'
Whip cream as left; fold in *4 tablespoons crushed peppermints* or *seaside rock* and omit vanilla essence.

BUTTER CREAM

450 g/1 lb icing sugar, sifted	In large bowl, with electric mixer (or spoon), beat icing sugar and butter until smooth, adding a little milk if necessary until butter cream is smooth with an easy spreading consistency.
300 g/10 oz butter, softened	
A little milk	

Lemon Butter Cream
Prepare as for Butter Cream, but substitute *lemon juice* for milk.

Mocha Butter Cream
Prepare as for Butter Cream, but add *45 g/1½ oz cocoa powder*; substitute *cold black coffee* for milk.

CHOCOLATE SOURED CREAM ICING

175 g/6 oz plain chocolate, broken into pieces	**1** In bowl over saucepan of gently simmering water, heat chocolate and butter until melted and smooth, stirring occasionally. Remove bowl from pan.
15 g/½ oz butter	
150 ml/¼ pint soured cream	**2** In medium bowl, with electric mixer, beat melted chocolate mixture, soured cream and icing sugar until smooth.
30 g/1 oz icing sugar, sifted	

SOFT CHEESE ICING

175 g/6 oz full-fat soft cheese, softened	**1** In small bowl, with electric mixer, beat soft cheese and milk just until smooth.
2 tablespoons milk	
225 g/8 oz icing sugar, sifted	**2** Beat in icing sugar and vanilla essence until blended.
1½ teaspoons vanilla essence	

Coffee Soft Cheese Icing
Prepare as for Soft Cheese Icing, but add *4 teaspoons instant coffee powder* with icing sugar; omit vanilla essence.

COFFEE FUDGE ICING

90 g/3 oz butter	**1** In medium bowl, put butter, sifted icing sugar, milk and coffee essence.
225 g/8 oz icing sugar, sifted	
1 tablespoon milk	**2** With electric mixer or spoon, beat ingredients until smooth and with an easy spreading consistency.
1 tablespoon coffee essence	
60 g/2 oz walnut pieces, pecans or hazelnuts, finely chopped	**3** To icing, add finely chopped walnuts, pecans or hazelnuts; fold in until evenly distributed.
Walnut or pecan halves, or shelled whole hazelnuts for decoration	**4** After spreading icing on cake, immediately press walnut or pecan halves or shelled whole hazelnuts into icing, around edge of cake or in attractive design over top. Leave to set before serving cake.

DARK CHOCOLATE ICING

175 g/6 oz plain chocolate, broken into pieces	**1** In heavy non-stick saucepan over low heat, or in double boiler over hot, not boiling, water, heat chocolate and butter until melted and completely smooth, stirring occasionally. Remove from heat.
30 g/1 oz butter	
2 tablespoons golden syrup	**2** With wire whisk or fork, beat in golden syrup and milk until mixture is smooth. Spread while icing is still warm.
3 tablespoons milk	

MOCHA ICING

350 g/12 oz icing sugar	**1** Into large bowl, sift icing sugar, cocoa and coffee powders; stir well to mix.
4 tablespoons cocoa powder	
1 teaspoon instant coffee powder	**2** Gradually add *about 3 table-spoons warm water*, mixing until icing has a coating consistency; stir in vanilla essence.
1½ teaspoons vanilla essence	

CHOCOLATE ICING

350 g/12 oz icing sugar	**1** Into large bowl, sift icing sugar and cocoa powder.
2 tablespoons cocoa powder	**2** Gradually add *about 3 table-spoons warm water*, mixing until icing has a coating consistency.

GLAZES

These recipes make enough for a 33 x 23 cm/ 13 x 9 inch or a 20-23 cm/8-9 inch round cake.

LEMON GLAZE

175 g/ 6 oz caster sugar
Juice of 1 1/2 lemons

1 In bowl, mix sugar and lemon juice until sugar dissolves.

2 With back of spoon, spread glaze over warm plain cake. Heat of cake causes lemon juice to run, giving cake a lovely lemon flavour and making it moist; sugar remains on top as a shiny crust.

RICH CHOCOLATE GLAZE

275 g/9 oz plain chocolate, broken into pieces
2 tablespoons icing sugar, sifted
3 tablespoons orange liquer
3 tablespoons milk
1 teaspoon instant coffee powder

1 In bowl over saucepan of gently simmering water, heat all ingredients until chocolate melts and mixture is smooth, stirring constantly.

2 Remove bowl from pan. Leave glaze to stand at room temperature to cool slightly until of spreading consistency, then spread while still warm.

Spreading chocolate glaze over cake: *stand cake on wire rack over sheet of greaseproof paper; spread glaze over top and sides with palette knife, letting excess glaze drip on to paper*

DECORATIVE TOUCHES

It is easy to add decorative touches to cakes that are covered in icing. To make spiral patterns below left, place cake on a turntable if you have one.

 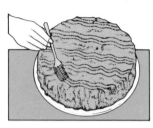

Press tip of palette knife into centre – turn cake, slowly moving knife outwards

Draw prongs of fork across icing in parallel rows; repeat rows at right angles

GLACÉ ICINGS

You only need a very small amount of glacé icing to make a plain cake look special.

GLACÉ ICING

60 g/2 oz icing sugar
Food colouring (optional)

1 Into bowl, sift icing sugar.

2 Gradually add about 1 1/2 teaspoons warm water, beating vigorously until icing reaches a coating consistency. Beat in a few drops of food colouring, if you like.

Coffee Glacé Icing
Prepare as for Glacé Icing, but substitute *1 teaspoon coffee essence* for the same amount of water.

Lemon Glacé Icing
Prepare as for Glacé Icing, but substitute *lemon juice* for water; use *yellow food colouring,* if you like.

Liqueur Glacé Icing
Prepare as for Glacé Icing, but use *liqueur of your choice* instead of water.

Orange Glacé Icing
Prepare as for Glacé Icing, but substitute *orange juice* for water; use *orange food colouring,* if you like.

TOPPINGS

Each of the following recipes makes enough to spread on top of a 33 x 23 cm/13 x 9 inch cake.

NUTTY FUDGE TOPPING

250 ml/8 fl oz double or whipping cream	1 In non-stick saucepan over medium-high heat, bring first 5 ingredients to the boil, stirring constantly.
100 g/3 1/2 oz caster sugar	
30 g/1 oz butter	2 Reduce heat to medium and cook for 5 minutes, stirring constantly. Remove pan from heat. Cool slightly, about 10 minutes, then stir in nuts.
1 tablespoon golden syrup	
120 g/4 oz plain chocolate, broken into pieces	3 Quickly pour topping evenly over cake, allowing some to run down sides. Refrigerate until topping is firm, about 1 hour.
200 g/7 oz shelled nuts, finely chopped	

PRALINE AND COCONUT TOPPING

120 g/4 oz butter	1 Start to prepare topping about 10 minutes before end of cake's baking time. In medium saucepan over low heat, melt butter.
100 g/3 1/2 oz desiccated coconut	
90 g/3 oz shelled nuts, finely chopped	2 Stir in coconut, chopped nuts and sugar. Remove saucepan from heat.
165 g/5 1/2 oz soft brown sugar	3 When cake is done, spread coconut mixture over hot cake. Grill cake for 2 minutes or until golden.

CRACKED CARAMEL

60 g/2 oz sugar	1 In small heavy saucepan over medium heat, heat sugar until melted and a light brown colour (about 6 minutes), stirring constantly.
	2 Immediately pour caramel on to greased baking sheet; cool.
	3 With rolling pin, crack caramel. If not using immediately, store in tightly covered container.

FILLINGS

Each of the following recipes makes enough filling for a 20-23 cm/8-9 inch sandwich cake.

ALMOND FILLING

120 g/4 oz blanched almonds, toasted	1 In food processor, finely grind toasted almonds.
120 g/4 oz icing sugar, sifted	2 In bowl, mix ground almonds with remaining ingredients until evenly blended, adding enough orange juice or liqueur to reach an easy spreading consistency.
60 g/2 oz butter, softened	
About 2 tablespoons orange juice or orange liqueur	

VANILLA CUSTARD FILLING

450 ml/ 3/4 pint milk	1 In non-stick saucepan, stir together all ingredients except vanilla essence.
50 g/1 2/3 oz caster sugar	
25 g/ 3/4 oz cornflour	2 Over medium-low heat, cook until mixture thickens and coats back of spoon well, about 20 minutes (do not boil or mixture will curdle). Stir in vanilla essence. Cool, then chill for 30 minutes.
2 egg yolks	
1 teaspoon vanilla essence	

FRESH LEMON FILLING

1 tablespoon grated lemon zest	1 In small saucepan over medium heat, stir all ingredients except butter with *125 ml/4 fl oz water* until well blended. Cook until mixture thickens and boils, stirring.
4 tablespoons lemon juice	
50 g/1 2/3 oz caster sugar	
4 teaspoons cornflour	2 Reduce heat; simmer for 1 minute, stirring occasionally. Remove from heat; stir in butter. Allow mixture to cool at room temperature.
15 g/ 1/2 oz butter	

Fresh Orange Filling
Prepare as for Fresh Lemon Filling, but substitute *orange zest and juice* for lemon zest and juice.

PASTRY-MAKING

You can make your own 'designer' pies, tarts and flans with the recipes and ideas on these pages. Pick a pastry to make the crust for any type of pie, whether served hot or cold; or choose a crumb crust to hold chilled fillings prepared separately. (An unbaked crumb crust, incidentally, is the quickest pie shell you can make.) The basic pastries for sweet pies are on pages 134-135; for tarts, flans and tartlets on page 159. These can be filled with fruit, custard, ice cream or mousse and then given the decorative touches – edges, tops, decorations, arrangements – that make a pie, tart or flan your very own creation. If you take a short cut and use bought frozen pastry, follow the same techniques for rolling and using the dough in double or single crust pies and tarts and flans.

EQUIPMENT

Using the right utensils can help make pastry-making easy and quick. Here are some of the most useful items. The pastry blender is a very clever invention, available at most good kitchenware shops; it is an excellent tool for cutting fat into flour.

Rolling pin: *choose the widest possible pin for easy rolling out of dough*

Pastry scraper: *use for scraping off any dough that sticks to work surface*

Pastry wheel: *straight or ripple-edged wheel with handle, which speeds cutting of pastry dough*

Pastry blender: *for cutting fats evenly into dry ingredients*

Pastry brush: *for brushing on egg and milk glazes, or jam glaze on fruit flans*

PASTRY-MAKING TECHNIQUES

ROLLING OUT DOUGH

Dough should be rolled with floured rolling pin on lightly floured surface. Slightly flatten ball of dough and roll it out, moving from centre to edge, keeping it circular. Push sides in occasionally by hand, if necessary, and lift rolling pin slightly as you near edge to avoid making dough too thin. Lift dough occasionally to ensure that it is not sticking. If it does stick, loosen it with pastry scraper and sprinkle more flour on surface underneath. Mend any cracks in dough as they appear, patching with dough cut from edge. Moisten torn edges, lay patch over tear and press it into position.

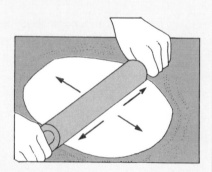

Rolling out dough: roll dough from centre to edge, keeping it circular. Push sides in occasionally by hand, if necessary, and lift rolling pin slightly as you near edge to avoid making dough too thin

LINING PIE DISHES AND TINS

If you are making a double crust pie, divide dough into 2 pieces, 1 slightly larger than the other. Use larger piece for lining pie dish or tin.

Roll out dough into round about 3 mm/$\frac{1}{8}$ inch thick and 4 cm/1 $\frac{1}{2}$ inches larger all round than upside-down pie dish or tin. Roll dough loosely round rolling pin and lift on to dish. Unroll and ease into dish, pressing on to bottom and up side with fingertips. Do not stretch dough; it will shrink back while baking. Make Decorative Pastry Edge (pages 136-137) and fill pie, or make top crust if it is a double crust pie.

PIE DISHES

Be sure your pie dish or tin is size specified in recipe. To check size, if it has not been marked on pie dish or tin by manufacturer, use a ruler to measure dish or tin from inside edge to inside edge.

Pie dishes of the same diameter may differ in capacity; the recipes in this book are for shallow pie dishes.

For nicely browned pastry top and bottom, use metal such as anodized aluminium, tin or enamel pie dishes and tins.

Don't grease pie dishes or tins unless recipe says to do so. Most pastry contains enough fat to keep it from sticking to pie dish or tin.

BAKING BLIND

A pie, tart or flan shell may be baked blind, that is, baked first without a filling. If it is to be filled with a very juicy filling, it should not be pricked with a fork before baking. Instead, after lining the pie dish or tin with dough and making a decorative edge, cut a sheet of foil and place it in the pie shell, pressing it gently on to the bottom and side. Then, according to recipe instructions, half fill the foil-lined shell with dried or baking beans or uncooked rice. Bake in preheated 220°C/425°F/gas 7 oven for 10 minutes; carefully remove foil, with beans or rice if used, and continue baking pie shell until golden. Cool pie shell completely before filling. Dried and baking beans and rice can be stored, after cooling, in covered container and used time and again for baking blind; do not use in cooking.

Half filling foil liner with dried beans for baking blind

A BAKING PRECAUTION

Sometimes, despite the cook's best efforts, juices from very ripe fruit will bubble over the rim of the pie dish on to the oven floor. If you are using very juicy fruit and suspect that this might happen, tear off a 30 cm/12 inch square of foil and turn the edges up 1 cm/½ inch on all sides; place on another oven rack directly below the pie to catch any dripping juices, and bake the pie as directed. Even if the pie does bubble over, the foil should catch all the drips and save on oven cleaning.

GLAZING AND BAKING

For a golden glaze, brush top crust (not edge) with milk, undiluted evaporated milk, or lightly beaten egg white; sprinkle crust with sugar, if you like. If pie crust edges begin to brown too much during baking, cover them with strips of foil to prevent burning. If top crust seems to be browning too much, cover pie loosely with foil for the last 15 minutes of baking time.

Covering pie crust edges with strips of foil to prevent burning

FREEZING PASTRY

Uncooked Pastry Dough
Roll out pastry dough into rounds 4 cm/1 ½ inches larger all round than upside-down pie dishes or tins, stack with 2 sheets of greaseproof paper between each, wrap and freeze. Use within 2-3 months.

To use, place round of dough on pie dish or tin; thaw for 10-15 minutes before shaping.

Pie Crusts
Freeze baked or unbaked shells in their dishes or tins, or in reusable foil pie tins. Store baked shells for 4-6 months; thaw, unwrapped, at room temperature for 15 minutes. Store unbaked shells for 2-3 months.

To use, prick unfilled shells well with fork and bake, without thawing, for about 20 minutes in preheated 220°C/425°F/gas 7 oven; or fill and bake as instructed in individual recipes.

Fruit Pies and Tarts
Freeze baked or unbaked fruit pies for 2-3 months. To freeze unbaked fruit pies, if fruit is very juicy, add 1-2 tablespoons extra flour or cornflour to filling. Do not cut slits in top crust. Wrap and freeze. Or, if pie is fragile, first open freeze until firm, then cover top with paper plate for protection, wrap and return to freezer.

To cook unbaked fruit pie, unwrap, cut slits in top crust and bake in preheated oven from frozen, allowing 15-20 minutes additional baking time or until fruit is hot and bubbling.

Thaw baked pies, unwrapped, at room temperature for about 30 minutes, then bake in preheated 180°C/350°F/gas 4 oven for 30 minutes or until warm.

Frozen Fillings
Pies with ice cream or frozen fillings will not only be easier to cut when serving, but also have more flavour, if they are allowed to stand at room temperature for about 15 minutes after removal from freezer. Unwrap them first so that any decoration will not be spoiled.

STORING PASTRY

Most fruit pies and flans can be kept at room temperature overnight, even in warm weather, covered with foil once cold. For longer storage (2 or 3 days), refrigerate; then freshen by warming them in oven.

Pies and tarts with cream, custard, whipped cream or soft cheese filling or fillings set with gelatine should be refrigerated and used within a day or so.

Balls of unbaked pastry dough may be wrapped in either greaseproof paper or foil, and stored in the refrigerator for a day or two.

HINTS AND TIPS

Here you'll find some do's and don'ts of good cooking, selected to help you make the recipes in this book with the least time and effort, and the greatest of ease. One very important rule should be observed with every single recipe: before you start to cook, read the recipe through to make sure you understand the instructions; then assemble ingredients and equipment to make sure you have everything you need.

Finally, treat your book as a 'working manual'; keep a pencil at the side and if you find a cake takes 20 minutes to cook in your oven rather than the recommended 30 minutes, jot this down by the recipe, together with any other useful comments – for example, which dish you used, whether you added pecans rather than walnuts, and so on.

GENERAL HINTS

• When recipe calls for butter or margarine, it refers to solid, block form. When cake recipe calls for soft margarine, use the soft tub variety (it has air beaten in). Don't use low-fat margarines and vegetable oil spreads, which contain more water and less fat; they may give different results.

• Brown sugar stored in freezer will be soft and usable when thawed. If brown sugar sticks together in lumps, soften in the microwave for a short time.

• When softened butter or margarine is needed in a hurry, cut the amount called for into small pieces; it will soften more quickly at room temperature than a large piece.

• Dry ingredients – flour, sugar, baking powder, bicarbonate of soda – should be kept in airtight containers in a cool, dry place.

• To cut sticky foods like candied peel, glacé cherries or dates, keep dipping knife or scissors in flour.

• When measuring ingredients to add to those already in mixing bowl, never hold a measuring spoon over the bowl. One slip of the hand and the recipe could be ruined by too much vanilla essence, baking powder or whatever.

• Place a folded damp tea towel or dish cloth under bowl when mixing by hand or folding ingredients into a mixture; bowl won't slip while mixing.

• To determine volume of mould, simply measure amount of water it takes to fill it to the brim.

• Use the right knife and cutting techniques, and slices will be perfect when you cut cakes and desserts.
For sandwich and layer cakes, use a well-sharpened chef's knife.
For meringue desserts and Swiss rolls, use a knife with a thin, sharp blade and wipe it with a damp cloth or kitchen paper after every cut.
Before cutting cheesecakes, mousse cakes and other 'sticky' desserts, dip knife blade in very hot water and dry quickly with kitchen paper. The heated blade will cut through without sticking.
In all cases, use a sawing motion and a light touch to avoid crushing the cake or dessert out of shape.

• If you have leftover whipped cream, pipe it or drop it by heaping spoonfuls on to a baking sheet and freeze. When cream is firm, loosen with a palette knife and store in polythene bag in freezer. To use, place frozen piped shapes or dollops on top of desserts; they will thaw in just a few minutes.

CUSTARDS AND CREAMS

• Stirring a little hot liquid into beaten eggs heats eggs so they will not curdle when added to more hot liquid.

• Always remove a custard mixture from the heat when checking to see if it is thick enough. Even just a few seconds extra cooking time could be too much.

• If custard is overheating, pour it quickly into cold bowl; whisk vigorously to prevent lumps forming.

• If custard has overheated, try dropping an ice cube into it, to rescue it from curdling.

• If cooked custard needs to cool before other ingredients are added to it, gently press dampened greaseproof paper on to surface of custard. Otherwise, a tough skin may form which will cause dessert to have a lumpy texture.

• A bain-marie helps custards bake evenly because it keeps the temperature constant and moderate, not too hot.

• To avoid spilling hot water when baking in a bain-marie, place filled ramekins or baking dish in large tin and centre tin on partially pulled out oven rack. Fill tin with hot water to come halfway up ramekins or dish, then gently push rack back into oven and bake custards as directed.

FRUIT AND NUTS

• An easy way to core apples and pears is with a melon baller. Just slice fruit in half and scoop out core in one smooth stroke.

• If using frozen raspberries to decorate top of dessert, take them from the freezer, spread them out on kitchen paper and thaw slowly in the refrigerator; they will retain their shape if used the moment they are thawed.

• When recipe calls for lemon or orange zest, that means thin yellow or orange outer layer of peel, not spongy white part (pith), which is bitter. Grate, using sharp grater, just before needed, because zest dries out quickly. Ideally, grate zest from unwaxed lemons and oranges.

• To get maximum amount of juice when squeezing citrus fruits such as oranges, lemons or limes, gently roll fruit on work surface, pressing lightly, before halving and squeezing.

• If you have a microwave oven, use it to help squeeze citrus fruit juice more easily. Place fruit on oven floor and heat on High (100% power) just until fruit feels warm to the touch.

• Store all nuts (whole or shelled) in the freezer for maximum freshness. Wrapped in freezer bags, whole nuts will keep fresh for 3 years; shelled nuts for 1 year; ground nuts for 3 months.

• Whole nuts in their shells are much easier to crack when frozen because they are more brittle.

• Delicate torte or gâteau recipes often call for 'finely ground nuts' to replace some of the flour. For successful results, nuts must be ground very finely, yet be dry and light. Be careful not to process nuts in food processor or blender for too long; if they're thick and pasty, they will be too oily and heavy. If you are grinding the nuts by hand, grind two or three times to achieve correct texture. Packets of 'ground' nuts are not fine enough and must be ground again.

CHOCOLATE

Plain chocolate is made from basic chocolate liquor, cocoa butter and other fats, cocoa powder and sugar. The more chocolate liquor, the darker the chocolate; the more cocoa butter, the richer it will be. Bitter-sweet chocolate contains less sugar.

• *Milk* chocolate contains chocolate liquor, cocoa butter and other fats, cocoa powder, sugar, milk and some-times cream. Because of the relatively low amount of chocolate liquor, milk chocolate cannot be substituted for plain or bittersweet chocolate.

• In recipes, use the best-quality plain dark chocolate you can find because it makes such a difference. Check the label before you buy, and choose the brand with the highest cocoa butter content. Most supermarkets and delicatessens stock good-quality plain chocolate; chocolat pâtissier is one of the best.

• *Plain chocolate flavour cake covering* is less expensive than real chocolate and does not have as fine a flavour. It contains less cocoa butter and more soft vegetable or nut fat. As a result, it is far easier to work with than real chocolate, especially when making chocolate decorations such as curls and caraque.

• *White* chocolate is really not chocolate at all, but a cooked-down mixture of fat, milk and sugar, with various flavourings added. Some white chocolate contains cocoa butter to give it a slight chocolate taste. White chocolate should only be used in recipes that specifically call for it.

• *Cocoa powder* is made from choco-late liquor that has had nearly all cocoa butter removed. *Drinking chocolate powder* contains dried milk, sugar and flavourings; it should not be substituted for cocoa powder in recipes because it is too mild and sweet.

• You can substitute cocoa powder for chocolate as follows:
For each 175 g/6 oz plain choco-late, use 6 tablespoons sifted cocoa powder plus 7 tablespoons caster sugar and 60 g/2 oz white vegetable fat or shortening.

• Store chocolate in cool, dry place. It keeps best if temperature is about 20°C/68°F, but not over 24°C/75°F.

• Chocolate stored in too cold conditions will 'sweat' when brought to room temperature.

• If chocolate is stored in too warm conditions, cocoa butter will start to melt and appear on surface of chocolate as a greyish-white coating. This does not affect flavour, and chocolate will return to its original colour when melted.

• Melting chocolate in the micro-wave oven: place 30 g/1 oz plain chocolate, broken into pieces, in small microwave-safe bowl. Heat on High (100% power) for 1-2 minutes, just until shiny (chocolate will still retain its shape). Remove bowl from the microwave and stir chocolate until melted and smooth.

• Melting chocolate in conventional ways: (1) Place in bowl over sauce-pan of gently simmering water. (2) Place in small dish or heatproof measuring jug and set in pan of hot water. (3) Place in heavy non-stick saucepan; melt over low heat – if pan is too thin, it will transfer heat too fast and burn chocolate. (4) For small amounts, leave chocolate in original foil wrapper; place on piece of foil and set in warm spot on cooker (not on burner).

• If chocolate does stiffen during melting, for each 90 g/3 oz of plain chocolate, start with 1 teaspoon and add up to 15 g/ ½ oz white vegeta-ble fat (not vegetable oil, butter or margarine, which contain moisture), stirring until chocolate liquefies again and becomes smooth.

• Stir chocolate after it has begun to liquefy. If melting more than 450 g/ 1 lb, start with 225 g/8 oz and add remainder in 60 g/2 oz amounts.

• To speed melting, break chocolate into small pieces and stir frequently.

• When adding liquid to melted chocolate, always add at least 2 tablespoons at a time, to avoid chocolate stiffening.

• When making chocolate decora-tions, work with chocolate as soon as it is melted and smooth. When heated too long it can become grainy.

• To avoid breaking chocolate curls, pick them up with cocktail stick.

BAKING

• If recipe says to preheat oven, allow at least 10 minutes for it to reach baking temperature.

• Make sure tins are size called for in recipe and prepare them before you start.

• If cake tins are to be greased with melted butter or margarine, use pastry brush, or crumpled grease-proof paper or kitchen paper. ➤

• Grease fluted tins and moulds very generously, especially the ridges up the side and the central funnel, so cake can be turned out easily. The best way to do this is to brush tin or mould with melted butter or margarine, vegetable oil or shortening.

• If you do not have a springform cake tin, use a tin with a removable base – and vice versa.

• Place tins on oven rack so they do not touch one another, or sides of oven.

• Wait until minimum baking time given in recipe has elapsed before opening oven door; opening it too soon can lower oven temperature and make cake mixtures and doughs fall.

CAKES

• For 3 or 4 cake layers, 2 oven racks are needed, placed so oven is divided into thirds; stagger tins so one is not directly underneath another.

• To line a tin with non-stick baking parchment, place tin on paper and trace round base with tip of small knife. Cut out tracing and place in greased cake tin; it will fit exactly.

• For chocolate cakes, dust bottom and sides of tins with sifted cocoa powder rather than flour – it will not leave white film on cake.

• Be sure to follow timing guide given in each recipe for beating cake mixtures. If not beaten thoroughly, ingredients will not be evenly distributed and cake will fall; if overbeaten, cake may be tough and dry and will not rise properly.

• When beating cake mixture, scrape bowl often with rubber spatula for even mixing.

• When folding in, always fold light, fluffy ingredient into heavier one. Whisking part of beaten egg whites into heavy mixture lightens it and makes it easy to fold in remaining whites without reducing volume.

• For even textured cakes without any large holes, cut through mixture in cake tins with rubber spatula to remove any air bubbles, or gently tap cake tin on work surface just before baking.

• Cakes are done when they shrink away from side of tin and top springs back when pressed with finger.

• After removing cake from oven, leave to cool in tin on wire rack for about 10 minutes before turning out. If cake is cooled completely in tin, it may stick to bottom and side and be hard to remove; however, if cake is removed from tin while it is too hot, it could break.

• When baking powder is called for in a cake recipe, always add the exact amount specified. Do not be overgenerous with baking powder as too much will cause cake to rise up beautifully in the oven and give you a false sense of security – cake will fall either just before it comes out of the oven or immediately after.

ICING AND FILLING

• For sandwich cakes, place first layer, top down, on plate; spread with filling, then place second layer, top up, on first, so flat bases of two layers face each other.

• Spread icing or firm filling to within 1 cm/½ inch of edge of cake, soft filling to 2.5 cm/1 inch of edge – weight of top layer will push it to edge.

• Spread cake with thin layer of icing first, to 'set' crumb, then ice again.

• When filling piping bag, stand narrow end in measuring jug or glass.

• To keep your piping bag sweet smelling, after each use, rinse it in warm water, then include it with a whites wash in the washing machine.

• A sturdy polythene bag makes a good piping bag. Fill, close with twist tie and snip small hole in corner.

FRUIT CAKES

• Line cake tin with foil to make cake easy to remove. Smooth out all creases, so side of cake will be smooth.

• Move oven rack to lower position to ensure whole cake is in middle of oven while baking.

• Mix dried fruit and nuts with a little flour before adding to mixture; this keeps them evenly suspended in mixture and prevents them from sinking to bottom while cake is baking.

• Spoon mixture evenly into tin and pack firmly to eliminate air pockets that will leave holes in baked cake.

• Test fruit cakes with a skewer or wooden cocktail stick inserted in centre; it should come out clean.

• Turn leftover fruit cake into an elegant dessert: slice cake into wine glasses, moisten with fruit juice or sherry and top with whipped cream.

PASTRY

• When making choux pastry dough, flour must be added as soon as liquid boils or water could evaporate and dough would not puff.

• Add flour for choux pastry dough all at once. Beat until smooth and formed into a ball that cleans side of saucepan.

• Pastries made with choux pastry dough should be eaten on the same day they are made, as pastry tends to soften quickly.

• Thaw frozen phyllo in its packet, otherwise it might dry out and crack.

• Once thawed, keep phyllo covered with damp cloth or cling film.

• Brush sheets of phyllo with melted butter – it adds flavour and keeps phyllo pliable so that it can be rolled or folded.

PIES

• What is the key to making good pastry? It is accurate measurement of ingredients, to ensure the correct balance of fat and flour, and not too much liquid. Too much flour makes tough pastry; too much fat results in a greasy, crumbly pastry. Too much liquid will require the excess flour that results in a tough crust.

• Roll out pastry dough on the coldest work surface possible – marble is ideal; granite and ceramic are also good.

• Roll out pastry as evenly as possible so edges are not too thin.

• When rolling out pastry dough, slide a pastry scraper or palette knife under it occasionally to make sure it is not sticking to the work surface. If it sticks, sprinkle work surface with more flour before continuing rolling.

• Never stretch pastry to fit into pie dish or tin; it will just shrink back when baking.

• After making a rope or fluted edge on a pie shell, hook points of pastry under rim of dish or tin so edge will stay in place as it bakes.

• For a shiny top, brush pastry with lightly beaten egg white. For a golden-brown glazed top, brush with beaten egg, egg yolk or milk.

• To help keep oven clean when baking fruit pie, place second oven rack below the one pie is on. Tear off sheet of foil, turn all edges up 1 cm/½ inch and place it on second rack to catch drips. Another way to catch drips from a fruit pie is to stand pie dish in a large roasting tin.

• To prevent soggy pastry in cream pies, try this: as soon as baked pie shell comes out of oven, brush it with lightly beaten egg white, making sure to cover areas pricked with fork. The heat from the hot pie shell will cook the egg white and form a protective seal to help eliminate sogginess after filling.

• If crumb crusts stick to pie dish or tin, set dish or tin on tea towel that has been wrung out in hot water and allow to stand briefly. It should then be easy to remove slices perfectly.

• After preparing your favourite pie, let your children use leftover pastry to make a special treat: get them to roll out dough and cut pretty shapes. While pie bakes, shapes can be browned in the oven at the same time, then spread with jam or sprinkled with cinnamon and sugar.

• When refrigerating a cream-topped pie, place it, uncovered, in a prominent position at the front of the refrigerator – this way everyone will notice it and it will not be knocked accidentally.

BISCUITS

• For a light texture, mix dough gently. Do not overwork dough or biscuits will be tough.

• No space to roll out biscuits? Shape dough into small balls, place 5-7.5 cm/2-3 inches apart on baking sheet and then press flat with bottom of a glass that has been dipped in caster sugar.

• Always start cutting at edge of dough and work towards centre, cutting biscuits as close together as possible to minimize scraps.

• Rehandling toughens biscuits, so press trimmings together – do not knead – before rolling again.

• Transfer fragile biscuits from board to baking sheet with fish slice to preserve shape.

• Always bake biscuits on heavy-duty baking sheets that do not bend or warp in the oven; silicone-coated baking sheets are now widely available, and are excellent for biscuit baking.

• Baking sheets should be at least 5 cm/2 inches smaller all round than your oven, so heat can circulate and biscuits can bake evenly.

• Always place dough on a cool baking sheet. It will spread too much on a hot one.

• Grease baking sheet only if recipe says so; very rich biscuits will spread too much if baked on greased sheets.

• After baking, transfer small biscuits at once from baking sheet to wire rack (they continue to bake on hot sheet).

• Cool biscuit bars completely in tin before turning out.

• Always cool biscuits completely before storing in airtight containers.

• When cutting up a tray of short-bread, cool to lukewarm, then mark into desired shapes and cut through; leave until almost cold before removing from tin. If you forget to mark and cut through, warm short-bread gently in oven again.

• Biscuits that are too hard can be softened by placing a slice of bread in the storage tin; change the slice every other day. A bread slice will also keep soft biscuits soft, just as it softens hardened brown sugar.

ICE CREAM AND FROZEN DESSERTS

• Ice cream, whether bought or home-made, keeps best in freezer at -18°C/0°F or lower.

• Ice cream will keep for 1 month in freezer compartment of refrigerator, or up to 2 months in home freezer.

• Do not re-freeze partially melted ice cream – a coarse, icy texture will result.

• To store open containers of ice cream, press cling film right on to exposed surface to protect ice cream from odours and prevent development of 'skin' or ice crystals.

• Partially frozen mixtures are ready for beating when firm 2.5 cm/1 inch round edge, though centre is still mushy.

INDEX

ACKNOWLEDGEMENTS

Photography   All photography by David Murray
Photographer's Assistant   Jules Selmes

Copy Editor   Norma MacMillan

Assisted by   Sally Poole, Diana Vowles

Typesetting   Rowena Feeny
Text film by   Disc To Print (UK) Limited
Production Consultant   Lorraine Baird
Reproduced by   Colourscan, Singapore

Home Economists
Step-by-steps and finished desserts   Elizabeth Wolf-Cohen
Finished desserts   Maxine Clark, Hilary Foster, Carole Handslip, Kathy Man, Janice Murfitt,
                       Berit Vinegrad, Mandy Wagstaff

Stylist   Angi Lincoln

The companies listed here very   **Arthur Price of England** p. 131 (fork and pie slice); p. 133 (pie slice);
graciously lent tableware   p. 138 (serving spoon); p. 143 (pie slice); p. 144 (napkin rings);
                       p. 154 (forks); p. 163 (napkin rings); p. 168 (pie slice);
                       p. 175 (sugar spoon); p. 181 (silver platter); p. 182 (pie slice);
                       p. 187 (fork); p. 235 (forks)

                       Classical Creamware Limited p. 77 (plate); p. 89 (plates, sugar bowl and shaker);
                       p. 105 (tea set and plate); p. 114 (plate); p. 124 (plate); p. 133 (plate);
                       p. 143 (plate); p. 148 (plate)

                       Dartington Crystal p. 179 (glass bowl)

                       George Butler of Sheffield Limited p. 132 (pie slice); p. 133 (forks); p. 139 (pie slice);
                       p. 141 (pie slice); p. 149 (forks); p. 161 (forks); p. 163 (pie slice and forks);
                       p. 166 (forks); p. 179 (forks); p. 181 (pie slice); p. 191 (pie slice)

                       Guy Degrenne p. 120 (pie slice); p. 157 (pie slice)

                       Josiah Wedgwood & Sons Limited p. 161 (plates); p. 173 (small plate); p. 180 (plates);
                       p. 187 (plate); p. 189 (coffee set and plates); p. 191 (tray and plate)

                       Villeroy & Boch Tableware Limited p. 103 (glass platter); p. 122 (glass platter);
                       p. 139 (glass platter); p. 154 (glass plates); p. 164 (glass platter);
                       p. 186 (plate); p. 194 (plate); p. 195 (plate)

Carroll & Brown Limited would   Corning Limited
also like to thank these   Neff U.K. Limited
companies for their assistance   Siemens Domestic Appliances Limited   40-373-3